D1329686

# MANAGERIAL THINKING:
## An International Study

# MANAGERIAL THINKING:
## An International Study

**MASON HAIRE**

**EDWIN E. GHISELLI**

**LYMAN W. PORTER**

*University of California, Berkeley*

JOHN WILEY & SONS, INC.

NEW YORK   LONDON   SYDNEY

Library of Congress Catalog Card Number: 66–21068
Printed in the United States of America

# Preface

This book discusses a variety of facets of trends of the times and of our hopes and beliefs. In the first place, it is an example of the growing penetration of the behavioral sciences into the problems of management. As such, it bears the stamp, both methodologically and in substance, of our professional commitment. We are psychologists, and we tend to approach problems and do research as psychologists do. In this case, it has meant, methodologically, the conviction that only the most precise and quantifiable knowledge possible is knowledge in the proper sense. At the same time, it is our conviction that present conditions and trends demand that we all know more about the rest of the people in the world with whom we live and deal. These two themes gave shape to the effort: The need for international knowledge and a belief in certain paths to knowledge.

It is always appropriate in a preface to point out the authors' indebtedness. It has never been more appropriate than here. No study would have been possible without the cooperation and forbearance of the more than 3,600 managers who responded to our inquiries. We thank them, collectively, since they must remain anonymous. Similarly, it would have been impossible for us to make contact with such a sample of managers in such a variety of countries without the help and goodwill of many individuals, firms, universities, management associations, and training centers. They, too, must be collectively thanked, since limitation of space does not permit us to list them here. It is worth saying, however, that a hopeful aspect of the problem of international amity and international understanding appears in the ready willingness and considerable effort shown by organizations all over the world. Finally, the Ford Foundation very kindly funded the project, and the Institute of Industrial Relations at the University of California (Berkeley) provided facilities and support for the work. Without these, too, the study would have been impossible. We express our deep gratitude to all these people and organizations.

No work like the one at hand is ever really finished. This book represents the barest scratching of the surface; it is tentative methodologically, and only titillating in terms of content. What importance there is here probably lies chiefly in the simple fact that it is among the first steps toward the establishment of a firm and precise empirical body of knowledge regarding international management. As such, we welcome any further investigations that will enlarge upon, and supplant it.

M. HAIRE
E. E. GHISELLI
L. W. PORTER

*Berkeley, California*
*April, 1966*

# Contents

## Map of the World

### after the Explorations of Haire, Ghiselli, and Porter

The map on the facing page is only partly facetious. It shows which countries are close to one another in terms of the similarities of managerial attitudes. This is exactly what the book is about: managers' thinking in different countries. The text will provide the detail for the groupings and distances we have represented, but the map does reasonable justice to the diversity. Unfortunately, the map is limited to two dimensions, whereas managerial views distribute themselves along a number of dimensions. In any case, it will probably do us all good to remember that, in addition to the geography of longitude and latitude, there is also a geography of motivation and attitude. As spatial geography shrinks with transportation and communication, it becomes doubly important for us all to concern ourselves with the psychological geography of neighborhoods and clusters.

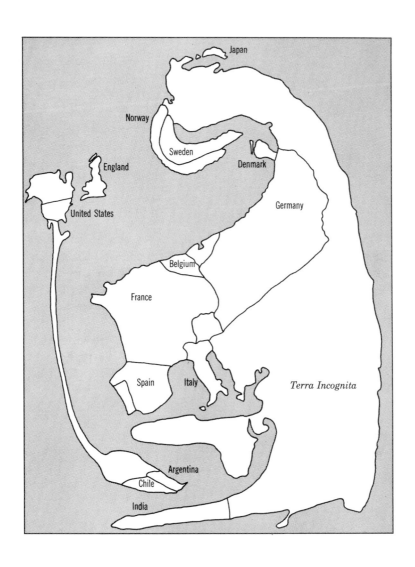

CHAPTER 1

# Introduction: The Nature of the Study and Its Findings

This book is the report of a research study on the attitudes of managers in various countries. It asks the questions: When managers think about managing, are their ideas all pretty much the same, or does managerial thinking differ from country to country? And, if it does differ, how do the countries group themselves together? Is there a readily discernible pattern in managers' responses by clusters or groups of countries? To answer these questions simply for the moment, it seems clear from the data reported here that there is a very high degree of similarity among managers' attitudes in all the countries studied. On the other hand, of all the differences observed among managers, about 25 percent of the variations were associated with national differences, so that there is an identifiable determinant of attitudes within each country. Furthermore, these national differences do tend to group themselves into intelligible patterns. These two points—the similarity and difference of managerial attitudes, and the clustering by countries—will, of course, have to be developed in considerable detail as the report progresses.

1

This introductory chapter will touch briefly on:

1. The form of the research instrument;
2. the problem of translation;
3. the sample surveyed; and
4. findings.

The reader can, if he likes, skip over the first three topics, since they are designed only to provide enough information to make the subsequent chapters on detailed findings more easily understood. If one wishes to avoid preliminaries, it is possible to plunge right into findings, and come back later, if necessary, to see how they were obtained. A more orderly method, however, would be to carry forward at least a cursory view of the research procedures.

### The Form of the Research Instrument

To answer the research questions stated above, we prepared a questionnaire which each manager–respondent could complete for himself. (A copy appears in Appendix A.) This form of tapping attitudes has real drawbacks—among them being that it makes it harder to go into great depth in the exploration of attitudes. Its virtue, however—and the consideration that seemed overriding in this case—is that it is possible to assure oneself that each respondent answered exactly the same questions, and that the results are strictly comparable from one group to another. This seemed an important exchange—giving up some depth for exactitude—in this case. As the problem of understanding managers' attitudes in other countries has grown, we have had a host of somewhat casual tourist-anecdotal reports on "What managers are like in Transylvania or Zenda." The problem in reading these reports is to know just what it is that one learns from them. Did the studies raise the same issues fom country to country? With the same kinds of people? Can the studies be compared with one another?

An impressionistic study—or even an interview study with a small, casually selected sample—of the way an institution is imbedded in a culture encounters real pitfalls. It is easy to bring to the fore the problems of capital formation in one country, the loose labor market in a second, and family succession in management in a third. Unless variables are checked in each country, however, their relative weights remain a puzzle. In one country, friendly government officials may be easy sources of information; in another, it may be managers of manufacturing; in a third, bankers. Are the observed differences characteristic of the country, or are they the somewhat inadvertent results of the kind of people chosen? Finally, the culture itself is hard to separate from the impression of the institution. The *gemütlichkeit* of one country, the *bonhomie* of a second, or the studied casualness of a third, may provide unwitting distortion in one's view of the scene. For all these reasons, a very careful attempt was made in this study to ask identical questions of each manager, and to ask them of the same kinds of managers in each country so that the answers could be compared with as little error as possible.

The content of the questionnaire was limited to three main areas: Leadership; the role of the manager in his culture; and the motives managers want to satisfy on a job and the degree to which managers feel these motives are satisfied. (This is the sequence in which these topics are treated in the text, although they appeared in a somewhat altered order in the questionnaire itself.)

The first set of questions—on leadership—consisted of 8 items to which the manager responded by checking on a 5-point scale ranging from "strongly agree" to "strongly disagree." The items were constructed logically to provide a series of steps from a somewhat unilateral, autocratic approach to management, to a more group-oriented team approach. They covered managers' beliefs in the capacity of subordinates, and their view of the efficacy of participation, of sharing information, and of providing opportunities for internal self-control on the job.

A second part of the questionnaire provided cognitive descriptions of the managerial role; they were obtained by use of a Semantic Differential format. The items in this section of the questionnaire will be described in more detail in Chapter 3.

Finally, a third part of the questionnaire, dealing with motivation, was made up of a series of 11 items designed to elicit responses geared to the Maslow hierarchy of needs for Security, Social needs, Esteem needs, and needs for Autonomy and Self-

Actualization. See p. 78, Chapter 4.) For each item, three questions were asked: How much is there now (of the opportunity to satisfy a given need)? How much should there be? And, how important is it? The respondent answered each question by checking a 7-point scale labeled from minimum to maximum. The difference between "How much is there now?" and "How much should there be?" provides a measure of the satisfaction of a need in question.

In addition to these three main parts of the questionnaire, a final page asked for demographic data relating to age of respondent, size of company, and the like.

### The Problem of Translation

The research was faced immediately with the problem of translating the questions, since they were, in each case, presented in the managers' own native language. Translation presents two special difficulties in such a comparative study: First, the language of management today is largely English—and American English at that; second, a study of cultures that approaches the comparative problem through language is immediately trapped in the fact that the language itself is part of the culture. To whatever extent one disregards the differences in connotation in the interest of comparability, one may be spuriously removing true cultural differences which are germane and important to the study itself. Questions in this study had to be rephrased or eliminated to meet this difficulty; and special steps had to be taken to try to assess the cultural loading on terms related to management.

Americans speak frequently of "leadership." The term itself, in any simple sense, is probably translatable only into the Scandinavian languages. The Latin countries tend to use the English word. Even before *Il Duce* and *Der Führer* gave special historical connotations to the term, it was not the same in direct translation. We also speak blithely in the United States about "the management team." The French would use the same word for "team" (*une équipe*) in sports that they would use for describing an hourly paid work group or gang; however, the word would sound distinctly odd if used to refer to the policy-making group.

Is this a difference in language alone, or is it a cultural difference reflecting part of the very comparative difference in management philosophy under study? To keep the responses comparable, words like "leader" and "team" had to be eliminated, even though their elimination may have resulted in the loss of some of the substance of the differences under investigation. The very word "manager" is almost impossible to translate simply. Its Latin root in *manus* makes it mean "to handle," but in the Latin languages the cognate word is used almost only to refer to the management of a horse by a rider. One "manages" the horse by tugging at the reins—a more unilateral and directive sense of the term than would be perfectly comfortable for most American managers. Even the British use of the term "managing director" implies partly a different corporate organization and partly a different view of the process of managing. The language of management is a problem for the research designer. For the person who wants some feeling for the meaning of the function of management in a culture, the variations in language provide a rich source of insights.

To deal with the problem of language, each questionnaire was translated from English into the language in question by a native of the country involved. The foreign-language version was then translated back into English, independently, by a second person to whom the language was native. This often led to a process of adjustment until a preliminary translation was obtained. This version was modified in the country of use (by conference with bilingual social scientists and managers) in order to get a formulation that was easy and idiomatic as well as linguistically correct. In the final stage of this process, the translated versions seemed reasonably satisfactory. The reader may check this point for himself in the translated versions appearing in Appendix A.

## The Sample Surveyed

The results of this study are based on a sample of 3,641 managers from 14 countries. The detailed breakdown of the sample appears in Appendix B. In each country, the sample is drawn from many companies and from various ages, levels of management, and sizes of companies. In general, nationalized and quasi-nationalized industries were excluded from the sample, though in some countries the defining line was so fuzzy that it was difficult to apply this criterion rigidly. Managerial cooperation in the research came through the medium of employers' associations, universities, management training centers, foundations, and individual companies. It is perhaps worth noting that in all the countries, managers were most cooperative in the study. In only two cases—one in England and one in the United States—did groups explicitly refuse to take part in the research.

Is this a representative sample of management? It is a broad and varied sample by which we attempted to represent the dominant dimensions of management in each country. It is not, however, strictly a representative sample. To produce such a sample, one might do one of two things. First, armed with a complete list of all the companies in a country, one might draw a random sample of them. Several things argue against this method. One is that no such list is generally available. Another is that if such a sample were drawn, there is no guarantee that the companies would all cooperate; and bias would be introduced, just as it is in our sample, because those companies who are willing to take part in studies of management probably have managerial attitudes different from those of companies who are less approachable. Finally, such a random sample would draw less heavily on large and medium-sized firms. While this would represent the population, it seems likely that these larger firms are opinion leaders in a sense that gives their responses greater diagnostic and predictive power than the responses of the more numerous tiny companies.

The second course in drawing a representative sample of management would be to sample proportionately along various dimensions—age, education, company size, etc.—in such a way as to reproduce the makeup of a country's population of managers. Unfortunately, again, no such knowledge of the distribution of the population of managers exists; nor even of the relevant dimensions along which the distributions should be made. Even in Sweden and the United States—probably the two most researched-upon groups of managers—we are painfully lacking in such demographic detail. Consequently, in the sample represented here, an attempt was made to sample different industries and different companies within an industry; different parts of the country; sizes of companies; and levels of management. It is not possible, therefore, to say that if another sample were drawn with the same rules we would expect the same results plus or minus a determinable error term. The sample was drawn impressionistically and sometimes opportunistically, but it is a broad and diverse group in each case, and probably comes close to representing the country involved. Of even more importance, where other studies of management exist, our proportions agree reasonably well with those reported by other research workers. The tables of demographic data in Appendix B show marked differences, in some cases, from one country to another. Are these to be interpreted as characteristic differences between countries, or as a failure of the sampling to draw upon a uniform population? Probably, to a large extent, they are characteristic differences. For example, in Spain, Italy, Belgium, and France, about 25 percent of the managers professed to have a major capital interest in the company they managed. In the other countries, this representation of equity was extremely rare. Clearly, to equate countries on this variable would vigorously distort the management community in many instances. Again, in most countries, the modal age of the managers surveyed was 35–45. In Germany, Italy, and India, it was 30–34; in Japan it was 50–54. It is not at all clear that the modal ages should be the same from country to country. In the exceptional cases noted here, major building or rebuilding of industry characterizes the postwar period, and one might expect these countries to differ from, for example, Chile, Argentina, and Spain. In a good many of the cases represented, the variation in demographic detail from country to country must probably be accepted as a characteristic of the country, and as one of the early steps toward a description of the population of managers.

## A Preliminary Look at Findings

As was suggested before, the two basic questions of our study are: Are the managers' attitudes the same or different? How do the countries cluster together? To these, a third can be added:

Within the segments of the study—leadership, the concept of the manager's role, and motivation—how do countries and managers differ from one another? In this chapter, the briefest possible report of the highlights relevant to these questions will be indicated without any of the supporting evidence or detail. For these supporting points, the reader should follow each of the issues through the chapter devoted to it.

To answer the question "Do managers from different countries differ from one another?" two figures were obtained. On any one of the scales in any of the three parts of the questionnaire, the total variation of the entire sample of 3,641 managers was computed. This figure—the standard deviation of the scores of all managers—gives an estimate of the difference observed among managers. On the other hand, the standard deviation of the means of countries gives an estimate of the differences among countries in the sample. If the standard deviation of the means of countries were to be as large as the standard deviation of all managers—so that the ratio of the two is 1.00—it would mean that all of the observed variation among managers was associated with national origin. In this case, the differences between managers could be completely accounted for by their country, with no room for individual differences of opinion of any other sort —a most unlikely situation. On the other hand, if all of the countries had the same average score, so that the standard deviation of their means was 0, it would signify that all of the observed variations in managers' attitudes were ascribable to individual differences, and none to country of origin. In this case, the ratio of the two standard deviations would be 0.

Among the three parts of the questionnaire the following ratios were obtained: Attitudes and assumptions underlying management practices, .32; cognitive descriptions of the managerial role, .26; needs and need satisfaction, .27—an average of .28. This means that of all the variation observed, about 28 percent was associated with national groupings; the differences among individuals are about 2½ times as great as the differences among countries. The three ratios reported here are remarkably similar, suggesting considerable stability in the pooled estimate. In each case, the ratio was made up of sub-parts: Four scores for attitudes and assumptions related to managerial practices, five factors in the descriptions of the managerial role, and three measures of motivation. These twelve measures also show rather close agreement, ranging from .17 to .48, with only three varying by more than .05 from the mean. The estimate seems reliable. If all differences arising from national origin were eliminated, the difference in managers' attitudes would be reduced by about 25 to 30 percent.

Is this difference arising from countries a big difference? It is, of course, impossible to answer this question in any absolute sense. The difference measured here is a relative one—the ratio of individual differences to national differences. However, two things can be said clearly: National differences make a consistent and substantial contribution to the differences in managers' attitudes. On the other hand, in terms of the possible differences in response to the items on the questionnaire, all of the responses tend to cluster fairly closely at one end of the scale. One might take the position that being a manager is a way of life and that, as such, a French manager might be expected to be more similar to an Indian manager, say, than to a French non-manager. The considerable similarity among managers' responses throughout the instrument lends some real support to this belief in the universality of managerial philosophy. On the other hand, one might believe that the fact of being a Frenchman, for instance, outweighs all else; so that a French manager is more like another non-managerial Frenchman in his attitudes about management than he is like an Indian manager. In support of this belief, there is the fact that 25 to 30 percent of the observed difference can be attributed to national origin. The cultural influence is present and substantial. It is not overwhelming.

This point about the simultaneous existence of similarity and diversity needs to be dealt with in a little more detail. It is an important point, and one that will come up again throughout the book. There is a very strong and consistent tendency for managers to express similar beliefs about management. In this sense, the values, perceptions, and attitudes of management can be said to be universal. To be a manager is to have a philosophy of management much like that of other managers everywhere. This similarity is so strong that the national groups, taken as units, tend to be remarkably similar. Popular stereotypes of the democratic Swedes, the Prussian mentality, and the tradition-ridden Japanese seem to demand widely and strikingly disparate scale positions on any measures of managerial strategy and tactics. These notions are not supported, insofar as they imply large and radical differences among the countries. Managers are so similar that countries find themselves, perforce, in the same region of the scale. However, in this considerable unanimity, a real diversity among countries exists. As has been mentioned, of all the differences among managers, 25 to 30 percent of the variation is associated with national origin. There are differences between countries, and the differences are real and substantial. Moreover, they cluster together in intelligible units which help to give us insight into the nature and origin of the observed differences.

In order to answer the second main research question—How do the countries group together?—each country's pattern of scores was compared with that of every other country. If, across a number of scales, country *B* is high when country *A* is high, and low when *A* is low, their scores are highly correlated and their patterns of response are similar. To the extent to which this tendency to vary together across a series of scales diminishes, the correlation and similarity diminish. In this manner, countries were compared each to each to see which ones are most similar to which other ones, and what clusters or groupings of countries come out of the data. The full table of intercorrelations among countries appears in Appendix C. One further technical word: In obtaining these correlations, a total of 94 scales was used from the three parts of the questionnaire, weighted to give each part —leadership, role descriptions, and motivation—equal representation. The scores used were standard scores of the entire population; they weighted countries equally, regardless of sample size.

The first thing that is clear from these intercorrelations is that some countries are much more similar to one another than they are to other countries. The correlations run from .89 (Argentina and Chile) to −.76 (India and Norway, and India and Sweden). These figures indicate, on the one hand, a very close similarity; and on the other, a rather high degree of dissimilarity. Of the 91 comparisons—the fourteen countries with each other—about 20 percent showed no consistent relationship (correlations between .15 and −.15); about 20 percent were very dissimilar (more than

—.40), and about 20 percent were fairly similar (more than .30). The countries are not all alike or uniformly scattered. Some of them are like others, and some are different from others. What patterns can we find in their relationships?

Major clusters of countries appear in a fairly simple way from these relationships: The Nordic-European countries (Norway, Denmark, Germany, and Sweden); the Latin-European countries (France, Spain, Italy, and Belgium); the Anglo-American pair; a group which might be called Developing countries (Argentina, Chile, and India); and, finally, Japan, which stands by itself and does not fit with any of the countries or clusters. These four clusters and one lone country have the following characteristic: Countries within a cluster are similar to one another and dissimilar to those in other clusters. Within a cluster, excluding Japan, the average correlation or similarity of one country to another is about .57. The average correlation with countries outside one's own cluster is —.38. In only two exceptional cases out of 37 possible comparisons is one country's correlation with another country outside its cluster higher than the average correlation within the country's own cluster. The conclusion is inescapable: There are groups of countries. The countries within each group are more like one another than they are like other countries. Moreover, it should be stressed that these clusterings are simple empirical facts which appear in the data when all the managers are asked the same questions. They are not a priori logical groupings forced on the data as a result of prejudged notions about relationships, but are the relationships which stand out from an analysis of the responses as they are.

The thing that emerges most clearly from the clusters is the strong pattern of cultural influence in these data. The first three clusters—Nordic, Latin, and Anglo-American—all include countries with strong bonds of similarity in language and religion; and with many common elements in their cultural background. Indeed, in one case, where a country was divided into two samples, the same trend was evident. In Belgium it was necessary to use a French-language questionnaire in the South and a Flemish one in the North. Even though the two parts of Belgium tended to go together, their differences tended to split along cultural lines. North Belgium, with its Protestant history, moved in the direction of the Nordic cluster, while predominantly Catholic South Belgium was more like the other Latin countries. The influence of cultural background and a broad sweep of values is unmistakable.

At first glance, the first three clusters seem to be language clusters, tempting one to ask: Is this merely an artifact of translation? Two responses seem clearly relevant here: First, one of the tightest clusters—Argentina, Chile, and India—is not a language cluster in that sense. Indeed, it cuts across two of the languages represented in earlier clusters. Clearly, the empirical findings do not support the explanation on the basis of language. Secondly, the close relation of language and culture, as was mentioned under the heading "The Problem of Translation," appears again here, as the two are, to some extent, inextricable.

At this point, let us consider another explanation that is often suggested in dealing with national differences in managerial styles. The bulk of comparative studies of management has been done by economists. As might be expected, they tend to find economic explanations for observed differences. As a result, there is a strong suggestion in these studies—though it is seldom stated or defended very explicitly—that differences in managerial style and strategy are primarily associated with differences in level of industrialization. The statement is usually made with a passing obeisance to the fact that cultural differences are present; but, after this brief mention, the cultural factor is ignored. The groupings of countries that emerge from these data fit remarkably poorly with any hypothesis flowing from the level of industrialization. The tight cluster of Spain, France, Belgium, and Italy, for example, or that of Norway, Sweden, Denmark, and Germany, provide a very mixed bag in terms of industrialization, but an understandable homogeneity in cultural strain. On any of the conventional measures of industrialization—percentage of non-farm workers, for instance, or production of fabricated goods—there is a wide gap between Spain, on the one hand, and France and Belgium, on the other; or between Norway and Denmark, and the more industrialized Sweden and Germany. Yet, in responding to questions about managing, these countries hang very closely together. In the Nordic cluster, for example, the average intercorrelation of each of the four countries with each other is about .40. Of the 40 correlations of these four countries with the ten others in the study, only 1 (Norway–England = .43) is of that order. Twenty-nine of the 40 correlations are negative. In the Latin cluster, similarly, the average intercorrelation is about .30. Of the 40 external comparisons only 3 are of that order; 29 are negative. The cultural groups are similar on these data, and different from the other countries.

This argument is not meant to suggest that the level of industrialization—or its history, pattern, and nature—are of no importance in determining managerial style and strategy. The data do not justify such a conclusion, and it does not seem useful to allow the explanation to degenerate into a simple *either-or* set of alternatives. Indeed, the Argentina-Chile-India cluster, cutting across language and cultural homogeneities as it does, is striking evidence of the effects of level of industrialization coming out in these data. What is clear, however, is the powerful strain of cultural differences in management thinking that appears repeatedly and consistently across these countries on these data.

### Some Areas of Implications

The cultural patterns in managerial strategy that emerge here would seem to have immediate and practical implications for managers, particularly for those interested in international business, in establishing operations in other countries, or in developing foreign nationals within their own organizations. Three main issues stand out: (1) The opportunity to examine and understand managerial attitudes in one's own country; (2) the implication for firms sending managers to work in foreign climates; and (3) the problems of executive development across cultures. Let us take them up briefly, one at a time.

The responses of managers from any one of the countries provide a kind of profile of the country's managerial attitudes. What does the manager think is the way to lead? What does he see to be the role of the manager? What does he hope for from his job? What does he get? How dissatisfied is he? How do variables such as age, ownership, education, level in the firm, size of company, and the like, cut across these attitudes? It would seem to be a worthwhile exercise for groups of managers in any country to examine these profiles and ask themselves: Is this the way it is here? Is this the way it should be here? And if it is not: What can we do about it? The possibility of comparing one's own profile with those of other countries, similar and different, goes a long way toward heightening understanding of the meaning of a particular pattern, and sharpening the evaluation of the observed state of affairs. In these days of an intensified competitive climate among countries in international business, such an analysis and understanding of one's own strengths and weaknesses is of special importance.

The proper training program for managers in overseas operations is intimately bound up with these cultural clusters, too. Many companies in the flush of international expansion feel that they have only enough time to pick the man with the right functional specialty, check to see that he has been relatively adaptable on his last few local assignments, and ship him off. What more can be done? If there is time enough, something on local competitive history, anti-trust or cartel climates, and a word on politics about does it. Typically, almost nothing is said about the relation between the culture to which the man is going and the managerial attitudes he will meet. The strong groupings of countries along cultural lines here suggest that this variable should not be neglected. A well-equipped manager should go into a country with some knowledge of the cultural streams relevant to management's thinking there. At the very least, some knowledge of the country's religious values, political climate, and literary traditions seems essential. More than that, however, he should be at home with a series of questions like: What is the meaning of egalitarianism and what form does it take? It there an elite? How is it recognized? What is honesty? How is it seen? What assumptions about the nature of human nature are implicit in, for instance, notions of original sin or of salvation—in a single-vote principle—in the role of caste or family? How are industriousness and self-actualization seen? How hard should one work? How much time should one invest in his family, his work, his friends? Questions like these are typically far removed from the portfolio of a manager going to a new country. Yet they are the clues to the cultural values which shape the managerial attitudes with which he will have to deal. The evidence of cultural clusters makes these questions imperative. So far, we have solved the problem by sending the best possible men and letting them learn the answers on the spot, or replacing them if they don't. The pressures of time and numbers mean that we can no longer afford this solution.

Finally, a consideration of the cultural influences on management's thinking leads us to the reverse process: Training foreign nationals for leadership positions. In many cases, the tacit assumption seems to have been made that one can take a man from whatever pattern of life one finds him in and add a set of managerial and industrial skills, leaving the rest of the organization of his life unchanged. The close relation suggested by our data between general cultural patterns and managerial style and strategy seems to deny this. The problem is not just to inject our techniques of leadership and control into an otherwise unchanged man, but to help him to develop the whole view and practice of life that goes with certain kinds of managerial philosophy. In a sense, you can't make a manager without making a man. To try to abstract a potential manager's general values of life, and to manipulate in a training program only the on-the-job practices of leadership and management, is a form of latter-day sociological colonialism which will probably have results similar to those of the geographical expansionist colonialism of an earlier day. Managerial strategy and practices are inextricably linked with general cultural values. To try to deal with one while keeping the other aloof and inviolate is, probably, eventually futile. It is necessary to go *all* the way in.

Subsequent chapters will cover more specifically—country by country and point by point—the manager's attitudes and assumptions underlying leadership techniques, his role, his motivations and satisfactions; the effects of his age and level, size of the firm, and the like. Through this wealth of detail, the reader is urged to keep in mind the central questions: How different are these managers' views from one another? What patterns are there to the differences? Where do the differences come from? In a sense, the respondents are all talking about the same thing—managing. Since we are all increasingly going to work together in these areas across countries, it becomes doubly important to recognize and understand the similarities and differences in managers' viewpoints.

CHAPTER **2**

# Attitudes and Assumptions
# Underlying Management Practices

Central to the act of managing is dealing with people. The way in which managers work with people presumably depends upon their assumptions about what people are like and how people can most effectively be led by a superior. We asked managers about such assumptions and attitudes, and found that in almost every one of the fourteen countries they held rather negative views about the average individual's capacity for initiative and leadership. At the same time, however, these managers felt that participative, group-centered methods of leadership are more effective than traditional directive methods. This seemingly paradoxical finding was more evident in some countries than in others; nevertheless, it was a finding universally present in each cluster of countries and in each individual country. The possible meaning and implications of this result will be discussed a bit later.

## The Importance of Such Assumptions and Attitudes

First, though, let us consider why it is important to ask managers about their assumptions concerning human nature, and their attitudes towards various management practices. In any manufacturing enterprise, the nature of the raw materials affects the procedures used to turn out the finished product. Likewise, in any type of organization, the nature and qualities of the individuals employed by the organization affect the procedures used to manage them. For example, if the workers are unskilled and have very little capacity for training, then the operations probably need to be fractionated into the smallest possible elements they can master. Only if they have some scope of intellectual and manual abilities can they be entrusted to carry out broader and more complex operations. Looking at managerial positions, if the ordinary person working in such a position possesses substantial capacity for initiative, for accepting responsibility, and for assuming leadership, then the organization can safely broaden spans of control, delegate considerable responsibility downward, and rely on the judgment and self-control of lower-level subordinates. However, if those qualities are rare among managers, or can be developed in them only with difficulty, and at great cost, then a more centralized and command-type organization is necessary. In other words, those in policy-making positions in a business or industrial establishment must structure its operations and procedures in logical accord with the abilities and qualities of the people who work for the organization.

The crucial point, here, is not what abilities and traits the employees actually have, but rather what their capabilities are as seen by their immediate and higher-level superiors. It is for this reason that it is important to learn about managers' assumptions concerning human nature and about their attitudes toward the way in which subordinates should be supervised. Their assumptions may be incorrect, and the management practices which they advocate may be ineffective, but, nevertheless, such assumptions and beliefs are likely to determine how organizations are, in fact, operated.

Classical or traditional organization theory, as many current writers in the field have pointed out, was based on certain assumptions, largely implicit, about the nature of people. At the risk of oversimplifying, we can say that the classical theorists assumed that the average employee inherently disliked his work, wished to avoid responsibility, lacked strong ambitions, was basically selfish and uncooperative, and was interested only in the money he could take away from his job. This is a picture of a fundamental lack of confidence in the abilities and intrinsic motivations of the average worker. It was from this conception of the typical employee that classical organization theory constructed a set of principles of organization that involved rigid chains of command, extreme specialization of functions, limited spans of control, and the like.

In contrast, many modern organization theorists base their ideas about how organizations should operate on an entirely different set of assumptions regarding human nature. These modern theorists begin by assuming that the average person does not inherently dislike work, that he can be taught to accept responsibility, that he does possess a certain amount of initiative and ambition and willingness to work with others, and, finally, that he is motivated by more than just monetary rewards. Building on these assumptions, modern organization theory stresses the importance of such practices as wide participation in decision making, the development of subordinate self-control, and the use of a variety of methods of influence; that is, they find these preferable to exclusive reliance on formal authority and economic sanctions as means of accomplishing the aims of the organization.

### The Items Used to Measure These Assumptions and Attitudes

It was with these contrasting assumptions between classical and modern organization theory in mind that we developed a series of 8 statements or items in one part of our questionnaire. Each item was relevant to an assumption or attitude on which the two types of theories differed, and respondents were asked to indicate (on a 1–5 rating scale) whether they agreed or disagreed with the statement as presented. For example, one of the 8 statements was:

> *"The average human being prefers to be directed, wishes to avoid responsibility, and has relatively little ambition."*

A manager who agreed with this statement was obviously taking a classical or directive viewpoint, whereas one who disagreed was responding more in line with modern organizational theory. (Four of the 8 items were stated in such a way that agreement indicated a classical viewpoint, and disagreement a modern viewpoint; the other 4 were stated in the reverse way, so that agreement to these items indicated the modern approach, and disagreement the classical approach.)

In preparing these 8 items, we attempted to cover four distinct areas of disagreement between the traditional-directive and the democratic-participative approaches. These four areas and the 2 items pertaining to each area are listed below:

1. *Capacity for leadership and initiative*

   - The average human being prefers to be directed, wishes to avoid responsibility, and has relatively little ambition.
   - Leadership skills can be acquired by most people regardless of their particular inborn traits and abilities.

2. *Sharing information and objectives*

   - A good leader should give detailed and complete instructions to his subordinates, rather than giving them merely general directions and depending upon their initiative to work out the details.
   - A superior should give his subordinates only that information which is necessary for them to do their immediate tasks.

3. *Participation*

   - In a work situation, if the subordinates cannot influence me then I lose some of my influence on them.

- Group goal-setting offers advantages that cannot be obtained by individual goal-setting.

4. *Internal control*

- The use of rewards (pay, promotion, etc.) and punishment (failure to promote, etc.) is *not* the best way to get subordinates to do their work.
- The superior's authority over his subordinates in an organization is primarily economic.

### Methodology

At this point, a brief note about methodology is necessary. As we indicated earlier, managers responded to each of the 8 items by using a 1–5 rating scale (running from "strongly agree" to "strongly disagree"). Since half of the items were framed to make positive statements with regard to the classical viewpoint, and the other half to make positive statements with regard to the modern approach, agreement with the former type of item would mean that the respondent favored the classical viewpoint; agreement with an item of the latter type would indicate agreement with the modern viewpoint. Thus, in order to construct our tables and charts we scored each question in such a way that a low score (i.e., towards 1) indicated a classical attitude and a high score (towards 5) indicated a modern attitude. In other words, in those tables and charts dealing with raw score means, the higher a mean value, the more the managers from a given country or cluster of countries favored a democratic-participative approach.

### The Major Finding and Its Implications

Now, returning once again to the substance of this chapter, what sort of findings should we expect? It seems likely that a manager's assumptions about human nature, and his attitudes toward the type of leadership practices likely to be most effective, should be affected to some degree by the broad stream of cultural traditions of the particular social environment (the country) in which he lives. It might be expected, for example, that Japanese and American managers would have quite divergent beliefs about the ordinary individual's capacity for initiative and leadership. The highly formal (and formerly feudalistic) structure and traditions which tend to exist in Japanese society would suggest that a business executive in that country would believe in a relatively narrow distribution of capacity for initiative and leadership on the part of the average individual. The diametrically opposite view might be expected of an American executive, growing up as he has with the social myth that any boy, potentially, can become President of the United States. Similarly, it might be anticipated that the German manager, living in a society with a rather strong authoritarian tradition, would be far less likely to advocate participation than would his counterpart in France, a country priding itself on its egalitarian traditions. As it turns out, this expectation tends to be confirmed, whereas our tentative prediction about the Japanese and American managers is partially invalidated. Throughout our study, certain findings seem right in line with the differences one might expect as a result of cultural dissimilarity; yet other such expectations are either not confirmed by the findings, or are actually disproved.

Despite the wide variety of cultures represented by the fourteen countries in our sample, there was considerable similarity among the managers from these various countries on the major finding from this part of our questionnaire: The tendency to disagree with the belief that the average individual has a capacity for initiative and leadership, and, at the same time, a tendency to agree that the best methods of leadership are the democratic-participative methods. Table 1 and Figure 1, which provide the raw score data, illustrate the universal nature of this finding. No matter how we group the data, the result is the same. In each country, in each group of countries, in all of the countries taken together, there is a relatively low opinion of the capabilities of the average person, coupled with a relatively positive belief in the necessity for democratic-type supervisory practices.

What is the meaning of this finding? In purely logical terms, positive attitudes in the first of our four areas of attitudes (see page 19)—capacity for initiative and leadership—would seem to be an essential foundation for positive attitudes in the other three areas dealing with leadership practices. The basic reason for adopting shared objectives, participation, and individual-oriented

TABLE 1. ATTITUDES TOWARD MANAGEMENT PRACTICES
(RAW SCORES *)

| | Capacity for Leadership and Initiative | Sharing Information and Objectives | Participation | Internal Control | N |
|---|---|---|---|---|---|
| Nordic-European Countries | | | | | |
| Denmark | 2.54 | 3.09 | 3.68 | 3.90 | 149 |
| Germany | 2.38 | 3.17 | 3.52 | 3.88 | 586 |
| Norway | 2.52 | 4.04 | 3.47 | 3.90 | 221 |
| Sweden | 2.22 | 4.01 | 3.35 | 3.88 | 342 |
| Average | 2.42 | 3.58 | 3.51 | 3.89 | |
| Latin-European Countries | | | | | |
| Belgium | 2.29 | 3.74 | 3.88 | 3.74 | 378 |
| France | 2.42 | 4.04 | 3.82 | 3.80 | 154 |
| Italy | 2.40 | 3.64 | 3.16 | 3.72 | 267 |
| Spain | 2.52 | 3.56 | 3.65 | 3.78 | 203 |
| Average | 2.41 | 3.75 | 3.63 | 3.76 | |
| Anglo-American Countries | | | | | |
| England | 2.72 | 3.78 | 3.48 | 3.56 | 239 |
| United States | 3.13 | 3.98 | 3.56 | 3.58 | 464 |
| Average | 2.93 | 3.88 | 3.52 | 3.57 | |
| Developing Countries | | | | | |
| Argentina | 2.64 | 2.96 | 3.31 | 3.62 | 198 |
| Chile | 2.80 | 3.08 | 3.32 | 3.65 | 159 |
| India | 2.81 | 2.96 | 3.35 | 3.38 | 114 |
| Average | 2.75 | 3.00 | 3.33 | 3.55 | |
| Japan | 2.88 | 3.58 | 3.98 | 3.77 | 165 |
| All Managers | 2.59 | 3.55 | 3.54 | 3.73 | |

* Higher mean values indicate stronger endorsement of democratic attitudes.

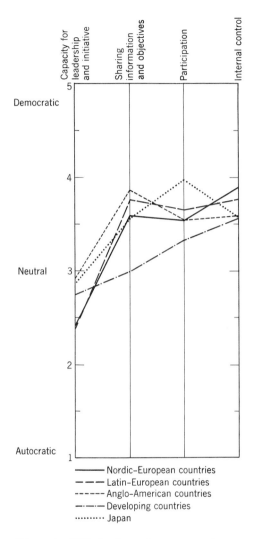

Figure 1. Attitudes toward management practices: by clusters of countries (raw scores).

self-control is the argument that subordinates fully possess the necessary capabilities for leadership and responsibility. After all, it would be absurd to have the lever which controls a machine require 200 lb. of pull to move it if workers are only strong enough to exert 100 lb. of pull. Similarly, it would seem illogical to install a set of procedures for sharing information, allowing self-control, and practicing participation, unless subordinates were capable of handling these types of situations. Yet, this is what the managers in our sample seemed to be advocating.

One interpretation of this finding is that it reflects a sort of partial digestion of the exhortations of group-oriented consultants and professors of management during the past decade. Participative and democratic approaches to leadership have been the *sine qua non* of executive development and training courses in recent years. It appears from our data that such ideas have received more or less universal lip service throughout middle and upper levels of management. At the same time, though, the supposedly necessary underlying assumptions concerning the average person's willingness and ability to assume responsibilities have, apparently, not been taken to heart. Thus, what seems to have emerged from these executive development programs and from various books and other writings on modern management is a situation where many managers want to build the techniques and practices of a Jeffersonian democracy on a basic belief in the divine right of kings!

Why is this the case? One obvious possibility is that managers do not really feel that positive benefits will be gained by the use of such democratic-type practices, but, nevertheless, feel that it is somehow old-fashioned or unorthodox these days not to endorse them. If this is so, then we would expect to find that although many managers subscribe to such beliefs in responding to an attitude questionnaire such as ours, they seldom put them into practice when dealing with subordinates in actual job situations. Certainly, this possibility may account for some of the support that was given on paper to this approach to managerial leadership.

Another possibility, however, is that many managers feel that certain benefits *are* gained by these methods, even though, at the same time, they believe the average individual lacks initiative and the willingness to accept responsibility. The major benefit to be gained from these methods would be a decreased resistance to the leadership of the superior. In other words, a manager might advocate these participative practices not because of a belief that he would obtain more initiative, innovation, and the like, but because of a belief that his subordinates would then be more likely to go along with his ideas about the goals of the organization and the way in which jobs should be carried out. In Lewenian terms, the manager would be voting for these practices because they serve to decrease or reduce any opposing forces. Seen in this light, then, a lack of belief that others have a great deal of unused capacity is not necessarily inconsistent with advocacy of group-centered, participative management practices.

Before we turn to a consideration of the differences among countries that did appear on this first part of the questionnaire, we should point out one other aspect of the major finding we have just been discussing. We have been emphasizing that managers in all countries had positive views concerning the use of participative methods of leadership. In so doing we should be mindful that most of our respondents were recruited through the cooperation of various management-training institutions or (in a few instances) with the help of several rather large progressive companies (as in India). It is entirely possible, even probable, that those who are inclined to cooperate in a study such as this are those managers (and companies) most in sympathy with the modern or human-relations-oriented management concepts. To the extent that this is true, the degree of pervasiveness of commitment to such practices is probably somewhat exaggerated. Nevertheless, the fact remains that there is a substantial segment of managers in a wide variety of companies and countries who are willing to endorse these methods. This, in itself, is a finding of considerable interest, for there were those who probably would have predicted a very low rate of acceptance of these ideas among managers in many of the non-United States countries.

Let us look in detail at the data presented in Tables 1 and 2 and Figures 1 and 2. First, we can consider Table 1 and Figure 1, which present the raw score findings. The raw score data allow us to study the "absolute" answers to the various questions comprising each scale, and to make comparisons of the findings on any one scale with those on the other scales. (Table 2 and Figure 2, which give the results in standard scores, are more appropriate for highlighting comparisons among countries on a given scale, and will be discussed later.) The bottom row in Table 1 shows the point we have already been discussing at some length in this chapter. This row, giving the mean values for each scale across the entire sample of 3,600 managers, shows that the mean endorsement of the 2 items dealing with capacity for leadership and initiative was 2.59, whereas for each of the other scales dealing with participative practices the values were 3.55, 3.54, and 3.73. Thus, we see that not only were the three administrative practices—sharing information and objectives; participation; and internal control—favored to a much greater extent than a belief in the capacities of the average individual; each of them was also endorsed to about the same degree as were the other two practices. The practice of fostering subordinate self-control rather than using external controls was only slightly more favored than were the practices of sharing information and using participation. This difference, therefore, was minimal compared to the large difference between adopting any of the three administrative practices, on the one hand, and believing in the capabilities of the employee, on the other.

Still focusing on Table 1 and Figure 1, we can note that the two Anglo-American countries and the three Developing countries come closest to matching their endorsement of democratic leadership practices with a faith in the average person. In the two English-speaking countries this relatively smaller difference occurs because the managers in these countries have a somewhat greater belief in subordinates' capacities than do managers in most of the other countries. In the Developing countries, the smaller difference is brought about more by a relatively weak endorsement of democratic-type administrative practices than by a positive belief in subordinates' capacities (although the Developing countries are somewhat above the average of all countries on this scale). The eight European countries, both the block of four Nordic countries and the block of four Latin countries, show rather similar patterns of clearly negative views of individuals' capacities for leadership and initiative, and strongly positive views of the modern management theory approach to administrative practices. It is the Europeans, then, who most strongly demonstrate the pattern of attitudes we have so far been focusing on in this chapter.

### Attitudes Toward Belief in the Average Person's Capacities

In the last few paragraphs we have been talking about the overall differences among clusters of countries in patterns of response to all four categories of items. We can now turn to an examination of differences among the countries in response to each of the four categories considered separately. To do so, the reader will find Table 2 and Figure 2 (which present the data in standard score form) most helpful because they allow quick comparisons of the attitudes of managers in any one country or group of countries with the total sample of managers for each of the four categories of questionnaire items. To prepare the data for Table 2 and Figure 2, we computed the mean and distribution of attitude scores for the total sample of 3,600 managers, letting each country carry equal weight in the distributions. Then, for each of the four response categories (i.e., for each column in Table 2 and Figure 2) the means of the various countries were expressed in terms of standard scores of the total sample of managers.[1] If the mean of a country were .00 in standard score terms, then, on the average, the attitudes of managers in that country would be precisely the same as the average of all managers. If the mean of a country were around 1.00, then, on the average, the attitudes of the managers in that country would be substantially higher than that of managers in general, falling at one standard deviation above the mean of the total sample of managers. Finally, if the mean of a country were around $-1.00$ the attitudes of the managers in it would be substantially lower than

[1] As most of our readers know, a standard score is obtained simply by subtracting the mean score of the total sample from the mean score for a group of respondents (in our case, a country) and dividing this value by the standard deviation for the total sample. For example, in the case of Chile, the mean score of 2.59 for the total sample was subtracted from the mean score of 2.80 for Chilean managers and this value of .21 was divided by the mean standard deviation of .74 for the total sample to give a final standard score value of .28, shown in Table 2.

Table 2. Attitudes Toward Management Practices
(Standard Scores *)

| | Capacity for Leadership and Initiative | Sharing Information and Objectives | Participation | Internal Control | N |
|---|---|---|---|---|---|
| **Nordic-European Countries** | | | | | |
| Denmark | −.07 | −.49 | .14 | .17 | 149 |
| Germany | −.28 | −.41 | −.02 | .15 | 586 |
| Norway | −.10 | .54 | −.07 | .17 | 221 |
| Sweden | −.50 | .51 | −.19 | .15 | 342 |
| Average | −.24 | .04 | −.04 | .16 | |
| **Latin-European Countries** | | | | | |
| Belgium | −.41 | .21 | .34 | .01 | 378 |
| France | −.23 | .54 | .28 | .07 | 154 |
| Italy | −.26 | .10 | −.38 | −.01 | 267 |
| Spain | −.10 | .02 | .11 | .05 | 203 |
| Average | −.25 | .22 | .09 | .03 | |
| **Anglo-American Countries** | | | | | |
| England | .17 | .25 | −.06 | −.17 | 239 |
| United States | .72 | .47 | .02 | −.15 | 464 |
| Average | .45 | .36 | −.02 | −.16 | |
| **Developing Countries** | | | | | |
| Argentina | .07 | −.63 | −.23 | −.11 | 198 |
| Chile | .28 | −.51 | −.22 | −.08 | 159 |
| India | .29 | −.64 | −.19 | −.35 | 114 |
| Average | .21 | −.59 | −.21 | −.18 | |
| Japan | .39 | .04 | .44 | .04 | 165 |
| All Managers | .00 | .00 | .00 | .00 | |

* Positive mean values indicate *relatively* democratic attitudes; negative values indicate *relatively* autocratic attitudes.

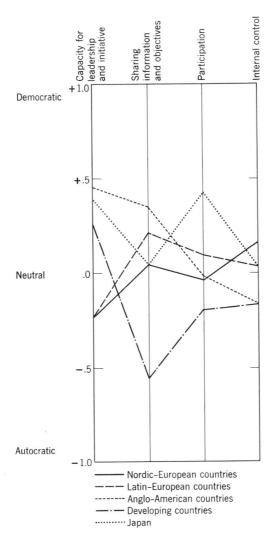

Figure 2.  Attitudes toward management practices:
by clusters of countries (standard scores).

that of managers in general, falling at one standard deviation below the total sample mean.

Let us first take up the category of items dealing with belief in the average person's capacity for leadership and initiative. It will be recalled that the 2 items in this category were the following (with the first item stated from the classical point of view and the second from the modern organization theory point of view):
1. "The average human being prefers to be directed, wishes to avoid responsibility, and has relatively little ambition." 2. "Leadership skills can be acquired by most people regardless of their particular inborn traits and abilities." We can see in the first column of Table 2 that managers from the United States were far more "democratic" in their viewpoints on this category of items than were managers from any other country. Since the United States is the home of most of modern organization theory, perhaps this finding is not too surprising. At any rate, it is one of the more striking of the specific findings of the study. Since the mean value for the American managers is so high, relatively speaking, and since the value for English managers is also on the plus side of the grand mean, the Anglo-American group of countries has the highest positive standard score for any of the five clusters of countries.

Surprisingly, Japan is the second highest scoring country with regard to a democratic-type view of the average person's capacities. The meaning of this finding is not immediately obvious. One possible explanation is that the Japanese managers, more than the other groups of managers in our sample, had a strong motivation to try to "please" the American researchers by giving them the response they thought the Americans wanted. In this connection, it can be noted that the Japanese managers were at or above the mean "democratic" score on the other three categories of items in addition to this category on individuals' capacity. It is also possible that because of their past traditions the Japanese, especially those managers sent to executive development programs, have a tendency to overreact to participative, democratic-oriented ideas and practices.

The other group of countries that has an overall standard score above the total sample mean on the capacity for leadership category is the cluster of Developing countries. For these countries, however, the relationship between their answers to items in this category and their answers to items in the other three categories is quite different from the Japanese pattern. While the Developing countries are above the mean in endorsement of a democratic belief in the capacities of the average individual, they are distinctly below the mean values in each of the other three categories dealing with the implementation of managerial action. Thus, managers in the Developing countries were not just routinely giving democratic answers to all of the questions. For the two South American countries in this cluster of Developing countries, there may be a ready explanation of their relatively positive attitudes towards the 2 questionnaire items dealing with individuals' capacities. In much of South America there exists a strong belief in the uniqueness and dignity of the individual. Thus, when questions are asked concerning what individuals are like, relatively positive responses might be expected. However, when the questions (as in the other three categories of Part I of the questionnaire) concern how individuals should be managed in a work situation, the answers would not necessarily be expected to be strongly democratic. The situation with regard to India, whose managers gave responses very similar to those of Chilean and Argentinian managers, is somewhat more difficult to explain. Perhaps the long association with English managers, plus a strong feeling that as a nation they have considerable untapped capacities, may have influenced the view of their managers on this attitude dimension.

The two groups of countries that had negative standard scores on the first category of items were the two European clusters, the Nordic- and the Latin-European countries. As Table 2 shows, Sweden and Belgium, especially, were well below the mean of the total sample of managers. Even more noteworthy, however, is the fact that all eight European countries we sampled were below the total sample mean. Such consistency from one country to another within Europe would argue strongly that cultural traditions, within society at large as well as within the business world, do have an impact on managerial philosophies and assumptions, especially with regard to something as basic as the nature of man.

## Attitudes Toward Sharing Information

Shifting our attention now to the second category of items (the second column in Table 2 and Figure 2), those dealing with the practices of sharing information and objectives, we see a rather different pattern of the relative responses from the five groups of countries. It will be recalled that the 2 items in this category were (both items being stated from a classical organization theory point of view): 1. "A good leader should give detailed and complete instructions to his subordinates, rather than giving them merely general directions and depending upon their initiative to work out the details." 2. "A superior should give his subordinates only that information which is necessary for them to do their immediate tasks." For this category of items, we find that the three Developing countries—Argentina, Chile, and India—hold decidedly negative views (relative to other countries) concerning this method of exercising leadership in a business organization. On the other hand, the four Latin-European countries view this practice relatively positively, whereas on the former category their responses were on the negative side. Perhaps the explanation of these shifts has something to do with managers' views concerning the expected reactions of subordinates to the sharing of information and objectives by superiors. In other words, the managers in Developing countries, while respecting the potentialities of the average person, nevertheless may feel that the typical subordinate or employee would not be accustomed, nor would respond favorably, to such sharing. Of course, they may be wrong in this belief, but the important point is that they seem to hold it. The managers in the Latin-European countries, on the other hand, may feel that their subordinates expect a certain amount of such sharing by the superior. It will be noted from Table 2 that managers in France feel especially positive toward this particular management practice, while those in Italy and Spain have views more nearly in line with the total sample.

The four Nordic-European countries show a sharp division among themselves on the idea of sharing information and objectives. Norwegian and Swedish managers were in relatively strong favor of the notion of sharing information and objectives. In direct contrast, the Danish and German managers were decidedly negative about the wisdom of this practice. Incidentally, this split between the two pairs of countries regarding this particular management practice was rather unique in that for most parts of the questionnaire the four Northern European countries tended to react similarly to the various questions.

Again, the two Anglo-American countries, for this category of items concerning the sharing of information and objectives, had the highest average positive scores. Their comparatively favorable stance on these items would seem to be related logically to their relatively positive belief in the capacities of the average individual. If the average subordinate can be trusted to assume a fair amount of responsibility, then it is reasonable to hold the view that information on objectives could be shared with him and that it is not necessary to give him detailed and complete instructions.

## Attitudes Toward Participation

Turning to the third category of items on this part of the questionnaire, items concerning participation and group goal-setting, we can see that the range of scores across the fourteen countries is narrower than was the case for the previous two sets of items. The 2 items in this third category were (both items being phrased in line with modern organization theory): 1. "In a work situation, if the subordinates cannot influence me, then I lose some of my influence on them." 2. "Group goal-setting offers advantages that cannot be obtained by individual goal-setting." The previous ranges for the fourteen individual country scores had been 1.22 (the difference between the largest positive standard score and the most negative standard score) for individuals' capacities, and 1.18 for sharing information. On this third category, the range is cut by a third to .82. The reduction of ranges of the scores for the four *groups* of countries (excluding Japan) is even greater, going from .70 and .95 for the first two categories to .30 for this third category concerning the advantages of using participation.

The reduced range of means for the third category of items indicates that any existing cultural differences or even differences in industrialization had less of an impact on this category than on the previous two categories. It appears that the nature of the situation (i.e., the business setting) operates to produce a certain uniformity of opinion among managers regarding just how much participation is likely to be effective. Also, perhaps, organization theorists and management trainers have tended to emphasize this particular management practice to such an extent in recent years that they have been partly responsible for managers in different countries being in fairly close agreement about the efficacy of participation.

The only countries that deviate to any extent from the total sample mean are Japan and several of the Latin-European countries. Japanese managers are the most favorable, of any nation's managers, toward the use of participation; they are followed by managers in Belgium and France. Italy deviates from the remainder of the Latin group of countries in that it is relatively negative towards participation. The Developing countries also are mildly negative, relatively speaking, toward this type of managerial practice. All other countries are very similar to each other in the degree of their endorsement of participation.

### Attitudes Toward the Nature of Supervisory Controls

The fourth category of items dealt with the nature of authority and control. The 2 items were: 1. "The use of rewards (pay, promotion, etc.) and punishment (failure to promote, etc.) is *not* the best way to get subordinates to do their work." 2. "The superior's authority over his subordinates in an organization is primarily economic." For this fourth category, the degree of homogeneity of mean responses from country to country was even greater than for the previous category concerning participation. The range of means among the fourteen countries was only .52, and for the four groups of two or more countries it was .32. Thus, again, for this category as for the previous one, the impact of cultural and industrialization differences was minimal. Of the fourteen countries, only India had a standard score that deviated more than .20 from the total sample mean. All other countries produced average responses that were relatively quite close to the overall mean. This similarity, rather than any differences among the various countries, is the major finding regarding these 2 items dealing with the topic of managerial controls.

CHAPTER 3

# Cognitive Descriptions of
# the Managerial Role

In Chapter 1 we talked about "the language of management" in connection with the practical problem of translating our questionnaire. In this chapter the language of management itself becomes the object of investigation. Specifically, we want to know how managers describe certain aspects of the managerial role.

When one sets out to describe a manager's role in an organization, he needs to say something about the types of action required of the manager and something about the position of the manager in the organizational hierarchy. This is essentially what we have asked our sample of managers to do in that part of our questionnaire that provides the data for this chapter. We asked them to indicate the meaning, to them, of several important actions relevant to the job of managing, and the meaning of status differences in managerial hierarchies. This was done by means of Osgood's Semantic Differential technique,[2] a tech-

[2] C. E. Osgood, G. J. Suci, and P. H. Tannenbaum, *The Measurement of Meaning*, University of Illinois Press, Urbana, Illinois, 1957.

nique involving some methodological intricacies that will be discussed at some length at a later point in this chapter.

## The Major Findings

A major focus in our attempt to get at cognitive descriptions of the managerial role was the differential meaning attached to the two concepts *to direct* and *to persuade*. In a sense, these two types of managerial action could be thought of as epitomizing the basic differences in approach to supervision between classical and modern organization theories, as discussed in Chapter 2. On the surface, at least, the concept *to direct* should imply a rather unilateral type of command to subordinates, a command backed up by the formal authority of the superior. *To persuade*, on the other hand, should imply a more give-and-take approach between the boss and the subordinate, an approach involving consideration of the subordinates' ideas, desires, and attitudes.

Overall, the findings, as supplied by the Semantic Differential technique, showed that *to direct* was viewed far more positively by most managers than was *to persuade*. The former type of action was regarded as having relatively more of the qualities of meaning of prestige, activity, and firmness. Furthermore, *to direct* was seen as being closer in meaning to the concepts of *to decide* and *to cooperate*. On the other hand, *to persuade* was considered closer in meaning to the more negative actions of reprimanding, making a mistake, and cheating. In other words, directing seems to be a "good" thing to do, while persuading seems to represent some sort of weakness or indecision on the part of the manager. This kind of finding on this part of the questionnaire may indicate that the sort of lip service paid to democratic methods of leadership in the first part of the questionnaire was just that—lip service. The differential meanings that managers attached to directing and persuading are more in line with their previously indicated low belief in the capacities of the average person for leadership and initiative.

Perhaps the most interesting, and most important, feature of the results regarding *to direct* and *to persuade* was not their overall difference in meaning across the entire sample of respondents, but rather the fact that this difference was much greater in some countries than in others. Managers in the Nordic-European countries in general, and in Germany in particular, saw very large differences in meaning between these two aspects of the managerial role. For them, directing has much greater prestige, and involves far more firmness than does persuading. In addition, directing is considerably more similar to the action of creating than is persuading; and much less similar to the concept of making a mistake than is persuading. Clearly, managers in these four countries, given a choice between directing or persuading subordinates, would prefer to direct them.

The other group of countries which described *to direct* and *to persuade* in fairly different terms was the cluster of Developing countries, especially India. Among the managers in the ten non-Nordic-European countries in our sample, Indian managers were closest to the managers in the Germany-Denmark-Norway-Sweden foursome in regarding direction and persuasion as different types of action. India, in turn, was followed by Chile in the overall size of difference in meaning between these two managerial concepts. Argentinian managers were, however, about in line with the remaining countries on this part of the questionnaire. For at least two of the three Developing countries then, the difference between directing and persuading is relatively large, but nowhere near as large as the difference obtained from the four Nordic-European countries.

The remaining countries—Japan, the two Anglo-American nations, and the four Latin-European countries—all perceive a relatively modest difference between directing and persuading. The two concepts are not identical in the eyes of the managers in these countries, but the amount of the difference between them is distinctly smaller than for the Nordic-European managers, and somewhat smaller than for the managers in the three Developing countries.

The most striking feature of the other part of the results reported in this chapter—the results concerning the meaning of hierarchical status differences—was the rather remarkable similarity of findings from country to country. These results are based on the differences in meaning attached to three relatively high-status positions in three types of hierarchies—factory manager, colonel, and bishop—compared to three relatively low-status positions—factory foreman, sergeant, and priest. The overall difference between these two sets of positions across the total sample of fourteen countries was relatively moderate. But more important, the results for any single country looked very similar to the results for all the other countries.

The overall differences—across all fourteen countries combined —between the three high-status and the three low-status positions indicated, as might be expected, that the higher positions were regarded somewhat more positively than the lower positions. For example, the higher positions were regarded as having slightly greater prestige and scope, and were seen as more similar than the lower positions to concepts such as *to decide, to create,* and *to direct.* At the same time, the high positions were seen as slightly less similar than the lower positions to the negative concepts of making a mistake and cheating.

## The Reasons for Using the Semantic Differential Technique

The way in which we attempted to get at differences in meaning between high- and low-status positions illustrates a very important feature of this (the Semantic Differential) part of our questionnaire. It was in this section of the questionnaire that we had something approaching a projective instrument. In the other two parts of the questionnaire—the part concerning attitudes and assumptions underlying management practices, and the part concerning motivations and satisfactions—the questions were direct and straightforward. The respondent clearly knew exactly what we were asking him. If he desired to give us an answer that he thought was "correct" rather than the answer he believed in, it was no problem for him to do so. On the Semantic Differential portion of the questionnaire, however, the ease with which the results can be "manipulated" is substantially (though, obviously, not completely) reduced. It would take a rather canny respondent, indeed, to deduce that one of the objectives of the researchers was to make comparisons of a combination of three high-status positions with a combination of three low-status positions. Even for the more direct comparison of *to direct* and *to persuade*, it is unlikely that many, if any, respondents consciously said to themselves when they came to the second of these two concepts (buried in a list of fifteen concepts, each to be rated on 9 scales): "Now let's see, they want to know how *to direct* compares in my mind to that earlier concept *to persuade.*"

It is also unlikely that very many managers had even a general knowledge of the purpose of this part of the questionnaire, such as: "The idea behind this part must be to see whether we see these various concepts in an old-fashioned or traditional way, or whether we see them in line with so-called 'modern' management principles." In fact, the very typical reaction we *did* get to this part of the questionnaire went something like this: "What kind of a crazy form of question have you got here? I don't understand the purpose of this part of the questionnaire."

It seemed clear, to us at least, that the Semantic Differential achieved our intended purpose of using it in the questionnaire; namely, it provided a format that obscured the focus of our subsequent analyses. In that sense, it functioned as a semi-projective device. At the same time, it created some practical problems in gaining subject cooperation because of its unique appearance to the vast majority of our respondents. It had the disadvantage of lowering our response rate to some (unknown) extent because a number of potential respondents glanced at this rather cryptic part of the questionnaire before filling it out, and decided that the entire questionnaire must have been poorly designed and, therefore, not worth the time or trouble it would take to complete it. We therefore sacrificed additional numbers of respondents so as to gain more projective material from those who were willing to fill out all parts of the questionnaire.

## Methodology

Since the Semantic Differential has seldom been used in a questionnaire study involving managerial respondents, we will go over the method in some detail for those who are interested in learning exactly how we analyzed the results in this part of our investigation. For those not interested in this more-or-less technical detail, pages 41–45 can be skipped, and the description of the results resumed on page 46.

The basic aim of the Semantic Differential method is to construct a kind of cognitive map. This map, in effect, says how far and in what direction each of a number of concepts is from every other concept. The meaning of a concept, then, is inferred from its position on this kind of map of cognitive space. The initial step in the construction of this cognitive map is to ask respondents to rate each concept being considered on a series of bipolar scales which remain the same across all concepts.

In our questionnaire, we asked respondents to rate fifteen different concepts on nine bipolar scales. Let us first identify the fifteen concepts: Eight of them concerned types of managerial functions; six of them concerned positions in organizational hierarchies; and the remaining one concerned an occupational position (the concept *physician*). (This latter concept, although included in the questionnaire, was not analyzed separately, and will not be further discussed in this chapter.)

The eight concepts representing managerial functions were composed of five types of action likely to be described in favorable terms,

> *to direct*
> *to persuade*
> *to decide*
> *to cooperate*
> *to create*

—and three types of action likely to be described in more neutral or even unfavorable terms,

> *to reprimand*
> *to make a mistake*
> *to cheat*

The intention in choosing the first five of these eight particular functions as concepts to be defined in Semantic Differential terms was to cover a fair cross section of more or less typical and frequent behavior patterns manifested by managers or persons serving in potential leadership roles in organizations. And, as we have already indicated, two of these five concepts—*to direct* and *to persuade*—were included specifically because they deal with rather different ways of approaching a leadership role in terms of managerial theories. The latter three of the eight functions, those having a somewhat more negative tinge, were included in order to have concepts which might provide some interesting contrasts in meaning. (For example, the inclusion of these three concepts helped determine whether *to direct* or *to persuade* had a relatively more positive image with our respondents.) All told, the positioning of these eight concepts into a cognitive pattern gives us some idea of a nation's view of what a manager does in his role as manager.

The six concepts representing positions in organizational hierarchies were composed of two positions from industrial organizations,

> *factory manager*
> *factory foreman*

two positions from military organizations,

> *colonel*
> *sergeant*

and two positions from religious organizations,

> *bishop*
> *priest*

The reader can immediately see that for each of these three institutions we have included a position relatively high and a position relatively low (but not the lowest possible) in the hierarchy. (It might be argued that a priest is at the bottom of religious organizations; however, when it comes to religious activities, the parishioners may represent the rank and file below the priest.) We do not claim, and it was not our intent to do so, that the three higher positions are exactly comparable from institution to institution; nor that the three lower positions are exactly equidistant from each of the higher positions. Rather, our purpose was to provide a set of three positions that are *relatively*, but unequivocally, higher in organizational hierarchies than a set of three other positions. In this way, we could determine the difference in meaning between a generalized concept of high organizational positions and a generalized concept of low organizational positions that would not be tied to any particular kind of organization.

Each of the fourteen concepts—the eight managerial functions and the six organizational positions—were rated on the same series of nine bipolar scales. The nine scales were chosen for inclusion on two bases. First, three of the scales (good-bad, active-passive, strong-weak) were included because they represent the three factors typically found in studies utilizing the Semantic Differential. Second, the other six scales were selected to sample different attributes that could easily be applied to describe either managerial actions or organizational positions. Since we felt it was necessary, in order to obtain a reasonable response rate, to use scales that would have a certain degree of "face validity" for managerial respondents, we purposely did not use some of the more abstract types of scales frequently found in investigations where the Semantic Differential technique is employed. The nine scales used were:

important—unimportant
profound—superficial
active—passive
wide—narrow
difficult—easy
good—bad
stable—changeable
interesting—uninteresting
strong—weak

In typical Semantic Differential style, each scale had seven steps and appeared like this on the questionnaire (see Appendix A for the format for this part of the questionnaire):

unimportant :___:___:___:___:___:___:___: important

A check mark close to one or the other end of the scale meant that the respondent felt that the concept being rated was well described by the word at that end of the scale, while a mark towards the middle meant the respondent was in more doubt as to which end of the scale was descriptive of the concept.

## How the Raw Data Were Analyzed

Our statistical analysis of the data from this part of the questionnaire followed procedures typically employed for Semantic

Differential data.[3] First, the intercorrelations among the nine scales were computed, and these intercorrelations then factor-analyzed. It is important to note that in the computation of the intercorrelations among the nine scales, each of the fourteen countries carried equal weight. That is, the intercorrelations were computed as if the numbers of managers in all countries were the same, the purpose being to cancel out the irrelevant fact that some countries (e.g., Germany) were represented by a dis-proportionately large number of respondents in our total sample. Our factorial analysis indicated that about 85 percent of the common variance could be accounted for by five independent and unrelated factors. These factors were subsequently rotated to a verimax solution to give us the loadings of each of the nine scales on each of these five factors. These loadings are shown in Appendix D.

From the loadings of the nine bipolar scales on the five factors, it appeared that the factors could be identified and defined as follows:

*Prestige.* The extent to which a concept is esteemed or admired.

*Scope.* The breadth, range, and latitude of a concept, as compared with its limitations and narrowness.

*Activity.* The degree of movement and change involved in a concept, as opposed to its tendency to be quiet or passive.

*Firmness.* Solidity, consistency, and steadiness of a concept, as compared to its instability and vacillation.

*Difficulty.* The effort involved in actions relevant to the concept.

After having obtained the above five factors, we proceeded to develop sets of weights for the computation of scores on these factors. The factor scores were based on the factor loadings of the nine scales together with their intercorrelations. To make the scores on the five factors comparable, we transmuted the raw factor scores into standard scores, with each of the fourteen countries carrying equal weight in determining the means and standard deviations. The mean of the scores on each factor then is .00 and the standard deviation is 1.00.

[3] Osgood, *op. cit.*

The five independent factors which emerged from our multiple factorial analysis can be considered in Osgood's terms to be the five basic cognitive dimensions or qualities of meaning which underlie the particular nine scales and fifteen concepts used in our Semantic Differential. Since the dimensions are independent, they are orthogonal in a geometric sense and describe a five-dimensional semantic space.

The meaning of a concept (e.g., the meaning of *to direct*), insofar as the scales we used reveal it, is given by its position in that space. The degree to which the overall meaning of two concepts is similar or different is given by the distance between them in the semantic space. These distances are Osgood's *D* scores. When the distance between two concepts is small they have similar meanings, and when the distance is large they have dissimilar meanings. So, for the managers in any particular country, we could determine the extent to which two concepts are the same or different by calculating the difference between the average positions of the two concepts—their average distance, in other words—for these managers.

The specific connotations of a concept are given by its positions on each of the five dimensions or qualities of meaning. Since the scores on these dimensions are given as standard scores, if the value of a concept on a given dimension is high and positive it means that the concept connotes a high degree of that property. If the value is high and negative, it means that the concept connotes the opposite of that property. For example, if the average score of a group of managers for a given concept (e.g., *to create*) on the first dimension (*prestige*) were 1.00, this would mean that *to create* carries with it a substantial amount of prestige for these managers. On the other hand, if the average score for this group of managers were −1.00, it would indicate that *to create* not merely lacks prestige, but actually has the opposite quality of disrepute or opprobrium. For any national group of managers, the differences in meaning between two concepts could be given by the differences between their averages on each of the five dimensions or qualities of meaning.

It is also possible to gain additional understanding of the meaning of a concept for a given group of respondents by determining which member of a pair of concepts is more similar in overall meaning to a third concept. The distances in semantic space between each member of the pair and the third concept are first determined; then the difference between the two distances is obtained. If the difference between the two distances is 0, then both members of the pair are equally similar (or dissimilar) to the third. If the distance is greater for one member of the pair than for the other, then that member with the greater distance is more *unlike* the third concept than is the other member. This, as we said, provides further information on how a given group of respondents evaluates the meaning of particular concepts, and allows for additional comparisons between one group of respondents and another group.

## Comparisons Between *To Direct* and *To Persuade*

So much for the intricacies of our statistical handling of the Semantic Differential data. We have seen how the raw score ratings made by respondents on each of nine scales for each of fifteen different concepts were converted by factor-analysis methods into standard scores for each of five independent dimensions of meaning; and how these factorial standard scores could be used to obtain the cognitive meaning of each separate concept and to compare the relative semantic differences between and among concepts. We are now prepared to turn to a detailed description and interpretation of our findings from this part of the questionnaire. First, the results for the comparison of meanings of two key managerial leadership actions, *to direct* and *to persuade*, will be analyzed. This will be followed by an analysis of the results concerning differences in meanings between the combination of relatively high organizational positions and relatively low positions. We thus proceed from some of the functional aspects of the managerial role to some of its structural features.

The story of the difference between *to direct* and *to persuade* will be told by making use both of tables and of graphs. To start, the reader is asked to look at Table 3. This table shows the overall difference in meaning—across all five semantic dimensions—between these two concepts, *to direct* and *to persuade*. As indicated in the note at the bottom of the table, the larger the value in Table 3, the greater the dissimilarity in meaning between the

TABLE 3. SIMILARITY OF THE CONCEPTS *To Direct* AND *To Persuade* *

|  | Differences | Number of Cases |
|---|---|---|
| Nordic-European Countries |  |  |
| Denmark | 1.03 | 130 |
| Germany | 1.99 | 578 |
| Norway | 1.16 | 217 |
| Sweden | 1.02 | 335 |
| Average | 1.30 |  |
| Latin-European Countries |  |  |
| Belgium | .51 | 374 |
| France | .37 | 153 |
| Italy | .31 | 265 |
| Spain | .57 | 201 |
| Average | .44 |  |
| Anglo-American Countries |  |  |
| England | .45 | 239 |
| United States | .43 | 459 |
| Average | .44 |  |
| Developing Countries |  |  |
| Argentina | .43 | 198 |
| Chile | .60 | 154 |
| India | .87 | 111 |
| Average | .63 |  |
| Japan | .40 | 156 |
| All Managers | .72 |  |

* Small values indicate similarity; large values indicate dissimilarity.

two actions. (The values given in Table 3 represent *D* scores, previously discussed on page 45.) Two conclusions are obvious from Table 3. First, all countries see some difference between *to direct* and *to persuade,* although the two concepts are by no means thought of as opposite in meaning (since the mean value for all managers, .72, could have been much larger). Second, there is considerable variation from one group of countries to another, and especially from one individual country to another, in the size of the difference in meaning between directing and persuading.

Figure 3 graphically illustrates the variation of average values among the four groups of countries and Japan. The reader can best appreciate the idea that this variation among groups of

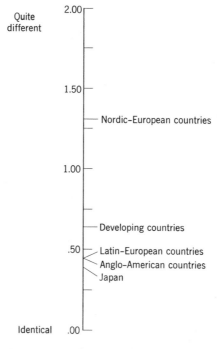

Figure 3. Similarity of the concepts *to direct* and *to persuade:* by clusters of countries.

countries is relatively large for the differences between *to direct* and *to persuade* by comparing Figure 3 with the later Figure 6 which shows the variation for differences between higher and lower organizational positions. Clearly, groups of countries differ more on the distinctions they make between directing and persuading than on the distinctions they make between a generalized concept of high-status positions versus a generalized concept of low-status positions. This would indicate that cultural and industrialization differences have a more pronounced effect on the meaning of contrasting methods of leadership than on the meaning of contrasting positions within organizational hierarchies. In other words, the functions of management seem to be more subject to cultural and national differences than are the structural aspects of management. Obviously, our data are not at all conclusive on this point, but they are at least suggestive.

The variation of differences between directing and persuading among the fourteen individual countries in our sample is shown in Table 3. The values shown in this table illustrate the relatively large variation that exists from country to country in the difference that managers see between the idea of persuading and the idea of directing. Again, for the sake of comparison, the reader is asked to contrast the individual-country values in Table 3 with the analogous values in Table 6. The relatively much larger variation for the results on the two managerial functions is again apparent.

Using the data given in Table 3 and illustrated in Figure 3, let us take up the question of which groups of countries and which individual countries perceived the largest differences in meaning between *to direct* and *to persuade*. It is apparent from Table 3 and Figure 3 that the Nordic-European countries constitute the cluster of countries where managers report the greatest differences between these two concepts. Their average of 1.30 is double that of the next closest cluster, the Developing countries, and triple the values for the other two clusters and Japan. All four of these Northern European countries have values of over 1.00, indicating that in an absolute as well as a relative sense they attach different meanings to these two types of leadership actions. On the basis of these findings for the Nordic-European countries, one would be tempted to conclude that cultural factors are exerting a strong influence here.

Of the managers in these four countries, it is the Germans who see the most decided difference between direction and persuasion. Their difference of 1.99 is, in fact, exceptionally large. Certainly (from an American viewpoint at least), it is not surprising to find that German industrial managers react rather differently to the concept of directing than to the concept of persuading. This finding would fit in with the average American's stereotype of Germany as being preoccupied with aspects of authority. In fact, some of the remarks by Heinz Hartmann, in his chapter on "Management in Germany" in Harbison and Myers' *Management in the Industrial World*, are quite relevant here. Hartmann points out that:

> . . . German management is very much concerned with its authority. If there is a difference between concepts of authority in Germany and in other industrialized countries, it seems to be in the substance of definitions and in methods of identification. Whereas management elsewhere describes its authority largely in terms of knowledge and technical skill . . . the German executive's system of authority consists of value-oriented or non-functional definitions. . . .[4]

When we examine, at a later point, Tables 4 and 5, we shall be able to see in exactly which ways German managers differentially defined the terms *to direct* and *to persuade*—terms that are logically relevant to the concept of authority.

The fact that the three Scandinavian countries also perceive a large difference (though not as large as that for Germany) between direction and persuasion indicates that for these countries also the concepts are salient to their views of leadership. The nature of this difference for the three Scandinavian countries will be outlined when we come to Tables 4 and 5.

Following the four Nordic-European countries is the bloc of Developing countries in terms of the size of the semantic difference between directing and persuading. Among the managers from these three countries, which share a relatively common stage of industrialization, it is the Indian managers who make

[4] F. Harbison and C. A. Myers, *Management in the Industrial World*, McGraw-Hill, New York, 1959, p. 270.

the greatest distinction between the two concepts. The value for Indian managers, .87, is above the .60 value for Chile, and well above the .43 difference for Argentinian managers, but considerably below the average of 1.30 for the four Nordic-European countries. (Incidentally, it is worth noting that the .87 value for India is substantially higher than the values of .45 and .43 for England and the United States, respectively. This is only one of a number of places throughout the questionnaire where the Indian managers give responses markedly different from those of English or American managers. The import of this finding is that it demonstrates that the results obtained for inter-country comparisons are not solely a function of the language of the questionnaire *per se*—the English, American and Indian samples all used the identical English-language questionnaires—but rather that they reflect cultural or industrialization differences over and beyond language differences.) Developing countries, then, make greater distinctions between persuasion and direction than do most of the countries in our sample, except for Germany and the three Scandinavian nations. This would seem to make some intuitive sense, because business operations in the three Developing countries have traditionally had more autocratic overtones than those in most of the more industrially advanced countries. Hence, it is not too surprising to find that managers in these Developing countries draw a fairly sharp distinction between *to direct* and *to persuade*.

Table 3 shows that the other seven countries—the four Latin-European nations, the two Anglo-American countries, and Japan —ascribe about the same degree of difference between the two concepts, directing and persuading. This difference is relatively small compared to the difference for the other countries previously discussed, but is definitely not a 0 difference. In other words, *to direct* is distinguished from *to persuade* in these countries, though not to a great degree.

We can now turn our attention to Table 4 and Figure 4, which show the comparative meanings of *to direct* and *to persuade* on the five semantic dimensions that emerged from our factor analysis. Looking at the bottom line of Table 4 we can see that the two concepts differed most on the dimensions of *prestige, activity,* and *firmness.* In each case, *to direct* was higher on the dimension,

TABLE 4. DIFFERENCES BETWEEN THE CONCEPTS *To Direct* AND *To Persuade* ON FIVE SEMANTIC DIMENSIONS *

| | Prestige | Scope | Activity | Firm-ness | Diffi-culty | Number of Cases |
|---|---|---|---|---|---|---|
| Nordic-European Countries | | | | | | |
| Denmark | .41 | .24 | .11 | .72 | −.56 | 130 |
| Germany | 1.35 | −.13 | .70 | 1.25 | −.27 | 578 |
| Norway | .90 | .10 | .32 | .63 | −.14 | 217 |
| Sweden | .77 | .12 | .31 | .56 | −.16 | 335 |
| Average | .86 | .08 | .36 | .79 | −.28 | |
| Latin-European Countries | | | | | | |
| Belgium | .22 | .01 | .30 | .35 | .05 | 374 |
| France | .08 | .21 | .19 | .22 | −.05 | 153 |
| Italy | .06 | −.01 | .22 | .21 | −.03 | 265 |
| Spain | .23 | .33 | .39 | .12 | .02 | 201 |
| Average | .15 | .14 | .28 | .23 | .00 | |
| Anglo-American Countries | | | | | | |
| England | .11 | .08 | .27 | .32 | −.10 | 239 |
| United States | −.02 | .03 | .17 | .36 | −.16 | 459 |
| Average | .04 | .06 | .22 | .34 | −.13 | |
| Developing Countries | | | | | | |
| Argentina | .13 | .06 | .36 | .06 | .18 | 198 |
| Chile | .20 | .14 | .37 | .38 | −.13 | 154 |
| India | .41 | .17 | .53 | .35 | −.40 | 111 |
| Average | .25 | .12 | .42 | .26 | −.12 | |
| Japan | .08 | −.01 | .14 | .35 | −.11 | 156 |
| All Managers | .35 | .10 | .31 | .42 | −.13 | |

* Positive values indicate *to direct* is higher on a dimension; negative values indicate *to persuade* is higher.

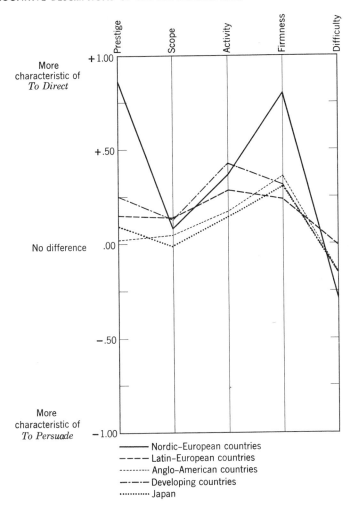

Figure 4. Differences between the concepts *to direct* and *to persuade* on five semantic dimensions: by clusters of countries.

i.e., better described by the dimension, than was *to persuade*. On the other two dimensions—*scope* and *difficulty*—there was little difference between directing and persuading, although *to direct* was regarded as involving slightly more *scope* and less *difficulty* than *to persuade*.

It seems apparent from our findings that the leadership method of directing is distinctly more positively valued than the method of persuading. Directing has greater prestige in thirteen of the fourteen countries (the fourteenth being the United States, where managers regard the two terms as almost exactly equal in prestige), more scope in eleven of the countries, more of the character of action in all fourteen countries, greater firmness in all fourteen countries, and is seen as not being as difficult as persuasion in eleven of the countries. We have, therefore, a highly consistent picture across quite different types of cultures and degrees of industrialization. The implication here seems to be that our semi-projective device, the Semantic Differential, has been sensitive enough to pick up some real differences in meaning between these two contrasting managerial methods, directing and persuading. When we get managers to compare these two methods via the Semantic Differential we find that directing is regarded in a distinctly more favorable light. On the other hand, when we used the less projective and more straightforward questioning techniques described in the preceding chapter, we found that managerial practices relevant to persuading seemed to be more favored than those relevant to directing. Thus, we have something of a paradox. We do not have enough additional kinds of data to allow us to resolve this paradox, but the findings from the Semantic Differential certainly indicate that one should proceed with caution if he thinks that at the present time most managers throughout the world strongly prefer democratic-persuasive methods to more autocratic-directive methods of leadership. At the very least, our findings in this part of the questionnaire indicate that the act of persuading has more of the connotations of weakness, passivity, and lack of importance, than does the act of directing. When faced with a decision as to which type of action to take, the preference of the typical manager in our sample seems clear.

Figure 4 graphically illustrates the variation among the four clusters of countries and Japan on the meaning of directing and persuading for each of the five semantic dimensions. The Nordic-European countries see *to direct* as having far more *prestige* than *to persuade*. The other three clusters and Japan regard direction as having slightly or moderately greater *prestige* than persuasion. On the dimension of *scope*, the managers in the four clusters agree that *to direct* is slightly higher, while Japanese managers see the two concepts as almost equal. For *activity* and *firmness*, all cluster averages show *to direct* as being better described by these two qualities, with the managers in the Developing countries being most convinced for *activity*, and the Nordic-European managers seeing the greatest distinction on the *firmness* dimension. On the *difficulty* dimension, Japan and three of the clusters regard *to persuade* as better described by this quality, while the Latin-Europeans see no difference between directing and persuading with regard to their degree of *difficulty*.

Individual-country results for the difference in meaning between the two methods of managerial leadership on the five semantic factors are shown in Table 4. Considering first the factor of *prestige*, Table 4 shows that all fourteen countries, except for the United States, felt that *to direct* has greater *prestige* than *to persuade*. This differential in favor of directing was, by far, larger in Germany and the three Scandinavian countries than in any of the other individual countries. For United States managers, there was virtually no difference in *prestige* between the two types of action, although the value for the United States was a shade in favor of persuading having more *prestige*. Looking at the picture for the *scope* dimension, we can see that the countries were rather tightly bunched around the point of no difference, although more of them fell to the plus (i.e., favoring *to direct*) side than to the other side of this point. Somewhat surprisingly, in light of the rest of the results in this section, German managers felt that directing had less *scope* than persuading, in contrast to the opinion of most of the other managers. On the *activity* dimension, all countries felt that *to direct* was better described by this connotation than was *to persuade*, with German and Indian managers being most emphatic about this, and Danish and Japanese managers least sure of the difference. For the dimension of *firmness*, again all fourteen countries felt the same way; namely, that directing connotes *firmness* more than does persuading. German, Danish, Norwegian, and Swedish managers were the firmest about *firmness*, while Spanish and Argentinian managers reported the smallest differences between directing and persuading on this dimension. Finally, for the factor of *difficulty*, the average manager in most countries apparently feels that *to direct* a subordinate is somewhat, though not drastically, easier than *to persuade* him. This was most true of managers in Denmark, India, and Germany; and least true of those in Argentina, Belgium, and Spain. In these latter three countries, there was a very slight tendency for managers to consider directing as being more *difficult* than persuading.

The comparative meanings of *to direct* and *to persuade* were measured not only by their scores on the five semantic factors emerging from the nine bipolar rating scales, but also by their relative similarity in meaning to six other concepts. These six other benchmark concepts were: *to decide, to create, to cooperate, to reprimand, to make a mistake,* and *to cheat.* The results for the comparisons of the two managerial functions to these other concepts are presented in Table 5 and Figure 5.

The bottom line of Table 5 will show us how *to direct* and *to persuade* compared to each of the other six concepts across all fourteen countries. The summary figures in this row indicate that directing was seen as more similar to deciding and cooperating than was persuading, while persuading was seen as more similar than directing to the concepts of reprimanding, making a mistake, and cheating. The actions in question were about equally similar to the concept of creating. Again, these specific results strongly reinforce our earlier stated interpretation that *to direct* was regarded in a much more positive fashion than *to persuade.* By any reasonable yardstick, the concepts of deciding and cooperating carry more favorable connotations for the average person than do the concepts of reprimanding, making a mistake, and cheating. Thus, on this point the results seem quite clear and consistent. In fact, the findings are especially remarkable when one stops to think that, on the surface at least, *to direct logically* should be related more closely to *to reprimand*, and should be less closely related to *to cooperate* than should *to persuade.* As it turned out, *psychologically* speaking, the act of directing was regarded as closer than persuading to the positive concept of cooperating, and more distant than persuading from the more negative concept of reprimanding. Without the benefit of a somewhat subtle device, such as the Semantic Differential, it is unlikely that these kinds of beneath-the-surface results would have been un-

| | To Decide | To Create | To Coop- erate | To Repri- mand | To Make a Mistake | To Cheat | Num- ber of Cases |
|---|---|---|---|---|---|---|---|
| **Nordic-European Countries** | | | | | | | |
| Denmark | .62 | .42 | .96 | −.70 | −.26 | −.25 | 130 |
| Germany | 1.79 | 1.01 | 1.52 | −.68 | −1.56 | −.44 | 578 |
| Norway | .49 | .57 | .81 | −.91 | −.80 | −.47 | 217 |
| Sweden | .92 | .51 | .80 | −.62 | −.59 | −.38 | 335 |
| Average | .96 | .63 | 1.02 | −.73 | −.80 | −.39 | |
| **Latin-European Countries** | | | | | | | |
| Belgium | .16 | −.23 | .18 | −.44 | −.46 | −.49 | 374 |
| France | .10 | .00 | .11 | −.27 | −.24 | −.17 | 153 |
| Italy | .18 | −.12 | .09 | −.21 | −.22 | −.91 | 265 |
| Spain | .11 | .07 | .13 | −.52 | −.34 | −.25 | 201 |
| Average | .14 | −.07 | .13 | −.36 | −.32 | −.46 | |
| **Anglo-American Countries** | | | | | | | |
| England | .31 | −.16 | .23 | −.23 | −.23 | −.26 | 239 |
| United States | .20 | −.31 | .25 | −.19 | −.16 | −.12 | 459 |
| Average | .26 | −.24 | .24 | −.21 | −.20 | −.19 | |
| **Developing Countries** | | | | | | | |
| Argentina | .10 | .14 | −.05 | −.25 | −.34 | −.29 | 198 |
| Chile | .42 | −.03 | .34 | −.53 | −.41 | −.39 | 154 |
| India | .60 | −.18 | .69 | −.73 | −.64 | −.68 | 111 |
| Average | .37 | −.02 | .33 | −.50 | −.46 | −.45 | |
| Japan | .17 | −.04 | .20 | −.26 | −.27 | .00 | 156 |
| All Managers | .44 | .12 | .45 | −.47 | −.47 | −.36 | |

* The higher the positive value, the more the comparison concept is similar to the concept *to direct;* the higher the negative value, the more the comparison concept is similar to the concept *to persuade.*

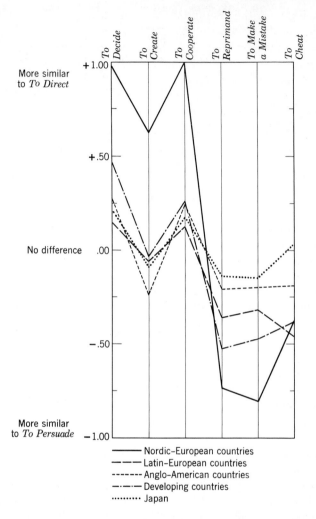

Figure 5. Comparative similarity of various concepts to the concepts *to direct* and *to persuade:* by clusters of countries.

covered. That they were discovered turns out to be a revealing piece of information. It indicates that the endorsement of democratic approaches to managerial problems may be more superficial than we would otherwise suspect.

In Figure 5 the results for the four clusters of countries and Japan are illustrated graphically. The immediate thing one notices about this figure is the rather wide separation of the Nordic-European bloc of countries from the other blocs on five of the six columns in the graph. Especially noticeable is the deviation of the Nordic foursome from the other groups on the first three columns: Those dealing with the relative similarity of directing and persuading to the "favorable" concepts of *to decide, to create,* and *to cooperate.* It is obvious that the managers from the Nordic-European area regard the idea of directing as much closer in meaning to these three concepts, compared to managers from the other three clusters of countries and Japan. Although managers from these latter groups of countries feel that *to direct* is closer than *to persuade* to the concepts of *to decide* and *to cooperate,* their tendency in this respect is much less strong than that of the Nordic-European managers. Furthermore, in comparing the relative similarity of directing and persuading to *to create,* the managers in the non-Nordic clusters actually feel that creating is as close to persuading as to directing.

We can now briefly look at each specific column in Figure 5. When *to direct* and *to persuade* are compared in terms of their similarity to the concept *to decide,* the value for the Nordic countries is about 1.00, whereas the values for the other groups range from about .10 to .50. The bloc closest to the Nordic bloc is that composed of the three Developing countries. The results for similarity of the two key concepts to *to create* show that the four Northern European countries see directing as rather strongly associated with creating, while the other clusters of countries feel that directing and persuading are about equally close to creating. For the column pertaining to *to cooperate,* the story is much the same as in the first two columns. The Nordic group see directing as distinctly closer to this concept than is persuading, while the other clusters of countries, though giving results in the same direction, see a less clear-cut association. Here again, it is the Developing country group which responds most like the Nordic group.

The situation for the last three columns in Figure 5, pertaining to the three "unfavorable" concepts, is almost a perfect mirror image of the situation for the first three columns. Here we find the Nordic group quite convinced that reprimanding, making a mistake, and cheating, are more closely connected with persuading than with directing. The other groups of countries, though tending in the same direction, are somewhat less convinced of this association. Again, as for the first three columns, the Developing countries are closest in their responses to the Northern European group; and, in fact, for the last column dealing with *to cheat,* their value slightly exceeds that of the Nordic foursome. Japan and the two Anglo-American countries provide the least extreme values for the last three columns. Managers in these countries see relatively small differences between directing and persuading in terms of their closeness to reprimanding, making a mistake, and cheating.

Returning again to Table 5, we can look at the country-by-country picture of the results that we have been discussing above. Highlights of this table include the observations that German managers had by far the most negative views of persuasion, whereas American, French, and Japanese managers generally held, relatively speaking, the least negative views. That is, German executives felt that persuading was much less closely associated than directing with the three "favorable" concepts of *to decide, to create,* and *to cooperate,* and was in truth much more closely associated with the "unfavorable" concepts of *to reprimand, to make a mistake,* and *to cheat.* For the United States, France, and Japan, the results showed that in most instances the managers in these three countries saw little difference between the two key managerial actions in terms of their relative closeness to any of the six comparison concepts. (In fact, it should be pointed out that the most extreme value for the United States occurred on the second set of columns dealing with associations with *to create,* where the American managers saw this concept as closer to persuading than to directing. Hence, their deviation in this instance tended to favor persuading both relatively and absolutely, if *to create* is considered a "favorable" concept.) Other countries tending to follow the German pattern were the three Scandinavian countries, India, and Chile. Countries more or less following the United States–France–Japan pattern were England, Argentina, and the three other Latin-European countries of Belgium, Italy, and Spain.

The sum and substance of the foregoing is that there is a fair degree of diversity in how individual countries differentially compared *to direct* and *to persuade* to six other concepts—this spread is anchored on one end by Germany and on the other end by the United States, France, and Japan. As was discussed earlier in the chapter, these results, based on the Semantic Differential, may give us some indirect clues as to the ways in which management problems are approached in Germany (and, to a lesser extent, in Sweden, Norway, and Denmark) compared to the way they are handled in countries like the United States, France, and Japan. Seemingly, culture has had some kind of impact on managerial thinking.

## Comparisons Between "High" and "Low" Organizational Positions

We now come to the final section of this chapter, and here we will deal in detail with the data concerning differences in meaning between relatively high organizational positions and relatively low positions. As we explained earlier, the data represent an indirect method of determining the saliency of organizational status differences for the various national samples of managers. The results are considerably less striking than those just discussed concerning differences between *to direct* and *to persuade;* but, nevertheless, they provide some important information pertaining to the degree of the impact of culture on managerial thinking.

Table 6 and Figure 6 present the basic picture of the degree of perceived similarity between sets of higher- and lower-status positions. The reader will recall that the set of relatively high-status positions was composed of the concepts *factory manager, colonel,* and *bishop.* The set of relatively low-status positions was composed of the concepts *factory foreman, sergeant,* and *priest.* Thus, the findings presented in Table 6 and the accompanying figure are based on the semantic differences between these composite sets of concepts.

The most obvious finding to note in Table 6 is that the values for the fourteen countries are remarkably close to the overall value of .47 for all managers. In other words, there was very little variation among the countries in the size of difference perceived

TABLE 6. SIMILARITY OF HIGHER-STATUS POSITIONS TO
LOWER-STATUS POSITIONS *

|  | Differences | Number of Cases |
|---|---|---|
| Nordic-European Countries | | |
| Denmark | .42 | 130 |
| Germany | .30 | 578 |
| Norway | .52 | 217 |
| Sweden | .48 | 335 |
| Average | .43 | |
| Latin-European Countries | | |
| Belgium | .53 | 374 |
| France | .54 | 153 |
| Italy | .55 | 265 |
| Spain | .63 | 201 |
| Average | .56 | |
| Anglo-American Countries | | |
| England | .36 | 239 |
| United States | .49 | 459 |
| Average | .43 | |
| Developing Countries | | |
| Argentina | .40 | 198 |
| Chile | .53 | 154 |
| India | .34 | 111 |
| Average | .42 | |
| Japan | .46 | 156 |
| All Managers | .47 | |

* Small values indicate similarity; large values indicate
dissimilarity.

between higher- and lower-status positions. The size of the over-all value, .47, indicates that most countries did see some differ-ence between these two sets of concepts, but this difference was smaller than that between directing and persuading, where the overall value for all managers was .72. Figure 6 shows graphically the similarity of values among the four clusters of countries and Japan.

The question arises as to why there was so little variation among the countries with regard to the semantic differences between high- and low-status positions. It is impossible to answer this question in any definitive way. However, there are some plausible explanations that involve the methodology employed on this particular part of the questionnaire. First, there is the fact

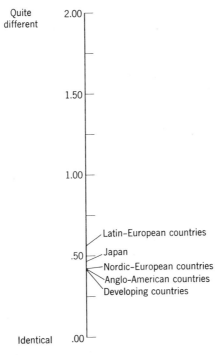

Figure 6. Similarity of higher-status posi-tions to lower-status positions: by clusters of countries.

that the values contained in Table 6 and represented in Figure 6 are based originally on raw data mean values for *composite* sets of high-status and low-status positions. In other words, since the raw score means for the two types of positions represent the average value for three specific concepts (e.g., for high positions, the concepts of *factory manager, colonel,* and *bishop*), there is the possibility of some small regression toward an overall mean value which would have the effect of reducing the difference between the two sets of concepts. However, such an effect, if any, was probably small. More important is a second aspect of the methodology. As the reader will remember, respondents were not asked to rate the meaning of "high-status positions" and "low-status positions" *per se.* They were asked, instead, to rate a number of specific positions in different types of institutions—three of the positions being relatively high ones and three being relatively low. It is entirely possible, even probable, that the major determinant of the subjects' responses to the specific concepts (e.g., *colonel*) was not the height of the position, but rather the type of institution (i.e., business, military, or church). Thus, for example, the responses to *colonel* and *sergeant* may have been similar primarily because the typical respondent was reacting in each case to a concept like *military man* rather than to *somebody in a high position* or *somebody in a low position.* In other words, the reaction to the type of institution may have overridden the reaction to status level, and resulted in a rather small perceived semantic difference. This, admittedly, is only speculation on our part, and such a possible reaction may or may not have been a major determinant of the results.

The differences between the higher- and lower-status positions on each of the five semantic dimensions are given in Table 7 and shown in the accompanying Figure 7. A glance at the bottom row of Table 7 will show for the total sample how the two sets of positions compared with each other on each dimension. From this bottom row it can be seen that higher-status positions were regarded as having more *prestige* and *scope* and as involving slightly more *activity* and *difficulty* than lower positions. There was no perceived difference between the two types of positions with regard to *firmness.*

The magnitudes of the values at the bottom of Table 7 for the

TABLE 7. DIFFERENCES BETWEEN HIGHER-STATUS POSITIONS AND
LOWER-STATUS POSITIONS ON FIVE SEMANTIC DIMENSIONS *

| | Prestige | Scope | Activity | Firmness | Difficulty | Number of Cases |
|---|---|---|---|---|---|---|
| Nordic-European Countries | | | | | | |
| Denmark | .30 | .12 | .27 | .03 | −.01 | 130 |
| Germany | .09 | .20 | .17 | .00 | .11 | 578 |
| Norway | .38 | .27 | .22 | .03 | .01 | 217 |
| Sweden | .22 | .13 | .37 | −.08 | .14 | 335 |
| Average | .25 | .18 | .26 | −.01 | .06 | |
| Latin-European Countries | | | | | | |
| Belgium | .24 | .32 | .05 | .03 | .34 | 374 |
| France | .22 | .48 | .11 | .00 | .03 | 153 |
| Italy | .51 | .11 | .08 | .03 | .14 | 265 |
| Spain | .84 | .31 | −.15 | .00 | .20 | 201 |
| Average | .45 | .31 | .02 | .02 | .18 | |
| Anglo-American Countries | | | | | | |
| England | .19 | .30 | −.06 | −.01 | .04 | 239 |
| United States | .24 | .39 | −.04 | −.12 | .11 | 459 |
| Average | .22 | .35 | −.05 | −.07 | .08 | |
| Developing Countries | | | | | | |
| Argentina | .16 | .22 | −.12 | −.09 | .25 | 198 |
| Chile | .39 | .31 | −.14 | .05 | .13 | 154 |
| India | .08 | .28 | .09 | .06 | −.14 | 111 |
| Average | .21 | .27 | −.06 | .01 | .08 | |
| Japan | .16 | .32 | .25 | −.05 | .14 | 156 |
| All Managers | .29 | .27 | .08 | −.01 | .11 | |

* Positive values indicate higher-status positions are higher on a dimension; negative values indicate lower-status positions are higher on the dimension.

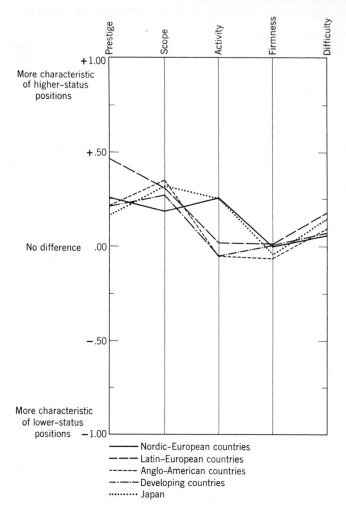

Figure 7. Differences between higher-status positions and lower-status positions on five semantic dimensions: by clusters of countries.

dimensions of *prestige, scope,* and *difficulty* are not great. However, what is impressive is the consistency of the direction of the findings from country to country for each of these three dimensions. Thus, for the first two columns in the table, those showing the values for *prestige* and *scope*, there was not a single national reversal of the overall trends; that is, in *all* fourteen countries, higher-status positions were thought of as possessing greater *prestige* and *scope*. Such consistency is well beyond chance levels of probability, and indicates that, psychologically speaking, positions that are relatively high in hierarchies have a different psychological connotation for managers, compared to positions that are relatively low. And, since the results are based on composite sets of positions, the findings indicate that the perceived difference is not confined to a particular type of institution. Likewise, for the last column in Table 7, which gives the data for the dimension of *difficulty*, the overall mean difference is quite small, 1.11; but 12 of the 14 values are in the same direction. Higher-status positions are thus seen rather consistently as being slightly more difficult than lower-status positions.

Figure 7 illustrates the variation among clusters of countries in the differences seen between the two types of positions on each of the five sematic dimensions. On three of the dimensions, the groups of countries have quite similar values. On the other two dimensions, those for *prestige* and *activity*, there is some degree of variation among the clusters. On the *prestige* dimension, the Latin-European countries perceive a somewhat sharper distinction between higher and lower positions than do the other groups of countries. However, as indicated in Table 7, this higher difference value for the Latin-European countries is due almost entirely to the Spanish managers. With regard to the *activity* dimension, all of the clusters have mean values indicating no difference between types of positions, with the exception of the Nordic-European countries and Japan. The reasons why these groups of countries differ from the others in their perceptions regarding the activity involved in higher versus lower positions is not immediately obvious.

Individual-country differences on the five semantic dimensions can be seen by looking back at Table 7. The table indicates how tightly bunched most of the individual countries are on the various dimensions. The greatest spreads, narrow ones at that, occurred on the *prestige* and *activity* dimensions. In only one instance, that of Spain on the *prestige* dimension, did an individual country really stand out from the other countries on any of

the five dimensions. The reader can appreciate the relative small-
ness of the variation among countries in Table 7 by comparing
this table with the comparable table for differences between *to
direct* and *to persuade* on the same five dimensions, Table 4.

As we have indicated earlier in this chapter, an excellent way
of learning more about the connotative meaning of concepts is to
determine their relative similarity to other concepts. Table 8 and
Figure 8 provide this type of information concerning higher-
versus lower-status positions. Each column in Table 8 indicates
which type of position is more similar to a given concept having
to do with some type of managerial action. The bottom row in
Table 8 shows these relative similarities across the total sample
of managers.

The picture we can draw from the values in Table 8 is quite
interesting. For seven of the eight columns in the table there is a
very high degree of consistency from country to country in the
direction of relative similarity of higher versus lower positions to
a given concept of managerial action. The first five concepts refer
to positive types of managerial action—deciding, creating, cooperating, persuading, and directing. Of the 70 values in these
columns (fourteen countries × five columns), 69 indicate that
managers regard these positive actions as being more clearly
associated semantically to higher- than to lower-status positions.
On the other hand, in the last two columns—representing two
negative actions, *to make a mistake* and *to cheat*—the situation is
exactly reversed. Out of 28 values (fourteen countries × two
columns), 24 are in the direction of *lower*-status positions being
more similar to these negative concepts. (The situation for the
column representing *to reprimand* does not give a consistent set
of values, although the tendency is for higher-status positions to
be regarded as more similar than lower positions to this concept.)
Thus, the picture that emerges is clear: Consistently, higher-
status positions are evaluated more positively than are lower-
status positions. This overall conclusion is hardly surprising, but
the consistency across nationalities and cultures (with one exception) is important to note and document.

The breakdown of our results by clusters of countries is illustrated in Figure 8. As can be seen here, most of the groups of
countries tend to have similar values on most of the dimensions.

TABLE 8. COMPARATIVE SIMILARITY OF VARIOUS CONCEPTS TO
HIGHER-STATUS POSITIONS AND LOWER-STATUS POSITIONS *

| | To De-cide | To Cre-ate | To Co-oper-ate | To Per-suade | To Di-rect | To Rep-ri-mand | To Make a Mis-take | To Cheat | Num-ber of Cases |
|---|---|---|---|---|---|---|---|---|---|
| **Nordic-European Countries** | | | | | | | | | |
| Denmark | .38 | .39 | .34 | .26 | .40 | −.01 | −.23 | .01 | 130 |
| Germany | .14 | .20 | .12 | .02 | .17 | .02 | −.05 | −.06 | 578 |
| Norway | .45 | .42 | .41 | .13 | .48 | −.09 | −.12 | −.31 | 217 |
| Sweden | .38 | .38 | .27 | .22 | .41 | .08 | −.19 | −.19 | 335 |
| Average | .34 | .35 | .29 | .16 | .37 | .00 | −.15 | −.14 | |
| **Latin-European Countries** | | | | | | | | | |
| Belgium | .30 | .38 | .29 | .35 | .38 | .16 | −.16 | −.17 | 374 |
| France | .41 | .36 | .49 | .38 | .53 | −.09 | −.03 | −.25 | 153 |
| Italy | .51 | .48 | .48 | .40 | .50 | .12 | −.05 | −.13 | 265 |
| Spain | .78 | .82 | .71 | .58 | .66 | .62 | −.02 | −.10 | 201 |
| Average | .50 | .51 | .49 | .43 | .52 | .20 | −.07 | −.16 | |
| **Anglo-American Countries** | | | | | | | | | |
| England | .24 | .29 | .04 | .26 | .28 | .01 | .10 | −.08 | 239 |
| United States | .25 | .41 | .27 | .38 | .34 | .25 | .20 | −.48 | 459 |
| Average | .25 | .35 | .16 | .32 | .31 | .13 | .15 | −.28 | |
| **Developing Countries** | | | | | | | | | |
| Argentina | .14 | .28 | .04 | .20 | .18 | .25 | −.04 | .09 | 198 |
| Chile | .46 | .46 | .36 | .44 | .46 | .21 | −.01 | −.26 | 154 |
| India | .28 | .12 | −.11 | .01 | .22 | −.18 | −.11 | −.03 | 111 |
| Average | .29 | .29 | .10 | .22 | .29 | .09 | −.05 | −.07 | |
| Japan | .34 | .34 | .31 | .36 | .14 | .10 | −.07 | −.46 | 156 |
| All Managers | .36 | .38 | .29 | .29 | .37 | .11 | −.06 | −.17 | |

* The higher the positive value, the more the comparison concept is similar to higher-status positions; the higher the negative value, the more the comparison concept is similar to lower-status positions.

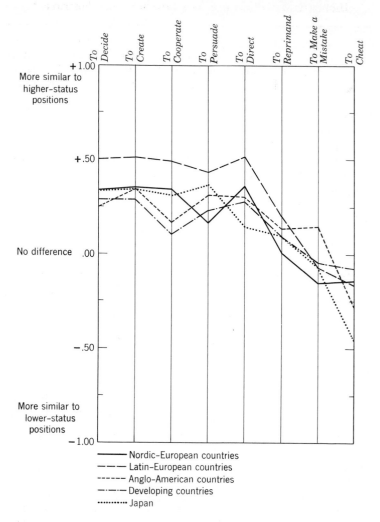

Figure 8. Comparative similarity of various concepts to higher-status positions and lower-status positions: by clusters of countries.

However, there are a few exceptions, the most notable being the relatively high value for the Latin-European countries on the first five concepts. This means that the Latin-European bloc tends to regard high-status positions as relatively more similar to the positive concepts of managerial actions (deciding, creating, etc.) than do other groups of countries. It must be pointed out, though, as can be seen in Table 8, that the relatively disparate value for the Latin-European group is due almost entirely to the Spanish section of that group. Other minor exceptions to the general similarity among groups of countries shown in Figure 8 are the relatively low values for the Anglo-American and Developing countries with regard to the similarity of the concept of high-status positions to the concept *to cooperate*, and the relatively high value for the two Anglo-American countries regarding the similarity of high-status positions to the concept *to make a mistake*. These exceptions appear to represent isolated deviations rather than any meaningful pattern of differences among the various groups of countries.

Finally, we can turn again to Table 8 to review the results for individual countries. The most visible finding here is the moderate but consistent deviation of Spanish managers on the first six concepts. It appears that, for Spain, hierarchical distinctions are much more prominent than they are for the other thirteen countries in our sample. Another interesting, though less obvious, fact to note in Table 8 is the *relatively* (though not absolutely) low position of Germany across the first five concepts. Germany is not very much lower than most of the other countries, but the fact that it is consistently low is surprising. Taken at their face value, the findings for Germany as shown in Table 8 would indicate that German managers see relatively small differences in the comparative similarity of high- and low-status positions to positive concepts of managerial action. This is surprising, inasmuch as the other results in our study—especially those reported in the first half of this chapter concerning differences in meaning between directing and persuading—pointed to a distinctly authoritarian orientation on the part of German managers. Because of these previous findings, it would be expected that German managers would have thought of high-status positions as clearly more associated in meaning with positive concepts, such as creating and directing, than low-status positions. But, as the table shows, this was not the case. However, the values for Germany were positive and were not very far below the average of all countries; therefore, probably not too much emphasis should be placed on Germany's relative position in this instance.

The great similarity in thinking (from nation to nation) for all of the countries on this part of the questionnaire can be better appreciated if the reader compares Table 8 with Table 5 (which showed the comparative similarity of directing and persuading to other concepts). Managerial distinctions among contrasting status positions seem to be much smaller than distinctions among contrasting types of leadership actions.

CHAPTER **4**

# Managerial Motivations
# and Satisfactions

Any job, be it that of an executive or that of the lowest-level clerk or blue-collar worker, requires something *from* the individual in the way of effort and the use of some capacities he possesses. At the same time, every job or position provides some degree of "return" *to* the individual in terms of some kind of need fulfillment. Thus, all jobs can be compared on either or both of these two kinds of variables: The input into the job and the outcome received from it. In this part of our study, we focused on the "outcome" from one's employment; that is, what the employee—in this case, the manager—gets from his job. With such information, we should have better insight into the impact of the job on the individual; and, with such insight, we should be able, ultimately, to make better utilization of managerial talent and abilities in any country or in any part of management.

Specifically, in this chapter, our results will deal with managers' perceptions of their need fulfillment, their satisfactions, and the importance they attach to different kinds of needs. We shall consider, for instance, such questions as whether managers in

**73**

Northern European countries see their jobs as more fulfilling than do managers in Southern European countries; and whether managers from "economically developed" countries, such as the United States and England, are more satisfied in their jobs than are managers from the Developing countries of India, Argentina, and Chile.

When we consider the various types of needs a person might attempt to satisfy through his job, we are faced with an almost infinite variety. Fortunately, the problem of classifying diverse kinds of needs into a reasonably small number of categories has been attacked by a number of psychologists. One of the most useful of such categorization schemes for the researcher interested in motivation in the work situation is the system proposed by A. H. Maslow.[5] Not only has Maslow presented a systematic classification of needs, he has also hypothesized a priority of ranking of the different types in terms of how essential they are to the individual. In our study, we adopted the Maslow classification system with some slight modifications, so that we ended up investigating five different types of needs. These needs, in the theoretical order of their priority or prepotency, were: Security, Social, Esteem, Autonomy, and Self-Actualization.

It is a surprising fact that only recently has factual evidence been obtained in this country concerning managerial perceptions of the amount of need fulfillment and need satisfaction that can be obtained from different types of managerial jobs.[6] When we turn to knowledge concerning the job satisfactions of managers in other countries, we find essentially no information at all. Therefore, one of the unique things about the present investigation was that it provided us with information where virtually none was available before. Obviously, our findings are not the final definitive answer to questions about managerial motivation throughout the world. They are, however, a first step in a direction that should prove to be an increasingly important area of research in the future.

[5] A. H. Maslow, *Motivation and Personality*, Harper and Row, New York, 1954.

[6] L. W. Porter, *Organizational Patterns of Managerial Job Attitudes*, American Foundation for Management Research, New York, 1964.

## The Major Findings

Our results point strongly to the relative salience of Self-Actualization and Autonomy needs for this international sample of managers. It appears obvious, from an organizational point of view, that business firms, no matter in what country, will have to be concerned with the satisfaction of these needs for their managers and executives. Both types of needs were regarded as relatively quite important by managers, but, at the present time at least, the degree to which they were fulfilled did not live up to their expectations. This gap between perceived actual fulfillment and expected fulfillment could of course be due either to unrealistic expectations on the part of managers, to actual inadequate fulfillment, or to a combination of both reasons. For managers in certain countries, at least, expectations did appear to be quite unrealistic, regarding the fulfillment of these needs to be provided from their jobs. It is unlikely, however, that unrealistic expectations were the whole answer in any country. It seems to be a tenable hypothesis that many business organizations in a number of countries are not doing as good a job of providing Autonomy and Self-Actualization satisfaction for managers as they should be, or at least not as good a job as they are doing in the areas of, say, Social and Esteem needs. The latter two types of needs, which were regarded by the managers as of relatively low importance, were also seen by them as relatively well satisfied. Organizations do not appear to have to pay additional attention to these kinds of needs, at least for their managers. (The situation for hourly rank-and-file workers, of course, may be substantially different from that for the managers in our sample.) It may be that, for managers, these needs, especially Social needs, are largely fulfilled off the job rather than at work.

The situation for Security needs was especially interesting. The 3,600 managers in our sample generally reported that the need for Security was relatively highly fulfilled, that the degree of fulfillment was in line with expectations (their satisfaction thus being high), and that they considered this an important need. The fact that Security needs seemed relatively well satisfied for managers may reflect the relatively good economic conditions existing in most of the countries at the time of our study. If a worsening of the world economic outlook were to cause many firms to retrench, it would be interesting to find out whether managers would still rate their fulfillment and satisfaction of Security needs as high as they did at the time our data were collected. In any event, it seems evident from the results for rated importance of needs that managers are concerned with Security, but, at the present time, they are finding this need adequately provided for by their various organizations in the different countries.

When we look at the overall differences among groups of countries with regard to motivations and satisfactions in the managerial job, we encounter fairly large variations in the patterns of motivational feelings. In certain countries, managers saw themselves as being very well off, so far as need fulfillment and satisfaction were concerned, whereas in other countries there was apparent dissatisfaction. The factors underlying these differences seem to be not only the degree of economic development of the country, but also the culture of the country in relation to business—one might say the "business climate." Thus, the United States and England are at least as well developed economically, or more so, than Denmark, Norway, and Sweden; yet the managers from the Scandinavian countries reported definitely higher need satisfaction. The explanation here would seem to involve cultural differences. Likewise, the fact that the four countries comprising the Latin-European group showed a great similarity in their responses to motivational questions, in spite of their differing degrees of economic development, would imply that culture had some influence. Nevertheless, it is also equally clear that culture cannot explain all the major differences in our results in this part of the study. It appears to be no accident that, in our sample, the least well-developed countries, economically speaking (Argentina, Chile, and India), were the countries with the least satisfied managers. Also, the fact of Indian managers responding very similarly to Argentinian and Chilean managers to most of the questions concerning need satisfaction and importance can hardly be ascribed to the similarity among cultures. The fact of India, Argentina, and Chile forming a clearly identifiable group of countries on this part of the questionnaire is probably best explained by their somewhat similar stage of economic development. It is at least a tenable hypothesis that where countries have not yet developed strong and flourishing economies, their firms and business organizations are, for the most part, not developed enough themselves to provide a high degree of managerial job satisfaction. This would seem to be especially true if one assumes that the reason why such things as modern techniques of leadership and managerial development are not as far advanced in these developing countries is because their firms cannot yet afford the "luxury" of devoting time and effort to activities they consider less essential than some of their other efforts more directly connected with the day-to-day affairs of running a business.

Having discussed some of the more important broad findings we obtained in the motivational area, we can now proceed to a more detailed review. To do so, the remainder of this chapter, following a short discussion of methodology, will be organized around the three major dependent attitude variables concerned with managerial motivation. First, we shall take up the question of *fulfillment*: How much of a need gratification does the manager feel he is actually receiving from his job? Second: How *satisfied* is the manager with this degree of fulfillment? Does it live up to his expectations, or does it fall short of what he thinks the job should supply in the way of need fulfillment? The third type of attitude to be discussed in this chapter concerns the degree of *importance* managers attach to each of the different types of needs. The chapter will conclude with a brief summary and an integration of the results concerning these three different aspects of managerial motivation.

## Methodology

To understand more fully the detailed data to be presented in the last part of this chapter, let us briefly outline the basic methodology used in this section of the questionnaire. As we mentioned earlier, we adopted Maslow's need-classification system —with a couple of minor modifications (no questions about biological needs, and a division of Maslow's Esteem category into Esteem and Autonomy). The five needs we investigated are listed below (in their theoretical order of priority); under each of the five headings, the specific questionnaire items used to measure these needs are listed also. These specific items total 11, and were arranged randomly in the questionnaire rather than in a theoretical order. The need categories and their specific items are as follows:

*Security*

- The feeling of security in my management position.

*Social*

- The opportunity, in my management position, to give help to other people.
- The opportunity to develop close friendships in my management position.

*Esteem*

- The feeling of self-esteem a person gets from being in my management position.
- The prestige of my management position inside the company (that is, the regard received from others in the company).
- The prestige of my management position outside the company (that is, the regard from others not in the company).

*Autonomy*

- The authority connected with my management position.
- The opportunity for independent thought and action in my management position.

*Self-Actualization*

- The opportunity for personal growth and development in my management position.
- The feeling of self-fulfillment a person gets from being in my management position (that is, the feeling of being able to use one's own unique capabilities, realizing one's own potentialities).
- The feeling of worthwhile accomplishment in my management position.

For each of these 11 items, the manager was asked the following questions and was to indicate his response on 7-point rating scales:

(a) How much of the characteristic *is there now* connected with your management position?

(b) How much of the characteristic do you think *should be* connected with your management position?

(c) How *important* is this position characteristic to you?

A check of 1 on a given rating scale meant there was a minimum amount, and a check of 7 meant there was a maximum amount (as perceived by the respondent).

To measure fulfillment, we used the response to question (a) for each of the 11 items.

To measure satisfaction, we used the response to question (b), minus the response to question (a), for each of the 11 items. In other words, our operational definition of need satisfaction was the difference between degree of expectation and degree of fulfillment with respect to a given need or aspect of a need.

To measure importance, we used the response to question (c) for each of the 11 items.

All of our results in the following sections of this chapter, and in the next chapter, will be presented in terms of the five categories of needs (Security, Social, etc.) rather than in terms of the 11 specific items used to measure the categories. Scores for an individual respondent for each category were obtained by averaging his responses to all of the items in a given category. Thus, for example, for the Esteem-need category, the responses to the 3 items in that category were summed and divided by three to obtain an individual's score for Esteem. In this way, scores from one need category could be compared directly to those from another category despite the fact that different numbers of items were used to measure the various categories.

In the pages to follow, the graphs and tables will be concerned with the mean scores for each country and each group of countries on each of the five categories of needs.

### Need Fulfillment

As we pointed out above, in measuring the degree of need fulfillment, we are asking the question: How much are you getting from your job? To emphasize what we have mentioned previously, fulfillment should not be confused with satisfaction, for satisfaction refers to the degree to which fulfillment meets expectation.

## Need Fulfillment of Managers in General

Table 9 and Figure 9 present the results for the individual groups of countries and for individual countries in terms of the mean *raw* scores for each of the five categories of needs. The first things to focus on at this point are the comparisons among the five different needs across all of the countries. The most obvious fact concerning this type of comparison is that there is a rather small difference in the degree of fulfillment from one need to the next. That is, managers in general regard their jobs as providing about the same degree of Self-Actualization needs as, for example, Esteem or Autonomy needs. The only two types of needs to deviate somewhat from this pattern of equal fulfillment are Security and Social needs. The most basic need (of the five studied in this investigation), Security, is seen as relatively more highly fulfilled compared to higher-order or less basic needs, while the next most basic type of need, Social, is seen as less well fulfilled than the higher-order needs. It appears, then, that if we combine results across countries (see the bottom row of figures in Table 9), there does not appear to be any direct relationship between the position of a need in the hierarchical system indicated by theory and its position in a ranking of the needs by degree of fulfillment.

One other point should be made concerning fulfillment of the various needs across all countries—that managers in general responded to the questionnaire by checking a relatively high degree of fulfillment. As can be seen from Table 9, all mean responses for all countries for each type of need are above 4.0, which is the midpoint of the rating scale. How much this pattern is due to a response-set to check the high end of rating scales and how much is due to a genuine high level of fulfillment is difficult to determine, of course, from our data.

## Variation Among Countries in Need Fulfillment

We can next turn our attention to the differences that exist among countries or groups of countries across all five needs. In other words, do managers from some countries report consistently

TABLE 9. NEED FULFILLMENT (RAW SCORES) *

| | Security | Social | Esteem | Autonomy | Self-Actualization | Number of Cases |
|---|---|---|---|---|---|---|
| **Nordic-European Countries** | | | | | | |
| Denmark | 5.51 | 4.56 | 4.87 | 5.45 | 5.43 | 149 |
| Germany | 5.48 | 4.27 | 5.23 | 5.32 | 5.22 | 586 |
| Norway | 5.53 | 4.79 | 5.17 | 5.44 | 5.29 | 221 |
| Sweden | 5.57 | 5.06 | 5.33 | 5.61 | 5.39 | 342 |
| Average | 5.52 | 4.67 | 5.15 | 5.45 | 5.33 | |
| **Latin-European Countries** | | | | | | |
| Belgium | 5.23 | 4.58 | 5.05 | 5.07 | 5.04 | 378 |
| France | 4.99 | 4.40 | 4.89 | 4.90 | 4.95 | 154 |
| Italy | 5.16 | 4.31 | 4.94 | 4.52 | 4.41 | 267 |
| Spain | 5.18 | 4.70 | 5.17 | 4.89 | 4.82 | 203 |
| Average | 5.14 | 4.49 | 5.01 | 4.84 | 4.80 | |
| **Anglo-American Countries** | | | | | | |
| England | 5.53 | 4.92 | 4.85 | 5.01 | 4.97 | 239 |
| United States | 5.25 | 5.11 | 4.81 | 4.80 | 4.96 | 464 |
| Average | 5.39 | 5.01 | 4.83 | 4.90 | 4.96 | |
| **Developing Countries** | | | | | | |
| Argentina | 5.50 | 5.08 | 5.43 | 4.95 | 5.07 | 198 |
| Chile | 5.28 | 4.83 | 5.22 | 4.81 | 5.06 | 159 |
| India | 5.67 | 4.50 | 4.72 | 4.46 | 4.67 | 114 |
| Average | 5.48 | 4.80 | 5.12 | 4.74 | 4.93 | |
| Japan | 5.50 | 5.10 | 5.17 | 5.26 | 5.54 | 165 |
| All Managers | 5.38 | 4.72 | 5.06 | 5.03 | 5.05 | |

* Higher values indicate greater need fulfillment.

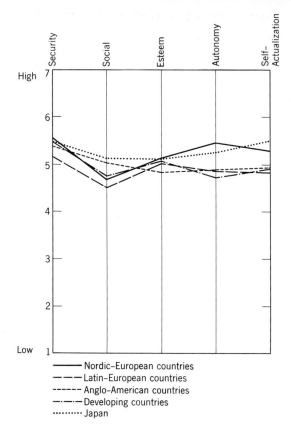

Figure 9. Need fulfillment: by clusters of countries (raw scores).

more need fulfillment than managers from other countries, regardless of the type of need being considered? To answer this question we can refer again to Table 9 and Figure 9 (for raw scores) and Table 10 and Figure 10 (for standard scores).

Let us first examine the differences among the groups of countries. Figures 9 and 10 show that there is no single cluster that is above all other clusters on all five of the types of needs. It would appear from Figure 9 that Japanese managers report the highest average level of fulfillment, if we average the results across the five needs. Even so, they are not the highest group in two of the

## Table 10. Need Fulfillment (Standard Scores) *

| | Security | Social | Esteem | Autonomy | Self-Actualization | Number of Cases |
|---|---|---|---|---|---|---|
| **Nordic-European Countries** | | | | | | |
| Denmark | .09 | −.14 | −.20 | .35 | .34 | 149 |
| Germany | .07 | −.37 | .18 | .24 | .15 | 586 |
| Norway | .11 | .05 | .11 | .35 | .21 | 221 |
| Sweden | .14 | .26 | .28 | .49 | .30 | 342 |
| Average | .10 | −.05 | .09 | .36 | .25 | |
| **Latin-European Countries** | | | | | | |
| Belgium | −.11 | −.12 | −.01 | .03 | −.02 | 378 |
| France | −.29 | −.26 | −.18 | −.12 | −.10 | 154 |
| Italy | −.16 | −.33 | −.12 | −.44 | −.59 | 267 |
| Spain | −.15 | −.02 | .11 | −.12 | −.22 | 203 |
| Average | −.18 | −.18 | −.05 | −.16 | −.23 | |
| **Anglo-American Countries** | | | | | | |
| England | .11 | .15 | −.22 | −.02 | −.08 | 239 |
| United States | −.11 | .30 | −.26 | −.26 | −.09 | 464 |
| Average | .00 | .23 | −.24 | −.14 | −.09 | |
| **Developing Countries** | | | | | | |
| Argentina | .08 | .28 | .38 | −.07 | .01 | 198 |
| Chile | −.08 | .09 | .17 | −.19 | .00 | 159 |
| India | .21 | −.18 | −.35 | −.49 | −.35 | 114 |
| Average | .07 | .06 | .07 | −.25 | −.11 | |
| Japan | .08 | .29 | .11 | .19 | .44 | 165 |
| All Managers | .00 | .00 | .00 | .00 | .00 | |

* Positive values indicate greater fulfillment of the need than for the average manager; negative values indicate lesser fulfillment.

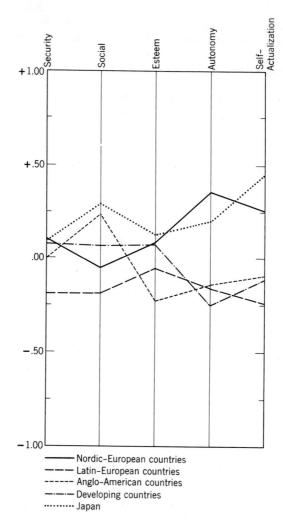

Figure 10. Need fulfillment: by clusters of countries (standard scores). *Note:* Positive values indicate greater fulfillment of a need than for the average manager; negative values indicate less fulfillment.

categories, Security needs and Autonomy needs. The other cluster that reports a fairly consistent pattern of high fulfillment is the Nordic-European group. This group, however, is not particularly high in the area of Social needs. The cluster with the lowest degree of fulfillment across all needs appears definitely to be the Latin-European cluster of Belgium, France, Italy, and Spain. They, as a group, report the lowest or next-to-lowest degree of fulfillment in each of the five need areas. Paradoxically, England and the United States, the most highly-developed countries, in terms of managerial training, have a cluster pattern that is fairly similar to that for the cluster of the least-developed countries, Argentina, India, and Chile. Both groups of countries, as can be seen especially in Figure 10, which reports the standard scores, are relatively high on the basic Security and Social needs, and relatively low on the two highest-order needs of Autonomy and Self-Actualization.

All in all, in terms of raw scores, the clusters of countries do not differ greatly in their degree of reported fulfillment of needs across all five needs. In terms of standard scores, however, there are some relative differences in their patterns, as we have noted.

We can now proceed to look at the differences among the individual countries. Looking at Table 9 for the data in raw score terms, and Table 10 for the data in standard scores, we see that Swedish managers report the most consistently high degree of need fulfillment among all fourteen countries studied. Norway and Japan are the only other countries, in addition to Sweden, which have positive standard score means in all five need areas. Other countries are high in particular need areas, but not in *all* areas as are the Swedes. For example, Argentinian managers are relatively high on Social and Esteem need fulfillments, but near the average in the other three need areas. On the other hand, Danish managers are relatively high in fulfillment of Autonomy and Self-Actualization needs, but considerably below average in Social and Esteem need fulfillments.

India and the United States show interesting patterns of fulfillment, because, as Table 10 indicates, each is among the very highest in certain need areas and among the very lowest in other areas. This pattern is especially noticeable for Indian managers. They report the highest degree of fulfillment of Security needs, compared to managers from any other country; the lowest degree of fulfillment of Esteem and Autonomy needs; and the second-lowest fulfillment of Self-Actualization needs, in comparison with managers from all of the other countries. The fact that the Indian managers can be so high on Security need fulfillment and, at the same time, so low on Esteem, Autonomy, and Self-Actualization need fulfillments is strong evidence that this part of the questionnaire was not evoking a simple response bias for a given group of managers to rate all items high or all items low.

### Need-by-Need Analysis

For a final look at need fulfillment, we can make a need-by-need analysis of the results. That is, we will focus on each need individually so as to determine the differences among clusters of countries and individual countries with respect to fulfillment of a particular need.

Starting with the most basic need of Security, we can see from Figure 10 for standard scores that all of the clusters of countries bunch around a standard score of .00, with the exception of the Latin-European group which has a small negative score. If we turn from the data for the clusters of countries to the data for individual countries, we see that, as noted above, managers from India report the greatest degree of fulfillment of Security needs, with the Swedish managers in second place. The lowest countries on fulfillment of this need are France, Italy, and Spain.

For Social needs, there is a somewhat greater spread among countries than was the case for Security needs, but it is still a relatively small spread. Japan and the two English-speaking countries are the groups with the highest degree of fulfillment of Social needs, and the Latin-European countries are again the lowest group, as they were for Security needs. In terms of individual countries, the United States, Japan, Sweden, and Argentina are relatively high, and Germany and Italy are relatively low.

In the Esteem need area, variation among clusters of countries is relatively slight, with no cluster being clearly higher than the others, and only the English-speaking group being relatively low. The highest individual countries on this need are Argentina and Sweden, and the lowest are India, the United States, England, and Denmark. Clearly, from these results, degree of economic development does not seem to be related to the amount of fulfillment of Esteem needs managers see themselves obtaining from their jobs. A somewhat wider dispersion among groups of countries can be seen with respect to Autonomy needs. The Scandinavian-German cluster reports the greatest degree of fulfillment of Autonomy needs, while both the Anglo-American and the Developing-country groups are lowest in this need area. All three of the Scandinavian countries report relatively quite high fulfillment of Autonomy needs. The individual countries with the lowest scores in this need area are India and Italy, especially the former.

Variation among clusters of countries on need fulfillment is greatest for Self-Actualization needs, as can be seen from Figure 10. The results here are quite similar to those for Autonomy needs. Japan and the Nordic-European countries are the groups with the greatest degree of fulfillment, and they are clearly separated (in standard score terms) from the other three clusters. Individually, Japanese managers indicate the highest level of fulfillment of Self-Actualization needs, followed, in order, by Denmark and Sweden. The lowest countries, again, as was the case for Autonomy needs, are Italy and India.

## Need Satisfaction

Although findings with respect to need fulfillment are interesting, the dependent attitude variable of need satisfaction would appear to be the most crucial of our three measures, in terms of its motivational implications. Since we have operationally defined the term "need satisfaction" as the difference between the perceived fulfillment and the perceived expectation of fulfillment, the results for need satisfactions are obviously not completely independent of those for fulfillment. Nevertheless, such results would seem to be more important for understanding managerial behavior because they are theoretically more likely to determine an individual's behavior. It is not how much of something we get that influences our behavior as much as it is what we think about what we get. For example, if one considers two individuals earning quite different salaries—say, $10,000 and $20,000—it is not at all certain that the higher-paid individual will look more favorably on his salary than the lower-paid individual will look on his. If the $10,000-man thinks that is about what he should be getting, he is more likely to be intrinsically satisfied with his salary and with that aspect of his job than the $20,000-man who feels he should be getting $40,000. Because of this dissatisfaction, the higher-paid individual is much more likely, presumably, to leave his present organization or job than is the $10,000-man. If this chain of reasoning is correct, the most important of all of our results in this part of the study will be the findings to be presented below concerning perceived need satisfaction.

### Need Satisfaction of Managers in General

As we did in discussing need fulfillment, we will first consider differences among the five types of needs in terms of how well satisfied they are across all fourteen countries. Table 11 and Figure 11 present the relevant raw score data for clusters of countries and for individual countries. One clear fact emerges if we look at the bottom row of Table 11 where the degree of dissatisfaction is averaged for each need across the fourteen countries: The three lower-order needs of Security, Social, and Esteem are seen as being better satisfied (less dissatisfied) than are the two higher-order needs of Autonomy and Self-Actualization. This fact indicates, therefore, that there is some relationship between the position of a need in the theoretical hierarchy and the degree to which it is seen as being satisfied in the job. In general, the more basic the need, the better it is satisfied in the management job, as the theory might predict. The relationship is clearly not perfect though, since Esteem, the middle need in the theoretical hierarchy, is seen as being better satisfied than the two lower-order needs, Security and Social. Esteem is, however, the only need that is out of line, in terms of the hypothesized hierarchy.

Overall, we can ask whether managers, regardless of their country of origin or the type of need being considered, are satisfied, in an absolute sense, with their jobs. In other words, should a measured dissatisfaction level between, say, .2 and 1.6 (in raw score terms by individual country) be considered a high or low amount of dissatisfaction? It is, of course, impossible to provide a definite answer to this question. If we consider that the maximum possible level of dissatisfaction on the scale we used was

TABLE 11. NEED SATISFACTION (RAW SCORES)*

| | Security | Social | Esteem | Auton-omy | Self-Actuali-zation | Number of Cases |
|---|---|---|---|---|---|---|
| Nordic-European Countries | | | | | | |
| Denmark | .60 | .54 | .32 | .58 | .75 | 149 |
| Germany | .77 | .52 | .62 | .86 | 1.02 | 586 |
| Norway | .57 | .41 | .32 | .40 | .87 | 221 |
| Sweden | .33 | .40 | .20 | .48 | .79 | 342 |
| Average | .57 | .47 | .36 | .58 | .86 | |
| Latin-European Countries | | | | | | |
| Belgium | .80 | .84 | .45 | .79 | 1.15 | 378 |
| France | .64 | .98 | .63 | 1.06 | 1.34 | 154 |
| Italy | .79 | .83 | .84 | 1.12 | 1.46 | 267 |
| Spain | 1.08 | 1.26 | .85 | 1.19 | 1.40 | 203 |
| Average | .83 | .98 | .69 | 1.04 | 1.34 | |
| Anglo-American Countries | | | | | | |
| England | .29 | .37 | .42 | .69 | 1.14 | 239 |
| United States | .29 | .38 | .60 | .93 | 1.20 | 464 |
| Average | .29 | .38 | .51 | .81 | 1.17 | |
| Developing Countries | | | | | | |
| Argentina | 1.15 | 1.18 | .89 | 1.34 | 1.51 | 198 |
| Chile | 1.10 | 1.14 | .81 | 1.13 | 1.25 | 159 |
| India | .72 | 1.19 | 1.12 | 1.52 | 1.58 | 114 |
| Average | .99 | 1.17 | .94 | 1.33 | 1.44 | |
| Japan | .52 | .59 | .56 | .55 | .58 | 165 |
| All Managers | .69 | .76 | .62 | .90 | 1.14 | |

* Higher values indicate greater *dis*satisfaction.

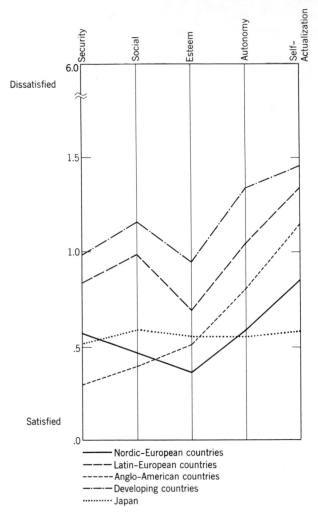

Figure 11. Need satisfaction: by clusters of countries (raw scores).

6.0, we might be inclined to say that managers are not very dissatisfied. However, if we look at the question from a different point of view—namely, that we are considering (for the most part) middle-level managers who *should* have quite satisfying jobs—the results indicate that managers feel there is definite room for improvement in their satisfaction. Thus, although absolute levels of dissatisfaction could have been much larger, they were still perceptibly higher than 0. Individuals are, of course, never perfectly satisfied with their jobs, but the data show that in managerial jobs some needs are relatively less satisfied than others. This would seem to hold especially true for the areas of Autonomy and Self-Actualization needs.

### Variation Among Countries in Need Satisfaction

Let us see what the differences were among the various clusters of countries in terms of overall levels of need satisfaction. As is so vividly shown in Figures 11 and 12, which give the raw and standard score results for the groups of countries, the Developing countries of Argentina, Chile, and India, and the Latin-European countries of Belgium, France, Spain, and Italy, are the two most dissatisfied groups of countries in each of the five need areas. This finding is especially interesting if these results for satisfaction are compared with those for fulfillment. (Compare Figure 11 to Figure 9 for raw scores, and Figure 12 to Figure 10 for standard scores.) Although generally on the low side in terms of fulfillment, neither of these two groups, especially the Developing countries, was lowest in fulfillment on all needs or even particularly below other countries on any given need. Thus, we can see that the Developing countries, and the Southern European countries, to some extent, have managers who are reasonably well fulfilled in their needs but who are not very satisfied with their degree of fulfillment. In other words, the *expectations* of managers in these two groups of countries, especially the Developing countries, are probably "unrealistically" high in the sense that they deviate more from a reasonable degree of obtained fulfillment than do the expectations of managers from the more developed countries, such as the United States and England. Certainly, this is a finding that has potentially some very interesting implications, and is, therefore, a finding that will receive additional attention later in this chapter.

There appears to be no one group of countries that is clearly more satisfied than all other groups on all types of needs. On some needs Japan is the most satisfied "cluster"; on other needs

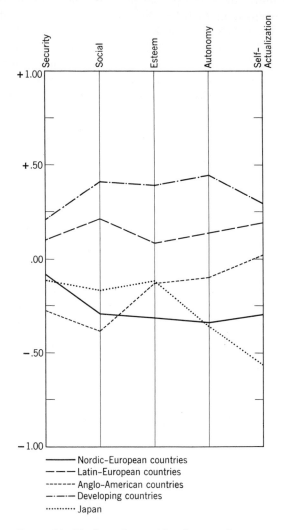

Figure 12. Need satisfaction: by clusters of countries (standard scores). *Note:* Positive values indicate greater *dis*satisfaction of a need than for the average manager; negative values indicate less *dis*satisfaction.

the England–United States duo is most satisfied; and on yet another category of needs the bloc of Northern European countries has the highest level of satisfaction.

One other feature of Figure 11 is especially worthy of note, and that is the comparisons of raw score profiles of dissatisfaction of the five clusters of countries across the five types of needs. Whereas the profiles for groups of countries were quite similar in terms of raw scores on need fulfillment (refer back to Figure 9), there are definite dissimilarities of profiles, in terms of need satisfaction raw scores. The profiles for the Developing countries and the Latin-European countries are the only two profiles that are similar to each other. The lines for these two clusters in Figure 11 start off (at the left, for the most basic needs) moderately low for Security need dissatisfaction, then decrease as they move to Esteem dissatisfaction, and later show relatively large increases in dissatisfaction from Esteem to Autonomy needs and large increases again from Autonomy to Self-Actualization needs. As can be seen, the Nordic-European group deviates from this pattern, in that the expressed dissatisfaction with Security needs exceeds that for Social needs. The English-American pattern also deviates, in that Esteem need dissatisfaction is greater in this group than is Social need dissatisfaction. Of particular interest is the fact that the pattern for the English-speaking group is in direct relationship to the theoretical ordering of needs in terms of their prepotency. That is, managers from England and America are most satisfied in the most basic needs, Security; then, most satisfied in the next most basic needs, Social needs; and so on, up to the least basic need of Self-Actualization which produces the least degree of satisfaction for them. Finally, the profile for Japan is completely different from that of any of the other four groups. The line for Japan is nearly a straight horizontal line, indicating that Japanese managers are about equally satisfied or dissatisfied in one need area as in another.

Individual country differences in satisfaction can be most easily seen in Table 12, which provides standard score means by countries. As is indicated by the high plus values (high degree of dissatisfaction) in Table 12, India, Argentina, Spain, Chile, and Italy are the countries which have the most dissatisfied managers. These are the five countries in Table 12 that have positive

TABLE 12. NEED SATISFACTION (STANDARD SCORES) *

| | Security | Social | Esteem | Autonomy | Self-Actualization | Number of Cases |
|---|---|---|---|---|---|---|
| **Nordic-European Countries** | | | | | | |
| Denmark | −.06 | −.22 | −.36 | −.33 | −.40 | 149 |
| Germany | .06 | −.24 | .00 | −.05 | −.13 | 586 |
| Norway | −.08 | −.34 | −.36 | −.52 | −.28 | 221 |
| Sweden | −.26 | −.36 | −.51 | −.43 | −.36 | 342 |
| Average | −.09 | −.29 | −.31 | −.33 | −.29 | |
| **Latin-European Countries** | | | | | | |
| Belgium | .08 | .08 | −.20 | −.11 | .00 | 378 |
| France | −.04 | .22 | .02 | .16 | .19 | 154 |
| Italy | .07 | .07 | .27 | .22 | .31 | 267 |
| Spain | .28 | .50 | .28 | .30 | .25 | 203 |
| Average | .10 | .22 | .09 | .14 | .19 | |
| **Anglo-American Countries** | | | | | | |
| England | −.28 | −.39 | −.24 | −.22 | −.01 | 239 |
| United States | −.28 | −.38 | −.02 | .03 | .05 | 464 |
| Average | −.28 | −.39 | −.13 | −.10 | .02 | |
| **Developing Countries** | | | | | | |
| Argentina | .33 | .42 | .33 | .45 | .36 | 198 |
| Chile | .29 | .38 | .24 | .23 | .10 | 159 |
| India | .02 | .43 | .61 | .63 | .43 | 114 |
| Average | .21 | .41 | .39 | .44 | .30 | |
| Japan | −.12 | −.17 | −.07 | −.36 | −.56 | 165 |
| All Managers | .00 | .00 | .00 | .00 | .00 | |

* Positive values indicate greater *dis*satisfaction than the average manager; negative values indicate less *dis*satisfaction.

standard scores (i.e., scores above the mean raw score dissatisfaction for all countries combined) in all five need areas. (France, also, almost makes it into that category of countries.) Indian managers are, relatively speaking, the most dissatisfied managers of any country, for three of the five needs; and the second most dissatisfied, for a fourth need. Only in the area of Security needs are Indian managers not dissatisfied. Argentinian, Spanish, and Chilean managers, in that order, are also very consistent in terms of a relatively high degree of dissatisfaction.

Looking at the other side of the coin, we see that the most satisfied managers in individual countries are the Swedish managers who rank among the three most satisfied national groups of managers in every need area. Other countries showing consistently high managerial job satisfaction across the various needs are the other two Scandinavian countries (Norway and Denmark), and Japan and England. United States managers are relatively well satisfied in the two basic need areas of Security and Social needs, but are about average among the various countries on each of the other three needs. Belgium and Germany tend to be near the mean of all countries on most of the needs, indicating that managers in these two countries are neither particularly satisfied nor dissatisfied.

### Need-by-Need Analysis

A need-by-need analysis of the satisfaction data shows the following (see Table 12 for the standard score results): The need for Security is seen as being best satisfied in England, the United States, and Sweden. This need is apparently least satisfied in the two South American countries (Argentina and Chile), and in Spain. In the area of satisfaction of Social needs, as in Security need satisfaction, the same three countries head the list; namely, England, the United States, and Sweden—plus, this time, Norway. The dissatisfied countries in this need area are again those most dissatisfied with Security need fulfillment; namely, Argentina, Chile, and Spain. Also high on dissatisfaction with Social need fulfillment is India.

For Esteem needs, the list of most satisfied countries is altered slightly, with Sweden, Norway, and Denmark leading this time. The fact that the three nations highest in Esteem need satisfaction are the Scandinavian countries may indicate something about the relative importance of business activities in this particular culture. The dissatisfied countries in the Esteem need area include Argentina, Chile, India (again), and Italy. Indian managers are especially dissatisfied in this need area. In fact, their dissatisfaction, expressed in standard scores, is more than one whole standard score away from the most satisfied country, Sweden.

In the Autonomy need area, Sweden and Norway continue to be the most satisfied countries, and Argentina and India the most dissatisfied. Finally, for Self-Actualization needs the picture changes somewhat, with Japanese managers expressing the greatest degree of satisfaction, followed, in order, by Denmark and Sweden. In this area, India and Argentina, along with Italy, again head the list of dissatisfied countries. Note that in these last three need areas—the areas of Esteem, Autonomy, and Self-Actualization satisfactions—United States managers were very close to the mean for all managers in the entire sample of 3,600 managers.

### Variation Within Countries

The last set of data on satisfaction that we should examine are the data concerning the standard deviations of managers within each country for each type of need (see Table 13 for individual country values, and Figure 13 for values by cluster of countries). First, comparing one need with another, it is apparent that the need producing the greatest dispersion in satisfaction among managers is Security. This high degree of variation may be due to the fact that only one item in the questionnaire was used to measure this need; however, since there does not seem to be any correlation of degree of dispersion and number of questionnaire items for the other four needs, this may not be an important consideration. In any event, for each country, there was a greater variation among managers within the country on Security need satisfaction than for any of the other four needs. The need producing the least dispersion was Esteem. The other three types of needs—Social, Autonomy, and Self-Actualization—were quite similar to each other in showing less dispersion than for Security needs, but more dispersion than for Esteem needs.

We can see from Figure 13 that managers in Japan and in the

TABLE 13. NEED SATISFACTION: STANDARD DEVIATIONS

| | Security | Social | Esteem | Auton- omy | Self- Actuali- zation | Number of Cases |
|---|---|---|---|---|---|---|
| **Nordic-European Countries** | | | | | | |
| Denmark | 1.40 | .86 | .73 | .75 | .75 | 149 |
| Germany | 1.27 | 1.09 | .76 | .97 | 1.02 | 586 |
| Norway | 1.28 | .71 | .64 | .69 | .81 | 221 |
| Sweden | 1.24 | .77 | .65 | .70 | .75 | 342 |
| Average | 1.29 | .86 | .70 | .78 | .83 | |
| **Latin-European Countries** | | | | | | |
| Belgium | 1.32 | 1.08 | .75 | .91 | 1.02 | 378 |
| France | 1.62 | .96 | .77 | .97 | .90 | 154 |
| Italy | 1.41 | .98 | .82 | 1.06 | 1.18 | 267 |
| Spain | 1.58 | 1.05 | .91 | 1.15 | .97 | 203 |
| Average | 1.48 | 1.02 | .81 | 1.02 | 1.02 | |
| **Anglo-American Countries** | | | | | | |
| England | 1.47 | .80 | .71 | .87 | .99 | 239 |
| United States | 1.49 | .80 | .80 | 1.04 | 1.09 | 464 |
| Average | 1.48 | .80 | .76 | .96 | 1.04 | |
| **Developing Countries** | | | | | | |
| Argentina | 1.41 | 1.06 | .80 | 1.14 | 1.01 | 198 |
| Chile | 1.37 | 1.06 | .89 | 1.09 | 1.02 | 159 |
| India | 1.22 | 1.12 | .87 | 1.06 | .98 | 114 |
| Average | 1.33 | 1.08 | .85 | 1.10 | 1.00 | |
| Japan | 1.11 | .83 | .76 | .80 | .79 | 165 |
| All Managers | 1.37 | .94 | .77 | .94 | .94 | |

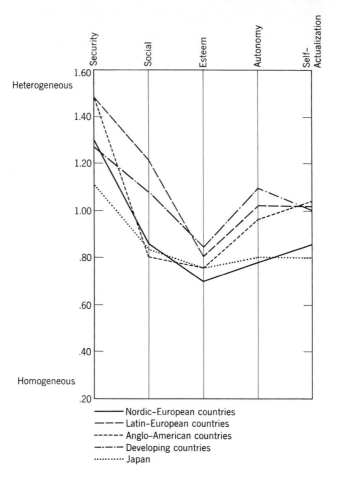

Figure 13. Need satisfaction: by clusters of countries (standard deviations).

Nordic-European bloc of countries were the most homogeneous groups of managers, while the Latin-European nations and the Developing countries were the most heterogeneous. These facts concerning relative degrees of dispersion of satisfaction scores among managers within particular groups of countries may reflect, in a larger cultural sense, the degree of homogeneity of individuals in particualr countries. Certainly, one would expect, on a purely cultural basis, that countries such as Sweden and Denmark would have greater homogeneity among individuals than would countries such as Belgium and France. It will be interesting to examine the dispersion data in our next section dealing with the importance of needs, because answers concerning need importance are more likely to reflect differences among individuals' values than are satisfaction data that concern descriptions of the job—that is, descriptions of the environment.

## Need Importance

Up to this point, we have looked at the questions of how fulfilled various needs are from country to country, and how satisfied managers in different countries are with the degree of fulfillment they think they are getting from their jobs. In this section, we will take up the question of *how important* are the different needs to managers in the different countries.

### The Importance of Various Needs for Managers in General

To begin with, we might examine the last line of Table 14 which gives the raw score means for all countries combined. This row of figures in Table 14 provides us with an opportunity to compare one need with another in terms of its importance to the total sample of managers. Here, it is evident that the five types of needs are *not* seen as of equal importance. Clearly, the most important of the needs studied was the need for Self-Actualization. Somewhat lower in importance were, in order, Autonomy and Security needs. If the reader now turns back to the last row in Table 11, which gives the mean satisfaction of the five types of needs across all countries, he will see that there is a fairly close relationship between the importance of a need and the degree to which it is *dis*satisfied. For both sets of data, Self-Actualization heads the list: Self-Actualization needs are seen as the most important and the least satisfied type of needs. Autonomy needs are seen as the second most important needs (just above Security needs) and, clearly, the second least satisfied needs. The third need in importance, Security, is fourth among the five needs in terms of degree of dissatisfaction. On the other hand, Social

TABLE 14. NEED IMPORTANCE (RAW SCORES) *

|  | Security | Social | Esteem | Autonomy | Self-Actualization | Number of Cases |
|---|---|---|---|---|---|---|
| Nordic-European Countries |  |  |  |  |  |  |
| Denmark | 5.53 | 4.96 | 4.50 | 5.65 | 6.00 | 149 |
| Germany | 6.04 | 4.66 | 5.28 | 5.96 | 6.19 | 586 |
| Norway | 4.80 | 4.93 | 4.76 | 5.54 | 6.05 | 221 |
| Sweden | 5.52 | 5.19 | 4.89 | 5.96 | 6.10 | 342 |
| Average | 5.47 | 4.93 | 4.85 | 5.77 | 6.08 |  |
| Latin-European Countries |  |  |  |  |  |  |
| Belgium | 5.70 | 5.32 | 4.95 | 5.87 | 6.24 | 378 |
| France | 5.22 | 5.08 | 4.83 | 5.83 | 6.35 | 154 |
| Italy | 5.68 | 5.18 | 5.73 | 5.72 | 6.17 | 267 |
| Spain | 6.07 | 5.86 | 5.58 | 5.86 | 6.13 | 203 |
| Average | 5.66 | 5.36 | 5.27 | 5.82 | 6.22 |  |
| Anglo-American Countries |  |  |  |  |  |  |
| England | 5.56 | 5.08 | 4.89 | 5.88 | 6.23 | 239 |
| United States | 5.30 | 5.37 | 5.09 | 5.80 | 6.30 | 464 |
| Average | 5.43 | 5.22 | 4.99 | 5.84 | 6.26 |  |
| Developing Countries |  |  |  |  |  |  |
| Argentina | 6.49 | 6.18 | 6.15 | 6.36 | 6.59 | 198 |
| Chile | 6.31 | 5.94 | 5.97 | 6.10 | 6.48 | 159 |
| India | 6.42 | 5.66 | 5.82 | 6.16 | 6.37 | 114 |
| Average | 6.40 | 5.92 | 5.98 | 6.20 | 6.48 |  |
| Japan | 5.81 | 5.83 | 5.23 | 5.99 | 6.30 | 165 |
| All Managers | 5.74 | 5.37 | 5.26 | 5.90 | 6.25 |  |

* Higher values indicate greater importance.

needs, regarded as fourth in importance, rank third in degree of dissatisfaction. So, Security needs and Social needs exchange places in the rankings of the needs on importance and satisfaction. Esteem needs are ranked last in importance and in degree of dissatisfaction. All in all, the data, looked at in this way, point to a correlation between importance and dissatisfaction. However, this correlation can be somewhat misleading, since there is another way in which the degree of relationship can be considered; namely, by comparing the ranks of the fourteen countries within a given need on satisfaction, on the one hand, and importance, on the other hand. Viewed in this manner, the data still show a positive relationship between perceived importance and perceived dissatisfaction; however, the relationship is less strong than that found in comparing ranks among the five needs across all fourteen countries for the satisfaction and importance data. Summing up, it seems clear that there is a fairly strong, if by no means perfect, tendency for the perceived importance of needs and the perceived degree of dissatisfaction to vary together.

### Variation Among Countries in Importance of Needs

Next we can examine the differences among the clusters of countries across the various needs. Here, Figures 14 and 15 will be most helpful, especially the latter, which graphs the data in standard scores. The top and bottom clusters stand out clearly in this figure. The Developing countries, across all five needs, consistently attach more importance to the needs than do managers from any other group of countries, whereas the Northern European managers attach the least importance to all of the need areas, with the exception of Security needs. Japanese managers follow the managers from the Developing countries in the amount of importance they attach to the various needs. The Latin-European group of countries is about at the middle across all of the needs, whereas the Anglo-American group attaches relatively low importance to Security needs and moderately low or average importance to the other needs.

Moving from the data by clusters of countries (as shown in Figures 14 and 15) to the data by individual countries (as shown in Table 14 for raw scores, and Table 15 for standard scores), we note a number of interesting findings. Using Table 15 (giving

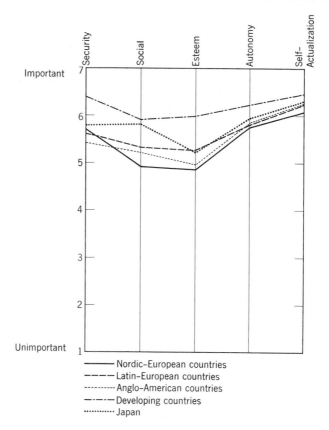

Figure 14. Need importance: by clusters of countries (raw scores).

standard scores) to illustrate the differences among countries, we can see that Argentinian managers attach more importance to each of the five needs than do the managers from any of the other 13 countries. In several instances, Argentinian managers are not only highest among the fourteen countries, but highest by a fairly sizeable degree. How should one interpret this finding? Perhaps it represents only a simple response bias to check rating scales at the extreme high end regardless of the specific stimulus presented, and, hence, is nothing more than a spurious

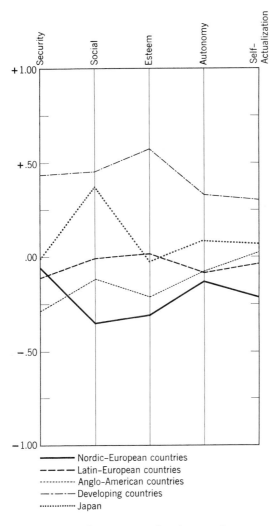

Figure 15. Need importance: by clusters of countries (standard scores). *Note:* Positive values indicate greater importance attached to a need than for the average manager; negative values indicate lesser importance.

TABLE 15. NEED IMPORTANCE (STANDARD SCORES) *

| | Security | Social | Esteem | Auton-omy | Self-Actuali-zation | Number of Cases |
|---|---|---|---|---|---|---|
| Nordic-European Countries | | | | | | |
| Denmark | −.21 | −.34 | −.60 | −.27 | −.33 | 149 |
| Germany | .16 | −.58 | .01 | .06 | −.08 | 586 |
| Norway | −.01 | −.37 | −.39 | −.38 | −.26 | 221 |
| Sweden | −.22 | −.15 | −.29 | .06 | −.20 | 342 |
| Average | −.07 | −.36 | −.32 | −.13 | −.22 | |
| Latin-European Countries | | | | | | |
| Belgium | −.09 | −.04 | −.24 | −.04 | −.01 | 378 |
| France | −.44 | −.24 | −.34 | −.08 | .13 | 154 |
| Italy | −.10 | −.15 | .37 | −.19 | −.10 | 267 |
| Spain | .18 | .40 | .25 | −.05 | −.16 | 203 |
| Average | −.11 | −.01 | .01 | −.09 | −.04 | |
| Anglo-American Countries | | | | | | |
| England | −.19 | .24 | −.29 | −.03 | −.03 | 239 |
| United States | −.38 | .00 | −.13 | −.11 | .07 | 464 |
| Average | −.29 | −.12 | −.21 | −.07 | .02 | |
| Developing Countries | | | | | | |
| Argentina | .49 | .66 | .69 | .48 | .45 | 198 |
| Chile | .36 | .47 | .55 | .21 | .30 | 159 |
| India | .44 | .23 | .44 | .27 | .16 | 114 |
| Average | .43 | .45 | .56 | .32 | .30 | |
| Japan | −.01 | .36 | −.03 | .08 | .07 | 165 |
| All Managers | .00 | .00 | .00 | .00 | .00 | |

* Positive values indicate greater importance attached to a need than for the average manager; negative values indicate lesser importance.

finding. This is quite unlikely to be the whole answer (although it may contribute to the finding) if one looks back at the results for need fulfillment which are likewise based on ratings in answer to a single question (How much is there now?). These fulfillment data (as shown in Table 10, which is the comparable standard score table to Table 15 for the importance data) show that while the Argentinians rated themselves high on fulfillment for two of the five needs, they rated themselves very near the average of all the countries on the other three needs. Therefore, it does not seem that a simple response tendency to mark all scales high is the entire answer to why Argentinian managers rate every need higher in importance than do managers from any other country. However, it is still possible for a somewhat more specific response bias to be operating; that is, Argentinians (and perhaps managers from other South American countries, since Chilean managers also rate the importance of most needs quite highly) may have a tendency not to distinguish among different types of needs in terms of importance, and therefore respond by saying "everything" is important to them. It is impossible, from our data, to say whether this type of response bias is occurring. It can be noted, though, that Table 14, which gives the raw score means, shows that the Argentinians did not give equal raw score answers to every need area. Looking across the row for Argentina, in Table 14, one can see that managers in this country rated the importance of Social and Esteem needs as clearly less than the importance of the other three types of needs. In any event, and for whatever reason, Argentinian managers attached a very high level of importance to all of the types of needs studied in this investigation.

Getting back to the picture for other individual countries (as shown in Table 15) we see that Chilean managers were second to Argentinian managers in the importance ratings they gave across all five needs. The same is true for the third nation of the Developing-country group, India. It is clear that the three members of our Developing-country bloc are alike, in that they attach uniformly high importance to the various needs. Whether this similarity represents some common response bias (which is probably unlikely), whether it is in some way connected to the relatively low need satisfaction that managers from these countries see themselves getting from their jobs, or whether there is some broad basis in the fact of their relatively low stage of economic development—these are all questions that we cannot answer from our data with any degree of confidence. This is one of a number of facets in this study that would merit further research efforts. The present finding is clear; the interpretation, difficult.

If we look at the individual countries attaching lowest importance across the needs, we can see (from Table 15) that each of the three Scandinavian countries is at or near the bottom for most of the needs. On particular needs, however, other individual countries join the Scandinavian group. For example, on Security, the two lowest among the fourteen countries are France and the United States, and, on Social needs, the lowest country by far is Germany.

### Need-by-Need Analysis

For the importance data, analysis of the results need by need (as was done for the fulfillment and satisfaction data), would add little to what we have already pointed out, since there is such a strong tendency for the same countries that are high or low on one kind of need to be high or low on another need.

### Variation Within Countries

To wind up this section on the importance data, we can note briefly the results for the degree of variation among managers within a country and for particular needs. These data are presented in Table 16 and Figure 16. Figure 16, giving a picture of the results by cluster of countries for the five types of needs, perhaps best sums up the findings with regard to variation on importance. As this figure clearly shows, there is greatest disagreement concerning the need for Security and the greatest agreement concerning the need for Self-Actualization. Japan and the three Developing countries tend to be the most homogeneous nations. Surprisingly, the Northern European nations are not among the relatively more homogeneous countries. This not only conflicts with the comparable findings for the satisfaction data, but also does not correspond to what one might expect, knowing the relatively homogeneous makeup of the population of these

TABLE 16. NEED IMPORTANCE: STANDARD DEVIATIONS

|  | Security | Social | Esteem | Auton-omy | Self-Actuali-zation | Number of Cases |
|---|---|---|---|---|---|---|
| **Nordic-European Countries** | | | | | | |
| Denmark | 1.58 | 1.23 | 1.39 | 1.09 | 1.00 | 149 |
| Germany | 1.22 | 1.18 | 1.23 | .93 | .74 | 586 |
| Norway | 1.14 | 1.15 | 1.22 | .99 | .81 | 221 |
| Sweden | 1.13 | 1.09 | 1.07 | .81 | .69 | 342 |
| Average | 1.26 | 1.16 | 1.22 | .95 | .81 | |
| **Latin-European Countries** | | | | | | |
| Belgium | 1.38 | 1.13 | 1.22 | .89 | .73 | 378 |
| France | 1.47 | 1.15 | 1.26 | .82 | .63 | 154 |
| Italy | 1.54 | 1.37 | 1.23 | 1.03 | .84 | 267 |
| Spain | 1.43 | 1.12 | 1.22 | 1.10 | .84 | 203 |
| Average | 1.45 | 1.19 | 1.23 | .96 | .76 | |
| **Anglo-American Countries** | | | | | | |
| England | 1.51 | 1.26 | 1.27 | .99 | .80 | 239 |
| United States | 1.43 | 1.10 | 1.15 | .88 | .71 | 464 |
| Average | 1.47 | 1.18 | 1.21 | .93 | .75 | |
| **Developing Countries** | | | | | | |
| Argentina | 1.08 | 1.11 | 1.07 | .87 | .64 | 198 |
| Chile | 1.20 | 1.01 | 1.09 | .89 | .65 | 159 |
| India | .88 | 1.04 | 1.04 | .86 | .64 | 114 |
| Average | 1.05 | 1.05 | 1.06 | .87 | .64 | |
| Japan | 1.14 | .91 | 1.03 | .80 | .65 | 165 |
| All Managers | 1.29 | 1.13 | 1.17 | .92 | .74 | |

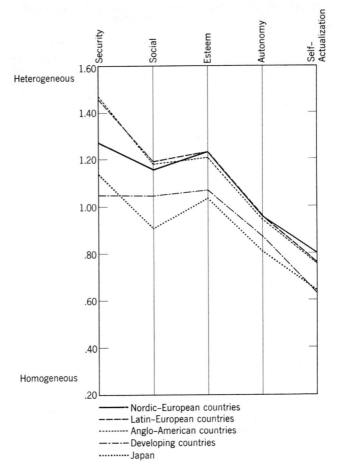

Figure 16. Need importance: by clusters of countries (standard deviations).

countries, especially the three Scandinavian countries. Therefore, the ideas we expressed tentatively in the previous section to explain the relative variations in need satisfaction are not confirmed by the importance data, which should be the set of data most sensitive to homogeneity among individuals, in terms of their personal values and beliefs.

## A Brief Overview and Integration

The past several sections of this chapter have been devoted to separate considerations of fulfillment, satisfaction, and importance. While convenient for descriptive purposes, this method of presenting the detailed findings neglects the interrelationships among these three dependent variables. Therefore, in this final section, we shall attempt a short integration of the motivational results. We will first focus briefly on findings concerned with comparisons among the different needs across all of the countries, and then follow with a longer summary of the findings concerned with differences among countries and groups of countries, regardless of kinds of needs.

In taking up the question of differences among needs, it will be helpful for the reader to refer to Summary Table A. This table is designed to indicate the relative rankings, from high to low, of the five kinds of needs for each of the three different kinds of attitudes concerning them: Fulfillment, satisfaction, and importance. Our attention will be directed largely to the last two columns in that summary table, the columns for satisfaction and importance.

If we look at the last two columns in Summary Table A, we see immediately that the two most critical types of needs are those for Self-Actualization and for Autonomy. Self-Actualization needs, though the least satisfied, are the most important needs; Autonomy needs are also regarded as relatively low in sat-

SUMMARY TABLE A.

SUMMARY RESULTS FOR DIFFERENCES AMONG NEEDS

| Need | Fulfillment | Satisfaction | Importance |
|------|-------------|--------------|------------|
| Security | High | Medium-High | High |
| Social | Low | Medium-High | Low |
| Esteem | Medium | Medium-High | Low |
| Autonomy | Medium | Low | High |
| Self-Actualization | Medium | Very Low | High |

isfaction and high in importance. On the other hand, Social and Esteem needs are highly satisfied, relatively speaking, and are regarded as relatively low in importance. The fifth type of need, the need for Security, shows a somewhat different combination of satisfaction and importance, compared to any of the other needs. In terms of satisfaction, Security needs are about as well satisfied as Esteem and Social needs; in importance, however, Security needs rank relatively high and, thus, close to the importance of Autonomy needs.

The implications of the summary findings shown in Summary Table A are obvious. For organizations in most of the countries in our sample—nations which, compared to all the other nations in the world, are relatively well developed economically—opportunities for increasing the motivational efforts of their managers lie in the Self-Actualization and Autonomy need areas. Since these are the areas regarded as being of high importance but relatively unsatisfied, the provision of additional avenues for fulfillment of these needs should result in improved managerial performance. However, this is a challenging task that organizations will not find easy to carry out in practice. It takes real thought and planning on the part of the topmost officials of firms to organize the work of their managerial forces in such a way as to grant the individual manager increased autonomy and self-actualization, and, at the same time, ensure that the total organization continues to operate as an integrated and coordinated unit. Rampant autonomy, for example, on the part of individual managers could result in adverse rather than beneficial effects. The achievement of meaningful increased opportunities for satisfaction of Self-Actualization and Autonomy needs, on the part of managers, will require considerably more than a mere superficial human relations "consideration" approach. It will require attention to the fundamental aspects of the ways in which companies are organized.

Let us now turn to the other major facet of the integration of the material of the preceding pages: The findings concerning differences among countries, especially groups of countries. To show the highlights of the results when analyzed in this manner, we have prepared another summary table, similar to Summary Table A. Summary Table B shows the relative rankings of the five clusters of countries for each of the three types of attitude variables: Need fulfillment, need satisfaction, and need importance.

It is readily apparent from Summary Table B that managers in the Northern European countries find themselves relatively well off, compared to managers from any other group of countries. These managers from Scandinavia and Germany report their needs to be both highly fulfilled and satisfied, and, in general, they rate the importance of these needs in their job situations as relatively low. Thus, for the managers from the Nordic-European countries, the job environment is, by and large, living up to expectations. The same conclusion seems to hold for Japan. The main difference between Japanese managers and those from Norway, Sweden, Denmark, and Germany is that the Japanese attach somewhat higher importance to the various needs than do the Nordic-Europeans. Thus, even though Japanese managers are more concerned about the various needs in their job environments, they find themselves to be receiving relatively high fulfillment, which, more or less, meets their expectations and therefore provides a moderately high level of satisfaction.

Managers in the United States and England, over all the five needs, appear to be about average in each of the three types of responses covered in our questionnaire. Reported need fulfillment is average to slightly below; satisfaction is average to slightly above; and importance is average to slightly below. However,

Summary Table B. Summary Results for Differences Among Clusters of Countries

| | Fulfillment | Satisfaction | Importance |
|---|---|---|---|
| Nordic-European | High | High | Low |
| Latin-European | Low | Low | Medium |
| Anglo-American | Medium-Low (changes by need) | Medium-High (changes by need) | Medium-Low |
| Developing Countries | Medium | Very Low | High |
| Japan | High | Medium-High | Medium-High |

more than is true for the other groups of countries, the results for United States and British managers are tied quite closely to the specific type of need being considered. That is, for the two lower-order needs, Security and Social, British and American managers' perceived fulfillment and satisfaction is relatively high, whereas, for the two highest-order needs, Autonomy and Self-Actualization, their perceived fulfillment and satisfaction is relatively lower (but not the lowest among the various groups of countries). Thus, to reiterate an earlier point, this pattern of need satisfaction is in direct correspondence to the theoretical hierarchy of needs. As we have stated elsewhere, this pattern indicates "either that the theory of prepotency of needs is particularly well adapted to organizational behavior in the United States and England, or that industrial firms in these countries have created conditions that fit the theory." [7] Again, though, one can say from an overall point of view that British and American managers are neither highly satisfied nor highly dissatisfied, and that the importance they attach to the various needs is about average.

The other two groups of countries, the Latin-European countries and the Developing countries, show a clearly different picture from the three groups of countries mentioned above. Both the mid-Southern European managers and the managers from the Developing countries report low to quite low satisfaction, and attach moderate to high importance to the various needs. Where these two groups differ from each other is, primarily, in the degree of reported fulfillment of needs. Somewhat surprisingly, the Developing-country managers report about average fulfillment (relatively speaking, compared to all countries) whereas the Latin-European managers indicate low need fulfillment as well as low satisfaction. It appears, therefore, that the reason for the managers in the Developing countries indicating low satisfaction is different from that for the managers in the countries of mid- and Southern Europe. Argentinian, Chilean, and Indian managers seem to be receiving fairly adequate need fulfillment, but they are dissatisfied with this degree of fulfillment because of exceptionally high expectations. In fact, one might say their expectations are unrealistic, since in many instances they exceed

[7] M. Haire, E. E. Ghiselli, and L. W. Porter, "Cultural Patterns in the Role of the Manager," *Industrial Relations*, Vol. 2, 95–117 (1963).

the expectations of managers in much more economically-developed countries, such as the Scandinavian countries and the United States. In the Latin-European countries, on the other hand, the relatively low satisfaction expressed by the managers seems to stem from relatively low fulfillment rather than from unreasonably high expectations.

Finally, we should point out again that relatively low need satisfaction, as we measured it, can be due either to low fulfillment, high expectations, or to both. The fact that managers in all three of the Developing countries, but especially Argentina and Chile, seem to have unrealistically high expectations may have some broad implications for management development in these economically developing countries. It may be that one of the most useful approaches to management training in the Developing countries, especially training directed to young and inexperienced managers, would be to help the trainees develop realistic expectations concerning the motivational satisfactions and frustrations they are likely to encounter in their jobs. It is possible that, because of the lack of an entrepreneurial tradition in many of these countries, young people deciding to go into industry have an overglamorized view of the rewards to be obtained in managerial jobs. At least, our results point to this possibility as one potential area of managerial training that deserves further attention.

CHAPTER 5

# Comparisons among Types
# of Managers

Like doctors, bank presidents, and professors, managers come in
a wide variety of types; that is, they and the positions they hold
can be classified into a number of different categories. Some
of these groupings are defined by the organizational characteristics of managers' positions, and other groupings by managers'
personal characteristics. We have chosen for examination two of
the former variables: Level of position within the organization,
and the size of organization for which a manager works; and one
personal variable, age. In this chapter, each of these three variables will be analyzed for relationships to the attitudes covered
by our questionnaire.

Comparisons of managers differing on each of the three afore-
mentioned variables can have important implications for organization theory. If there are attitudinal differences associated with
these organizational and personal variables that hold up consistently across various countries, then it would appear that there
are factors relevant to the structure and operation of organizations that transcend particular cultural influences. On the other

hand, if some of these variables have one type of impact in one group of countries and quite another direction of relationship in a second group, then this difference would reinforce the notion that cultural influences must be taken into account in the study of how managers approach their organizational responsibilities.

## The Major Findings

What, in fact, was found was that none of the three "independent" variables (level, size, age) had a strong effect on two of the three attitude areas covered by the questionnaire. Attitudes and assumptions underlying management practices (see Chapter 2) and cognitive descriptions of the managerial role (see Chapter 3) did not seem to be influenced crucially by a manager's level, the size of his organization, or his age. Nevertheless, as we shall see in detail later in this chapter, relationships between these three independent variables and the two attitude areas mentioned were not completely lacking. For example, of the three structural and personal variables, company size seemed to have the greatest impact on attitudes relevant to management practices. Managers from larger-size firms tended to have more favorable views concerning the use of participation, the sharing of information, and so forth. On the other hand, age seemed to be slightly more influential than either of the other two variables in determining cognitive descriptions of the managerial role. Older managers, in most countries, regarded the concepts of *to direct* and *to persuade* as more similar than did younger managers.

The one set of dependent attitude variables that did seem to be strongly affected by level, size, and age was the motivation-satisfaction area. The level at which a manager works was found to have a quite consistent relationship to perceptions of need fulfillment and need satisfaction, with the higher-level managers clearly indicating more favorable attitudes. Size of company also was related rather consistently to perceptions of fulfillment and satisfaction. However, in contrast to level-of-position effects, which were consistent across needs as well as across countries, the effects of size were consistent (though not universally so) across countries, but differed distinctly by type of need; that is, managers from large-sized companies reported more fulfillment and satisfaction of Security needs, while managers from small-sized firms were considerably more fulfilled and slightly more satisfied in Autonomy needs than were their large-company counterparts. Here, then, is a finding of considerable potential significance. The major implication would be that for most countries, as firms grow and increase in size (in terms of number of employees), they are likely to increase the feelings of security on the part of their managers but at the same time they run the risk of *decreasing* opportunities to fulfill Autonomy needs. When managers were compared by their ages, we found that older managers reported greater fulfillment of their needs but, surprisingly, felt slightly more dissatisfied with this fulfillment than did younger managers. In other words, older managers indicated they were receiving more psychological rewards from their positions than younger managers, but their expectations about what they should be receiving were so much greater than those of the younger managers that they were actually less satisfied. Again, this finding has important implications for companies throughout the world, in terms of their policies for dealing with their managers past the age of 40, regardless of their level in the firm.

These, then, are some of the key results when we compare different groups of managers. Detailed elaborations will be given in the sections that follow. The remainder of this chapter is organized around each of the three comparisons: Higher- versus lower-level managers, managers in larger companies versus those in smaller organizations, and younger managers versus older managers. Within each of these three sections, we shall examine the differences between the groups in their attitudes about management practices, their conceptualizations of the managerial role, and their motives and satisfactions.

## Methodology

In the tables and figures that accompany the text in this chapter, the differences between the various groups of managers are given as differences in *standard scores*. (To obtain these standard score differences we divided the raw score differences between the means of two groups by the standard deviation for all managers in the total sample.) The chief advantages to be gained by expressing the differences in standard scores are that their magnitudes can be better appreciated, and, especially, differences in one area can be compared with those in another area. One other methodological comment needs to be made here to facilitate a more meaningful interpretation of the findings reported in this chapter. Comparisons on each of the three variables (e.g., management level) were made without regard to the other two variables. This means that when we compared higher- versus lower-level managers we did not control for the fact that higher-level managers were undoubtedly older, and that, on the average, they probably came from relatively smaller companies. Thus, the relative magnitude of the differences between higher- and lower-level managers could be affected (either by reduction or enlargement) by contamination of the effects of the other two uncontrolled variables. Since one part of our data tends to show that older managers are less satisfied than younger managers, this means that the true differences between higher and lower managers in their perceptions of need satisfaction are probably somewhat larger than would appear from our tables and graphs. However, from previous extensive experience with attitudes of American managers [8] we know that level is more likely to affect size-of-company differences and age differences, than the reverse. Hence, the reader is especially cautioned to remember that level is not controlled when large-company managers (who probably come from a lower average level of management) are compared to small-company managers, or when younger managers (from a probably lower average level) are compared to older managers.

## Management Level

Generally speaking, it is the function of executives at the highest levels of organizations to set broad policies, while the chief

---

[8] L. W. Porter, "Job Attitudes in Management: I. Perceived Deficiencies in Need Fulfillment as a Function of Job Level," *Journal of Applied Psychology*, Vol. 46, 375–384 (1962); Porter, *op. cit.*: "IV. Perceived Deficiencies in Need Fulfillment as a Function of Size of Company," *Journal of Applied Psychology*, Vol. 47, 386–397 (1963).

functions of managers at middle and lower levels are to implement these policies and put them into action. This being the case, we divided our sample into top management, on the one hand, and middle and lower management together, on the other. (Since we had aimed at obtaining only middle- and upper-level managers as respondents, we had very few low-level supervisors in our total sample. Consequently, this was not a large enough group to place in a separate category and it was, therefore, combined with the middle-level group.) Thus, our higher-level managers tend to be policy makers and our (relatively) lower-level managers tend to be implementers of policy.

### Method of Classifying Managers by Level

Before examining the tables and graphs that present the results for managerial-level comparisons, we need to say a few words concerning how respondents were classified by management level. Any reader not interested in the details of this classification system may skip to the bottom of page 119.

To say of a manager that he is, for instance, at the third level of management in his organization does not, in and of itself, indicate how high or low he is in the hierarchy. If there are only three managerial levels in his organization, then, clearly, he holds a lower managerial position; if, however, there are twelve managerial levels, then obviously he is high in the hierarchy. Consequently, to describe quantitatively the level of a manager's position, it is necessary to express it as a ratio of the number of levels above him to the total number of levels in the organization.

For this ratio to be meaningful, it is necessary to think of the levels in an organization as a continuum. Each level, then, is taken to be an interval in this continuum. In an organization in which there are three levels, those managers who are in the top level would be thought of as falling in the top third of the scale; those in the second level as falling in the middle third of the scale; and those in the third level as falling in the lower third of the scale. Similarly, in an organization in which there are six levels, those managers in the top level would be thought of as occupying the top sixth of the scale, those in the second level as occupying the next sixth of the scale, and so on.

Therefore, in any organization, regardless of the number of managerial levels in it, the top level would cover 0–1 on the scale, the second level 1–2 on the scale, the third level 2–3 on the scale, and so on. As a representative value for the managers at any level, the midpoint of their interval can be assigned. Thus, managers in the top level would be assigned a level value of .5 (which is the midpoint of the interval 0–1); managers in the second level would be assigned the level value of 1.5 (which is the midpoint of the interval 1–2); managers in the third level would be assigned the level value of 2.5 (which is the midpoint of the interval 2–3), and so on.

By dividing the level by the total number of levels, a value is obtained which indicates the percent position of the individual in the managerial hierarchy. The lower a manager's ratio is, the higher he is in the hierarchy; and the higher his ratio, the lower he is in the hierarchy. For example, the ratio for a manager in a three-level organization above whom there are two levels is 2.5/3 or .83, and the ratio for a manager in a six-level organization above whom there are two levels is 2.5/6 or .43. It is apparent, therefore, that even though there are the same number of levels above each manager, the first holds a lower job than does the second.

### Attitudes and Assumptions Underlying Management Practices

Table 17 and its accompanying Figure 17 present the results for a comparison of higher-level with lower-level managers in their attitudes and assumptions concerning managerial practices. As is immediately apparent, there is no overall trend in the data. The first three columns in Table 17 show that, in about half the instances, higher-level managers have more democratic or participative attitudes, whereas, in the other half of the instances, the reverse is true. In addition, specific differences (regardless of direction) for a given country on a given attitude dimension are generally quite small. Only very occasionally is there a relatively large difference, such as for the United States in column 1, where lower-level managers appear to believe more strongly than higher-level managers in the capacity of the average individual for leadership and initiative.

The one type of attitude covered in Table 17 that seems to show any consistency across countries is that of allowing subordinates to exercise internal or self-control (column 4). On this dimension, there is some consistent tendency, from country to country, for higher-level managers to be somewhat less authori-

TABLE 17. ATTITUDES TOWARD MANAGEMENT PRACTICES: HIGHER-LEVEL VERSUS LOWER-LEVEL MANAGERS (DIFFERENCES IN STANDARD SCORES) *

| | Capacity for Leadership and Initiative | Sharing Information and Objectives | Participation | Internal Control | Number of Cases | |
|---|---|---|---|---|---|---|
| | | | | | Higher Level | Lower Level |
| Nordic-European Countries | | | | | | |
| Denmark | .09 | −.13 | .04 | .07 | 36 | 97 |
| Germany | −.07 | −.10 | −.12 | −.01 | 178 | 386 |
| Norway | −.05 | .05 | .13 | .12 | 123 | 87 |
| Sweden | .01 | .12 | −.09 | .11 | 183 | 153 |
| Average | −.01 | −.02 | −.01 | .07 | | |
| Latin-European Countries | | | | | | |
| Belgium | .15 | −.02 | .00 | .15 | 171 | 197 |
| France | .06 | .08 | .11 | .14 | 85 | 67 |
| Italy | −.27 | −.04 | −.11 | .22 | 70 | 161 |
| Spain | −.18 | .18 | −.07 | .08 | 99 | 88 |
| Average | −.06 | .05 | −.02 | .15 | | |
| Anglo-American Countries | | | | | | |
| England | .15 | .21 | .20 | .16 | 44 | 189 |
| United States | −.41 | −.03 | −.09 | −.15 | 64 | 396 |
| Average | −.13 | .09 | .06 | .01 | | |

Table 17 (*continued*)

| | Capacity for Leadership and Initiative | Sharing Information and Objectives | Participation | Internal Control | Number of Cases | |
|---|---|---|---|---|---|---|
| | | | | | Higher Level | Lower Level |
| Developing Countries | | | | | | |
| Argentina | −.27 | .01 | .16 | −.43 | 48 | 153 |
| Chile | .01 | −.05 | .07 | .14 | 29 | 127 |
| India | .11 | −.15 | −.28 | .46 | 16 | 98 |
| Average | −.05 | −.06 | −.02 | .06 | | |
| Japan | −.01 | −.30 | .07 | −.08 | 58 | 94 |
| All Managers | −.05 | −.01 | .00 | .07 | | |

\* Positive values indicate the attitudes of higher-level managers are more democratic; negative values indicate those of lower-level managers are more democratic.

tarian in their outlook than are lower-level managers. However, even on this dimension, the summary value across all countries indicates a relatively small overall difference.

Interestingly, of all the fourteen countries in our sample, only managers from England and the United States seem to show fairly strong and consistent trends in a given direction across all four attitude dimensions covered in this part of the questionnaire. In addition, the trends for these two countries are exactly opposite in direction. In England, apparently, the higher the level of a manager's position, the more likely he is to adopt the democratic-participative type of attitude. In the United States, on the other hand, the higher a manager's position, the more likely he is to be relatively more authoritarian in his assumptions about people and in his attitudes towards managerial practices. These contradictory trends are somewhat surprising, since,

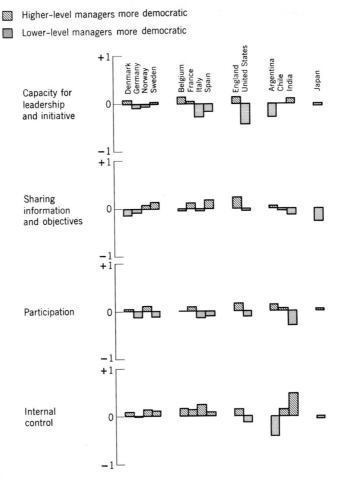

Figure 17. Attitudes toward management practices: higher-level versus lower-level managers.

throughout the data presented in the preceding chapters, English and American managers tended to demonstrate quite similar directions of attitudes. The findings shown in Table 17 would indicate that organizational level may have a differential effect in British business organizations compared to those in our own country, at least for certain types of attitudes.

### Cognitive Descriptions of the Managerial Role

The reader will recall that in this part of the questionnaire we ascertained the degree of difference seen by managers between the concepts *to direct* and *to persuade,* and the degree of difference seen between higher-status and lower-status positions in hierarchies. In Tables 18 and 19 and Figures 18 and 19 we have calculated, in standard scores, the difference between these differences when higher-level managers are compared to lower-level managers.

As both Tables 18 and 19 and their corresponding figures show, no overall trends were evident for one group or another of managers to see larger differences between either of these two sets of concepts. Again, though, there were a few specific exceptions where a rather large value was obtained in one table or another for a given country. Higher-level Norwegian managers perceived a much closer similarity between directing and persuading than did lower-level Norwegian managers, while the reverse trend was true for Italy. Likewise, German and French higher-level managers perceived a greater similarity of higher- and lower-status positions than did lower-level managers, whereas the reverse was again true for Italy. If there were any consistent trends for groups of countries in the results presented in Tables 18 and 19, they existed in the Nordic-European group, where, generally speaking, higher-level managers perceived less of a distinction between directing and persuading, and between high- and low-status positions, than did lower-level managers in these countries. This may indicate that in the Nordic-European countries higher-level executives have a slightly less authoritarian view of the managerial role than do lower-level managers. However, from these data on differences, this interpretation cannot be made with any degree of certainty.

### Need Fulfillment

Do higher-level managers feel they obtain greater need fulfillment from their jobs than do lower-level managers, as one would expect? The relevant data to answer this question are provided in Table 20 and Figure 20, which show the differences between the two categories of managers for each type of need within each country and group of countries.

TABLE 18. SIMILARITY OF THE CONCEPTS *To Direct* AND *To Persuade:* HIGHER-LEVEL VERSUS LOWER-LEVEL MANAGERS (DIFFERENCES IN STANDARD SCORES)*

|  | Differences Between Means | Number of Cases | |
|---|---|---|---|
|  |  | Higher Level | Lower Level |
| Nordic-European Countries | | | |
| Denmark | −.14 | 33 | 83 |
| Germany | −.27 | 174 | 381 |
| Norway | −.30 | 119 | 87 |
| Sweden | .05 | 179 | 150 |
| Average | −.17 | | |
| Latin-European Countries | | | |
| Belgium | −.01 | 167 | 195 |
| France | .05 | 83 | 68 |
| Italy | .23 | 69 | 160 |
| Spain | −.06 | 99 | 87 |
| Average | .05 | | |
| Anglo-American Countries | | | |
| England | −.06 | 45 | 188 |
| United States | −.04 | 63 | 391 |
| Average | −.05 | | |
| Developing Countries | | | |
| Argentina | .18 | 47 | 144 |
| Chile | .00 | 29 | 122 |
| India | .13 | 16 | 95 |
| Average | .10 | | |
| Japan | .15 | 56 | 88 |
| All Managers | −.01 | | |

* Positive values indicate the two concepts are more similar for lower-level managers; negative values indicate they are more similar for higher-level managers.

TABLE 19. SIMILARITY OF HIGHER-STATUS POSITIONS TO LOWER-STATUS
POSITIONS: HIGHER-LEVEL VERSUS LOWER-LEVEL MANAGERS
(DIFFERENCES IN STANDARD SCORES)*

| | Differ-ences Between Means | Number of Cases | |
|---|---|---|---|
| | | Higher Level | Lower Level |
| Nordic-European Countries | | | |
| Denmark | −.17 | 33 | 83 |
| Germany | −.26 | 174 | 381 |
| Norway | .09 | 119 | 87 |
| Sweden | −.08 | 179 | 150 |
| Average | −.11 | | |
| Latin-European Countries | | | |
| Belgium | −.04 | 167 | 195 |
| France | −.27 | 83 | 68 |
| Italy | .33 | 69 | 160 |
| Spain | −.04 | 99 | 87 |
| Average | −.01 | | |
| Anglo-American Countries | | | |
| England | −.08 | 45 | 188 |
| United States | .05 | 63 | 391 |
| Average | −.02 | | |
| Developing Countries | | | |
| Argentina | .02 | 47 | 144 |
| Chile | .04 | 29 | 122 |
| India | −.12 | 16 | 95 |
| Average | −.02 | | |
| Japan | .06 | 56 | 88 |
| All Managers | −.03 | | |

* Positive values indicate the two concepts are more similar for lower-level managers; negative values indicate they are more similar for higher-level managers.

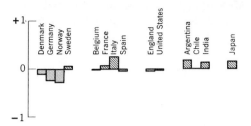

◪ The two concepts more similar for lower-level managers

◫ The two concepts more similar for higher-level managers

Figure 18. Similarity of the concepts *to direct* and *to persuade:* higher-level versus lower-level managers.

It is obvious from the findings that higher-level managers, as expected, consistently report greater degrees of need fulfillment than do lower-level managers. However, such differences stand out much more clearly in some need areas than in others, and in some countries more than in others.

Taking up, first, the differences among types of needs, we can see that it is the three higher-order needs of Autonomy, Esteem, and Self-Actualization, in that sequence, that produced the greatest divergence in perceived fulfillment between the levels of man-

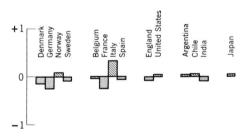

◪ The two concepts more similar for lower-level managers

◫ The two concepts more similar for higher-level managers

Figure 19. Similarity of higher-status positions to lower-status positions: higher-level versus lower-level managers.

| | Se-curity | Social | Esteem | Auton-omy | Self-Actuali-zation | Number of Cases | |
|---|---|---|---|---|---|---|---|
| | | | | | | High-er Level | Low-er Level |
| Nordic-European Countries | | | | | | | |
| Denmark | −.07 | −.11 | −.06 | −.15 | .10 | 36 | 97 |
| Germany | .07 | .23 | .42 | .35 | .35 | 178 | 386 |
| Norway | −.04 | −.01 | .14 | .25 | .13 | 123 | 87 |
| Sweden | −.05 | .10 | .16 | .30 | .26 | 183 | 153 |
| Average | −.02 | .05 | .17 | .19 | .21 | | |
| Latin-European Countries | | | | | | | |
| Belgium | .14 | .08 | .23 | .40 | .27 | 171 | 197 |
| France | .01 | −.04 | −.04 | .09 | .17 | 85 | 67 |
| Italy | .23 | −.06 | .09 | .18 | .09 | 70 | 161 |
| Spain | .49 | .40 | .39 | .74 | .29 | 99 | 88 |
| Average | .22 | .10 | .17 | .45 | .21 | | |
| Anglo-American Countries | | | | | | | |
| England | .04 | .04 | .22 | .09 | −.04 | 44 | 189 |
| United States | .26 | .10 | .46 | .38 | .30 | 64 | 396 |
| Average | .15 | .07 | .34 | .24 | .13 | | |
| Developing Countries | | | | | | | |
| Argentina | .37 | .28 | .47 | .54 | .32 | 48 | 143 |
| Chile | .12 | .23 | .42 | .62 | .24 | 29 | 127 |
| India | −.15 | .29 | .36 | .26 | .30 | 16 | 98 |
| Average | .11 | .27 | .42 | .47 | .29 | | |
| Japan | .81 | .24 | .84 | .85 | .63 | 58 | 94 |
| All Managers | .16 | .13 | .29 | .35 | .24 | | |

* Positive values indicate higher-level managers have greater need fulfillment; negative values indicate lower-level managers have greater
need fulfillment.

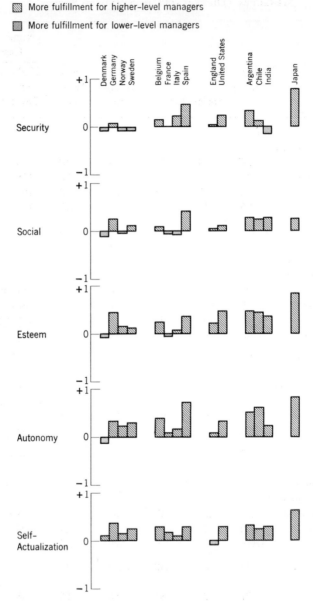

Figure 20. Need fulfillment: higher-level versus lower-level managers.

agement. For each of these three needs, no more than two countries showed reversals of the trend, and these reversals were quite small. To put it another way, out of forty-two possible comparisons for these three needs (three needs × fourteen countries), there were only four cases in which lower-level managers felt they received greater fulfillment when compared to upper-level managers. It is clear, therefore, that for Autonomy, Esteem, and Self-Actualization needs, there was a significant trend for higher-level managers to receive greater fulfillment—a trend that was consistent, almost without exception, from country to country.

For the other two needs, Security and Social, the same trend is present, but not in such strength nor with such consistency. The mean values of differences in favor of upper-level managers are smaller than for the three higher-order needs; and there are more instances of reversals. Nevertheless, for most countries, it is evident that higher-level managers feel they get more Security and Social need fulfillment than do lower-level managers.

Turning to the variation that exists among groups of countries in terms of the spread in need fulfillment between higher- and lower-level managers, we can see that organizational-level differences are least pronounced in the Nordic-European countries, and most pronounced in Japan. The differences between higher-level and lower-level managers are also large among the Developing countries. In more specific terms, the country with the least difference in fulfillment between upper-level and lower-level managers is Denmark, where, in fact, for four of the five needs, the lower-level managers actually report slightly greater fulfillment than do their colleagues at higher levels! Other individual countries that have quite small differences between the two levels of managers are France and England. At the other end of the scale, Japan is far and away the single country with the largest gap in fulfillment between the two management levels. Following Japan are Spain and Argentina. Germany, which often has results similar to those of the three Scandinavian countries, differs considerably from them on this variable of difference in fulfillment between upper-level and lower-level managers, in that in Germany the difference is relatively large. Considering these results for individual countries, one is certainly tempted to conclude that the degree of "democratic tradition" in the country is somehow related to the size of the difference in perceived need fulfillment between managers high in organizational hierarchies and those who are low. The only fact that seems to deviate from this conclusion is the relatively large difference that exists between upper-level and lower-level managers in the United States. Perhaps, in this country, which presumably has a long "democratic tradition," other factors are responsible for this relatively large separation.

### Need Satisfaction

Table 21 and Figure 21 give the results for need satisfaction in the same way that Table 20 and Figure 20 did for need fulfillment. It is necessary to keep in mind that in Table 21 positive values indicate degrees of dissatisfaction. Given the results we have just discussed for need fulfillment, it would be expected that the data for perceived satisfactions (the differences between need fulfillment and need expectations) would show a similar pattern of results, and this turns out to be the case. Out of seventy comparisons (five types of needs × fourteen countries), in only twelve instances do lower-level managers show less dissatisfaction than higher-level managers. Again, as with fulfillment, there is a clear and unmistakable trend for higher-level managers to perceive their jobs in a significantly different manner from lower-level managers.

If we look at the bottom line of Table 21, which gives the average degree of difference in dissatisfaction between higher-level and lower-level managers among all countries for each need, we can compare differences among the five types of needs. Such an inspection of Table 21 shows that there is a rather surprising similarity of degree of difference in dissatisfaction from one need to another. The three higher-order needs show only a slightly larger difference between the upper-level and lower-level managers than do the two lower-order needs. Hence, there appears to be more differentiation among the needs in terms of differences of fulfillment between the two levels of management than is the case for differences of satisfaction. However, for certain specific countries, there are some rather large variations in management-level differences, from need to need. For example, in Germany, the range of differences, expressed in standard scores, is from

TABLE 21. NEED SATISFACTION: HIGHER-LEVEL VERSUS LOWER-LEVEL
MANAGERS (DIFFERENCES IN STANDARD SCORES) *

| | Security | Social | Esteem | Autonomy | Self-Actualization | Number of Cases Higher Level | Lower Level |
|---|---|---|---|---|---|---|---|
| **Nordic-European Countries** | | | | | | | |
| Denmark | .09 | .17 | −.07 | .11 | −.09 | 36 | 97 |
| Germany | .00 | −.10 | −.24 | −.24 | −.33 | 178 | 390 |
| Norway | −.01 | .05 | −.04 | −.05 | .01 | 123 | 87 |
| Sweden | −.12 | −.13 | −.21 | −.23 | −.27 | 183 | 153 |
| Average | −.01 | .00 | −.14 | −.10 | −.17 | | |
| **Latin-European Countries** | | | | | | | |
| Belgium | −.09 | −.17 | −.11 | −.32 | −.27 | 171 | 197 |
| France | −.16 | −.03 | −.06 | .12 | −.08 | 85 | 67 |
| Italy | −.01 | .21 | .24 | .14 | .10 | 70 | 161 |
| Spain | −.29 | −.10 | −.18 | −.56 | −.18 | 99 | 88 |
| Average | −.14 | −.02 | −.03 | −.16 | −.11 | | |
| **Anglo-American Countries** | | | | | | | |
| England | .09 | −.05 | .00 | −.12 | −.07 | 44 | 189 |
| United States | −.31 | −.21 | −.18 | −.14 | −.20 | 64 | 396 |
| Average | −.11 | −.13 | −.09 | −.13 | −.14 | | |
| **Developing Countries** | | | | | | | |
| Argentina | −.31 | −.40 | −.45 | −.58 | −.28 | 48 | 143 |
| Chile | −.06 | .01 | −.15 | −.41 | −.05 | 29 | 127 |
| India | −.24 | −.48 | −.30 | −.26 | −.36 | 16 | 98 |
| Average | −.20 | −.29 | −.30 | −.42 | −.23 | | |
| Japan | −.50 | −.26 | −.33 | −.41 | −.44 | 58 | 94 |
| All Managers | −.14 | −.11 | −.15 | −.21 | −.18 | | |

* Positive values indicate greater dissatisfaction on the part of higher-level managers; negative values indicate greater dissatisfaction on the part of lower-level managers.

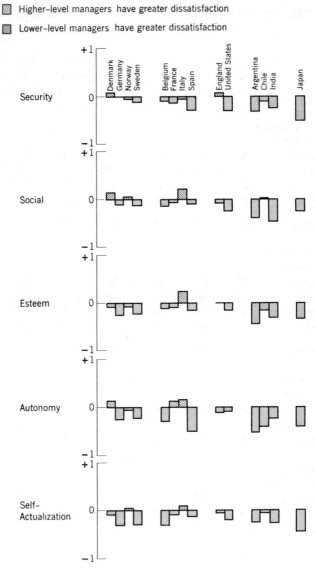

Figure 21. Need satisfaction: higher-level versus lower-level managers.

.00 (for Security needs) to .33 (for Self-Actualization needs). In Germany, it seems clear that for the two lower-order needs, Security and Social, lower-level managers are almost as satisfied as upper-level managers, but for the three highest-order needs, the lower-level managers are definitely more dissatisfied than their colleagues at upper levels. Spain is another example of a country where there are large differences among the needs in the degree to which upper-level managers differ from lower-level managers in satisfaction. Lower-level Spanish managers express consistently more dissatisfaction than upper-level managers for all five needs. For four of the five needs, the differences are not very great. However, for Autonomy needs, the difference is quite large (.56 in standard score terms). As a final example of a country where the various needs bring out differing degrees of difference in satisfaction between the two managerial levels, we can look at the case of India. Here, as in Spain, lower-level managers are consistently more dissatisfied in all need areas than are upper-level managers. In the Social need area, though, the size of the difference is considerably larger than in the other four need areas.

Turning to the overall differences among countries or groups of countries insofar as the comparisons of the satisfaction of upper- versus lower-level managers are concerned, we can see from Table 21 that the continental European countries (both northern and southern) and England generally show relatively small management-level differences, whereas the Developing countries and Japan show relatively large differences between levels. At one extreme is Italy, where lower-level managers actually are more satisfied than upper-level managers, and at the other, Japan and India, where the upper-level managers express much greater satisfaction than lower-level managers. In certain countries, such as Germany and Spain, as we have already noted, the two managerial levels have relatively small differences on certain needs and relatively large differences on other needs. On the whole, it appears that (with the possible exception of the United States) the countries with strong democratic traditions show the smallest differences in perceived need satisfaction between managers at relatively high levels in their companies and managers at relatively low levels.

*Need Importance*

The findings for differences between upper-level and lower-level managers in the importance they attach to various needs can be summarized succinctly: There are essentially no differences. This can be seen in Table 22 and Figure 22, which give the results for importance of needs. The bottom row of Table 22 shows that there is almost no variation in the size of upper- versus lower-level differences from need to need. As far as differences among groups of countries are concerned, there is also very little variation. The findings for individual countries are, of course, somewhat more variable. For example, in England there is a fairly strong trend for lower-level managers to attach more importance to the various needs across all five types of needs. In contrast, there is a trend in the United States (though neither as strong nor as consistent as in England) for higher-level managers to attach greater importance to the different needs. In general, though, the most noticeable conclusion is that organization level has relatively little effect on the amount of importance that managers attach to given needs.

There is one final, critical aspect of the findings to note with regard to the effects of managerial level on the perceived importance of needs. This concerns a comparison of the effects of level on perceived importance with its effects on perceived fulfillment of needs. Both perceptions were measured by exactly the same kind of scales (numerical rating scales ranging from 1–7). Therefore, assuming the variability of ratings to be roughly similar for fulfillment as for importance, we can determine by comparing Tables 20 to 22 whether management level had more of an effect on perceived fulfillment than on perceived importance. It is clearly evident from this comparison that the level on which a manager works in an organization has a much greater effect on his perceptions of the degree of need fulfillment he is receiving in his job than it does on his perceptions of the degree of importance he attaches to the various needs. This is one of the most striking findings of our entire study.

## Size of Company

Size is an organization structural variable that has been studied rather extensively. However, most previous research has focused

|  | Se-curity | Social | Esteem | Auton-omy | Self-Actuali-zation | Number of Cases | |
|---|---|---|---|---|---|---|---|
|  |  |  |  |  |  | Higher Level | Lower Level |
| Nordic-European Countries |  |  |  |  |  |  |  |
| Denmark | .09 | −.04 | −.13 | −.01 | −.26 | 36 | 97 |
| Germany | −.13 | −.05 | −.02 | .08 | −.14 | 178 | 386 |
| Norway | .04 | .04 | −.08 | .31 | .14 | 123 | 87 |
| Sweden | −.14 | −.07 | −.07 | .02 | .08 | 183 | 153 |
| Average | −.04 | −.03 | −.08 | .10 | −.05 |  |  |
| Latin-European Countries |  |  |  |  |  |  |  |
| Belgium | −.06 | −.06 | −.03 | −.01 | −.07 | 171 | 197 |
| France | −.23 | −.15 | −.32 | .03 | .24 | 85 | 67 |
| Italy | .14 | .13 | .11 | .31 | −.03 | 70 | 161 |
| Spain | .15 | .30 | −.10 | −.06 | .08 | 99 | 88 |
| Average | .00 | .06 | −.09 | .07 | .06 |  |  |
| Anglo-American Countries |  |  |  |  |  |  |  |
| England | −.07 | −.34 | −.10 | −.24 | −.28 | 44 | 189 |
| United States | .14 | −.10 | .08 | .01 | .12 | 64 | 396 |
| Average | .04 | −.22 | −.01 | −.12 | −.08 |  |  |
| Developing Countries |  |  |  |  |  |  |  |
| Argentina | −.07 | −.11 | .01 | −.02 | −.03 | 48 | 143 |
| Chile | −.07 | .15 | .05 | .25 | .16 | 29 | 127 |
| India | −.36 | −.04 | −.23 | −.05 | −.11 | 16 | 98 |
| Average | −.17 | .00 | −.06 | .06 | .01 |  |  |
| Japan | .20 | −.09 | .21 | .38 | −.08 | 58 | 94 |
| All Managers | −.03 | −.03 | −.04 | .07 | −.01 |  |  |

* Positive values indicate the need is more important for higher-level managers; negative values indicate it is more important for lower-level managers.

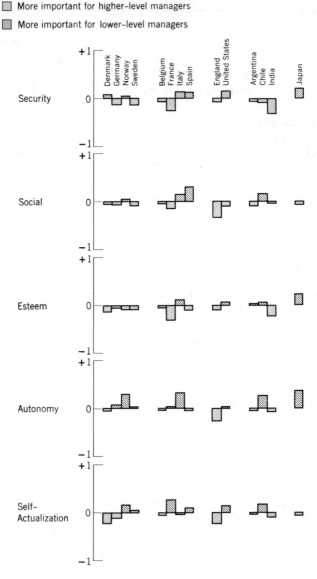

Figure 22. Need importance: higher-level versus lower-level managers.

on comparing small-sized *units within* organizations to large-sized units within these same or other organizations. (See Porter and Lawler [9] for a review of the literature pertaining to organization size in relation to job attitudes and job behavior.) There has been relatively little research, especially on managers, where size of company rather than size of unit within a company has been the independent variable. In this section, we shall compare the attitudes of managers working in relatively small companies with those of managers working in relatively large ones.

In making comparisons on the basis of organization size, categories representing different sizes must always be drawn along arbitrary lines. In a previous work on American managers,[10] three categories were formed: Small: 1–499; medium: 500–4,999; and large: over 5,000. However, in the worldwide sample represented by the fourteen countries in our present study, there were relatively few managers who worked for firms employing more than 5,000 individuals. (Exceptions to this, in our sample, were the United States, of course, and England, Germany, and India.) Therefore, we decided to form only two categories of size: "Small" companies employing 1–500 employees, and "large" companies employing more than 500 employees. The reader should keep clearly in mind that the large category was composed mostly of managers who worked in medium-sized firms with from 500–5,000 employees, rather than in really large firms with over 5,000 employees. In other words, although this category is correctly labeled "large" in a relative sense, it is essentially "medium" in an absolute sense.

### Attitudes and Assumptions Underlying Management Practices

Managers from larger companies in our sample consistently advocate more positive attitudes towards a democratic-participative approach to management, as can be seen clearly in Table 23 and Figure 23. Of the fifty-six differences shown in Table 23 (fourteen countries on each of four attitude dimensions), forty-one are in this direction. Note that the bottom row of the table,

---

[9] L. W. Porter and E. E. Lawler, "Properties of Organization Structure in Relation to Job Attitudes and Job Behavior," *Psychological Bulletin*, Vol. 64, 23–51 (1965).

[10] Porter, 1963, *op. cit.*

giving the averages across the fourteen countries, shows that, for
each of the four attitude dimensions, more democratic-type attitudes were expressed by the managers from the larger companies. The average differences across all countries were not
large, except for the area of sharing information and objectives;

TABLE 23. ATTITUDES TOWARD MANAGEMENT PRACTICES: MANAGERS
IN SMALLER VERSUS LARGER COMPANIES (DIFFERENCES
IN STANDARD SCORES)*

| | Capacity for Leadership and Initiative | Sharing Information and Objectives | Participation | Internal Control | Number of Cases | |
|---|---|---|---|---|---|---|
| | | | | | Small | Large |
| **Nordic-European Countries** | | | | | | |
| Denmark | .23 | −.02 | −.36 | −.26 | 69 | 80 |
| Germany | .11 | −.10 | −.04 | −.01 | 126 | 453 |
| Norway | .07 | −.39 | .08 | −.26 | 93 | 127 |
| Sweden | .10 | −.18 | −.17 | −.16 | 100 | 242 |
| Average | .13 | −.17 | −.12 | −.17 | | |
| **Latin-European Countries** | | | | | | |
| Belgium | −.11 | −.29 | −.24 | −.16 | 177 | 199 |
| France | .23 | −.10 | −.07 | .24 | 56 | 97 |
| Italy | −.20 | −.41 | −.12 | .09 | 95 | 171 |
| Spain | −.09 | −.13 | .11 | −.03 | 131 | 69 |
| Average | −.04 | −.23 | −.08 | .04 | | |
| **Anglo-American Countries** | | | | | | |
| England | −.04 | .09 | −.37 | −.12 | 24 | 213 |
| United States | −.46 | −.23 | −.20 | .19 | 20 | 441 |
| Average | −.25 | −.07 | −.29 | .04 | | |

Table 23 (*continued*)

| | Capacity for Leadership and Initiative | Sharing Information and Objectives | Participation | Internal Control | Number of Cases | |
|---|---|---|---|---|---|---|
| | | | | | Small | Large |
| Developing Countries | | | | | | |
| Argentina | −.14 | −.25 | −.04 | −.36 | 111 | 86 |
| Chile | −.28 | −.20 | −.21 | −.12 | 83 | 76 |
| India | −.09 | −.54 | .44 | .16 | 6 | 107 |
| Average | −.17 | −.33 | .06 | −.11 | | |
| Japan | .08 | −.32 | .04 | −.19 | 61 | 103 |
| All Managers | −.04 | −.22 | −.08 | −.07 | | |

* Positive values indicate managers in smaller companies have more democratic attitudes; negative values indicate managers in larger companies have more democratic attitudes.

but the averages are based on differences (from country to country) that are generally consistent in direction. Only on the questions dealing with beliefs in the capacity of the average individual for leadership and initiative was there a lack of consistency among the countries.

Looking in more detail at Table 23, we can see that in thirteen out of fourteen countries managers from larger companies were more in favor of sharing information; in ten out of fourteen countries they were more in favor of the use of participation; and also in ten out of fourteen countries they were more in favor of allowing subordinates to exercise self-control. In the fourth area— degree of belief in the capacity of the average person—managers from larger companies had a more positive attitude in eight countries; whereas the reverse was true in the other six countries. On this dimension, it was primarily in the Nordic-European coun-

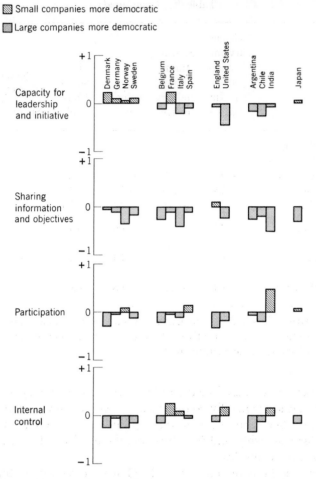

Figure 23. Attitudes toward management practices: managers in smaller versus larger companies.

tries that the smaller-company managers had greater faith in the average man's capacities than did the larger-company managers.

When comparisons are made among individual countries and among groups of countries across all four attitude areas in Table 23, there is no single country or group of countries in which managers from smaller companies consistently have more favorable attitudes towards democratic-participative approaches. For each individual country, and for each group of countries, either there is no trend or there is a consistent trend in favor of the larger companies.

These results for the comparison of attitudes towards management practices between managers from relatively small companies versus those from relatively larger companies should give pause to anyone who condemns, *a priori*, the practices of large organizations simply because they are large. Our evidence, of course, does not say anything about how organizations are actually run. We have data only on the attitudes of those people who run the companies; managers' actual practices may not necessarily conform to their attitudes. Nevertheless, in the absence of more definitive data (other than some writer's personal observations), our findings indicate that large companies are probably not any worse than smaller companies in their use of autocratic and authoritarian measures; perhaps they are even slightly better in this respect.

### Cognitive Descriptions of the Managerial Role

How similar are the concepts *to direct* and *to persuade* in the minds of small-company versus large-company managers? Table 24 and Figure 24 give the answer: Managers from the smaller companies are less likely to see a similarity between these two concepts. In other words, for these small-company managers, there is a more distinct semantic difference between direction and persuasion than there is for larger-company managers. This is true in ten of the fourteen countries, and, thus, is a fairly consistent finding, even though the overall difference across the fourteen countries is not large. The meaning of this finding is not perfectly clear, but it certainly is not inconsistent with the findings reported in the previous table showing that managers from smaller companies had more authoritarian attitudes. If a relatively larger difference is seen between directing and persuading, as is the case for small-company managers, this may imply that these managers have a tendency to see direction in a more favorable light. (This interpretation is based on the relevant information in Chapter 3, where the data indicated that

TABLE 24. SIMILARITY OF THE CONCEPTS *To Direct* AND *To Persuade:*
MANAGERS IN SMALLER VERSUS LARGER COMPANIES
(DIFFERENCES IN STANDARD SCORES)*

| | Differences Between Means | Number of Cases | |
|---|---|---|---|
| | | Small | Large |
| Nordic-European Countries | | | |
| Denmark | .18 | 55 | 74 |
| Germany | .19 | 122 | 449 |
| Norway | −.21 | 91 | 125 |
| Sweden | −.01 | 98 | 237 |
| Average | .04 | | |
| Latin-European Countries | | | |
| Belgium | .21 | 173 | 199 |
| France | .13 | 53 | 99 |
| Italy | .04 | 93 | 171 |
| Spain | −.10 | 128 | 70 |
| Average | .07 | | |
| Anglo-American Countries | | | |
| England | .02 | 24 | 213 |
| United States | −.07 | 20 | 435 |
| Average | −.03 | | |
| Developing Countries | | | |
| Argentina | .05 | 111 | 86 |
| Chile | .06 | 81 | 73 |
| India | .26 | 6 | 104 |
| Average | .12 | | |
| Japan | .09 | 55 | 101 |
| All Managers | .06 | | |

* Positive values indicate the two concepts are more similar for managers in larger companies; negative values indicate they are more similar for managers in smaller companies.

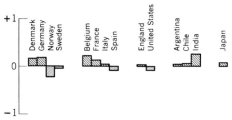

⬛ The two concepts more similar for managers in larger companies

⬜ The two concepts more similar for managers in smaller companies

Figure 24. Similarity of the concepts *to direct* and *to persuade:* managers in smaller versus larger companies.

when differences were perceived between these two concepts, *to direct* was regarded more favorably than *to persuade.*)

In Table 25 and Figure 25, the overall value across all fourteen countries shows a very slight tendency for managers in small companies to make a greater distinction between high- and low-status positions when compared to larger-company managers. However, there is relatively little consistency shown in the country-by-country values in this table. In the two European groups of countries there are practically no differences in the perceptions of the two categories of managers; on the other hand, in the Anglo-American and Developing countries, large-company managers are more likely to indicate similarity between high- and low-status positions. In general, then, to the extent that Table 25 shows any trends, they are trends consistent with those in the previous table dealing with the concepts *to direct* and *to persuade.*

### Need Fulfillment

Table 26 and Figure 26 present the results for the comparison of need-fulfillment attitudes of managers who work in relatively small organizations versus those who work in relatively large organizations. The general picture given in this table and figure is that there is no consistent trend in favor of either smaller or larger companies. For certain needs the small company seems to produce greater feelings of need fulfillment; for some other

TABLE 25. SIMILARITY OF HIGHER-STATUS POSITIONS TO LOWER-STATUS POSITIONS: MANAGERS IN SMALLER VERSUS LARGER COMPANIES (DIFFERENCES IN STANDARD SCORES) *

| | Differences Between Means | Number of Cases | |
|---|---|---|---|
| | | Small | Large |
| Nordic-European Countries | | | |
| Denmark | .00 | 55 | 74 |
| Germany | .00 | 122 | 449 |
| Norway | −.07 | 91 | 125 |
| Sweden | −.09 | 98 | 237 |
| Average | −.04 | | |
| Latin-European Countries | | | |
| Belgium | −.10 | 173 | 199 |
| France | −.02 | 53 | 99 |
| Italy | −.04 | 93 | 171 |
| Spain | −.04 | 128 | 70 |
| Average | −.05 | | |
| Anglo-American Countries | | | |
| England | .08 | 24 | 213 |
| United States | .23 | 20 | 435 |
| Average | .16 | | |
| Developing Countries | | | |
| Argentina | .17 | 111 | 86 |
| Chile | .35 | 81 | 73 |
| India | .33 | 6 | 104 |
| Average | .28 | | |
| Japan | .05 | 55 | 101 |
| All Managers | .06 | | |

* Positive values indicate the two concepts are more similar for managers in larger companies; negative values indicate they are more similar for managers in smaller companies.

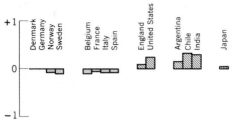

■ The two concepts more similar for managers in larger companies

■ The two concepts more similar for managers in smaller companies

Figure 25. Similarity of higher-status positions to lower-status positions: managers in smaller versus larger companies.

needs there is essentially no difference; and, for yet another type of need, the results favor the large company. Likewise, there is no country, except Argentina, in which there is complete consistency across all five types of needs for one size of company to produce greater fulfillment than the other size. Nevertheless, if one counts the number of plus (greater fulfillment in smaller companies) and minus values in Table 26, the overall edge, in a ratio of about 2–1, is in the direction of slightly greater need fulfillment in smaller companies. The fact that this overall advantage for smaller companies is not particularly great can be seen if one compares Table 26 with Table 20, for need fulfillment differences between different levels of management. Such a comparison demonstrates that managerial level has a greater effect on perceptions of need fulfillment than does the size of the company for which a manager works.

Returning to Table 26, we can begin our more detailed analysis of the results for company size by making comparisons of the effect of size among the five types of needs. As the bottom line of Table 26 indicates, there was virtually no difference in perceptions of fulfillment between large-company managers and small-company managers in two of the need areas—Social needs and Self-Actualization needs. The average difference between the two size groups in each of these two need areas was about as close to 0 as is possible to obtain. In the Security need area, the overall trend indicates greater fulfillment in larger companies,

## TABLE 26. Need Fulfillment: Managers in Smaller Versus Larger Companies (Differences in Standard Scores) *

| | Security | Social | Esteem | Autonomy | Self-Actualization | Number of Cases Small | Number of Cases Large |
|---|---|---|---|---|---|---|---|
| **Nordic-European Countries** | | | | | | | |
| Denmark | −.21 | .23 | −.07 | −.05 | .12 | 69 | 80 |
| Germany | .02 | −.10 | .19 | .01 | −.05 | 126 | 453 |
| Norway | −.08 | .17 | .10 | .21 | .15 | 93 | 127 |
| Sweden | −.33 | −.10 | .09 | .03 | .02 | 100 | 242 |
| Average | −.15 | .05 | .08 | .05 | .06 | | |
| **Latin-European Countries** | | | | | | | |
| Belgium | −.34 | −.32 | −.08 | .26 | −.13 | 177 | 199 |
| France | −.06 | .11 | .22 | .40 | .20 | 56 | 97 |
| Italy | −.03 | .26 | .40 | .39 | .15 | 95 | 171 |
| Spain | −.09 | .10 | .06 | .35 | .01 | 131 | 69 |
| Average | −.13 | .04 | .15 | .35 | .06 | | |
| **Anglo-American Countries** | | | | | | | |
| England | −.13 | −.48 | −.15 | .32 | −.08 | 24 | 213 |
| United States | −.73 | −.18 | .15 | .28 | −.14 | 20 | 441 |
| Average | −.43 | −.33 | .00 | .30 | −.11 | | |
| **Developing Countries** | | | | | | | |
| Argentina | .08 | .10 | .15 | .25 | .09 | 111 | 86 |
| Chile | .03 | .11 | .17 | .17 | −.02 | 83 | 76 |
| India | −.38 | −.26 | .18 | .03 | −.28 | 6 | 107 |
| Average | −.09 | −.02 | .17 | .15 | −.07 | | |
| Japan | .26 | −.10 | .40 | .48 | .14 | 61 | 103 |
| All Managers | −.14 | −.03 | .15 | .22 | .01 | | |

* Positive values indicate managers in smaller companies have greater need fulfillment; negative values indicate managers in larger companies have greater need fulfillment.

More fulfillment for managers in smaller companies
More fulfillment for managers in larger companies

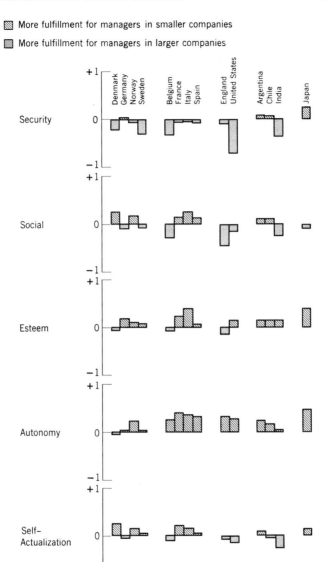

Figure 26. Need fulfillment: managers in smaller versus larger companies.

this being the direction of the difference in ten of the fourteen countries. On the other hand, in the other two need areas, Esteem and Autonomy, the trends are clearly in the opposite direction, with consistently greater fulfillment in the smaller companies. The trend in this direction is especially noticeable in the Autonomy need area where, although the average difference is not great, the direction of the difference favors the small-sized companies in thirteen of the fourteen countries. In summary, comparisons of the size of company differences among the needs show that the theoretical position of a given need in the hierarchy is not related to the difference favoring one or the other size of company. To illustrate this point, for the lowest-order need (Security), large-company managers are more satisfied; for a middle-order need (Esteem), small-company managers are more satisfied; for the highest-order need (Self-Actualization), there is no size-of-company difference. Thus, any trends in favor of one or the other size of company seem unrelated to the theoretical priority or prepotency of the different needs.

When the different countries are compared with each other, in terms of the degree of difference in need fulfillment between small-company managers and large-company managers, we can see from Table 26 and Figure 26 that every country except Argentina has at least one type of need that favors one of the size categories, and at least one other need that favors the other size category. In Argentina, smaller-company managers say they receive more fulfillment in each of the five need areas when compared to large-company managers. Other countries showing this same trend in favor of small companies, in four of the five need areas, are Norway, France, Italy, Spain, Chile, and Japan. In terms of groups of countries, the two European clusters and Japan all show small but consistent trends in the direction of greater perceived need fullfillment in smaller companies in all of the need areas, with the exception of Security needs. (In Japan, the exception is the Social need category rather than the Security category.)

The individual countries showing a trend more in favor of large companies are Denmark, Belgium, England, the United States, and India. However, it should be noted that each of these other countries, with the exception of Denmark, has relatively few managers in the small-company category in our sample. In terms of groups of countries, only the English-speaking duo of the United States and England (with very few respondents in the small category) seems to show a clearly definite trend toward greater need fulfillment in larger companies.

To emphasize, once again, the overall picture for fullfillment, there is a trend for smaller-company managers to report greater need fulfillment in their jobs. But this trend is quite weak, in that, the average difference in fulfillment between small- and large-company managers for a given need in any particular country is usually not very great. Furthermore, as we have pointed out previously, the small-company managers in our sample tended to come from higher organizational levels than did the large-company managers, and this fact probably resulted in their comparative fulfillment appearing to be relatively greater than it is in fact.

### Need Satisfaction

Shifting now to Table 27 and Figure 27, which present the differences in perceived satisfaction of needs between small- and large-company managers, we can see a clear contrast between these results and those for need fulfillment. Whereas the fulfillment results showed a weak trend in favor of smaller companies, the satisfaction results show a somewhat stronger trend in the opposite direction! That is, for four of the five needs and for eleven of the fourteen countries, there is greater dissatisfaction among small-company managers than among large-company managers. Thus, even though smaller-company managers report slightly greater degrees of need fulfillment (on the average), their dissatisfaction is greater because they have higher expectation levels than do large-company managers. If one accepts our operational definition of satisfaction—the difference between expected fulfillment and perceived actual fulfillment—our results show a clear overall trend for managers working in large companies to be more satisfied with the need fulfillment received in their jobs. Above all, this is true for Security needs, as will be shown.

The strength of the trend in the direction of greater satisfaction among managers in large companies varies, of course, with the type of need. In fact, for one of the five needs (Autonomy), small-company managers express slightly greater satisfaction than

| | Security | Social | Esteem | Autonomy | Self-Actualization | Number of Cases Small | Number of Cases Large |
|---|---|---|---|---|---|---|---|
| **Nordic-European Countries** | | | | | | | |
| Denmark | .22 | −.14 | −.15 | .01 | −.18 | 69 | 80 |
| Germany | −.03 | .01 | −.11 | .08 | .06 | 126 | 453 |
| Norway | .36 | .14 | .03 | .10 | −.02 | 93 | 127 |
| Sweden | .74 | .07 | .05 | .07 | .10 | 100 | 242 |
| Average | .32 | .02 | −.05 | .07 | −.01 | | |
| **Latin-European Countries** | | | | | | | |
| Belgium | .39 | .28 | .05 | −.13 | .05 | 177 | 199 |
| France | .96 | .11 | −.11 | −.13 | −.05 | 56 | 97 |
| Italy | .30 | −.16 | .10 | −.07 | .11 | 95 | 171 |
| Spain | .57 | .34 | .05 | −.23 | .07 | 131 | 69 |
| Average | .56 | .14 | .02 | −.14 | .05 | | |
| **Anglo-American Countries** | | | | | | | |
| England | .87 | .43 | .39 | −.04 | .07 | 24 | 213 |
| United States | 1.28 | .32 | .13 | −.27 | .43 | 20 | 441 |
| Average | 1.08 | .38 | .26 | −.16 | .25 | | |
| **Developing Countries** | | | | | | | |
| Argentina | .06 | .50 | .05 | −.16 | .01 | 111 | 86 |
| Chile | .00 | −.14 | .03 | .11 | .13 | 83 | 76 |
| India | .91 | .51 | .37 | .07 | .28 | 6 | 107 |
| Average | .32 | .29 | .15 | .00 | .14 | | |
| Japan | −.26 | −.04 | −.08 | −.22 | −.04 | 61 | 103 |
| All Managers | .46 | .16 | .06 | −.06 | .07 | | |

* Positive values indicate managers in smaller companies are more *dis*satisfied; negative values indicate managers in larger companies are more *dis*satisfied.

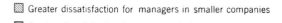

☒ Greater dissatisfaction for managers in smaller companies

☐ Greater dissatisfaction for managers in larger companies

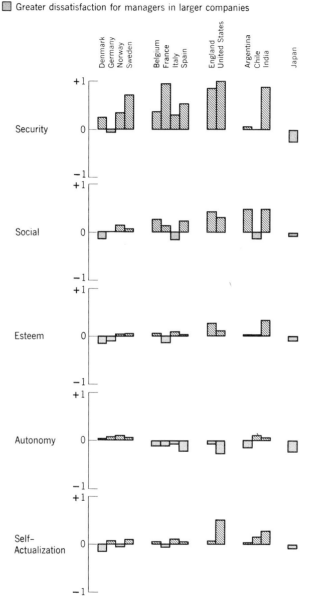

Figure 27. Need satisfaction: managers in smaller versus larger companies.

do large-company managers. The results for all of the other four needs, however, indicate that large-company managers receive greater satisfaction. This is especially true in the Security need area, where not only is there a large average difference between the two categories of managers (as shown in the bottom line of Table 27), but also a consistency of difference from country to country. The average strength of trends in the other three need areas (Social, Esteem, and Self-Actualization), is not high, but there is consistency from country to country in the direction of more satisfaction being expressed by the large-company manager.

In terms of individual country differences, only Japan seems to deviate markedly from the overall picture. In Japan, there is a consistent trend across all five types of needs for small-company managers to be more satisfied. Among the other thirteen countries, though, with the possible exceptions of Denmark and France, the picture is strongly in the direction of large-company managers expressing more satisfaction. Three groups of countries show average differences in favor of large companies in at least four of the five need areas. Such trends are most noticeable in the Anglo-American countries and in the Developing countries. Managers in the United States, for example, show definite trends in the direction of more satisfaction in large than in small companies, in all need areas except Autonomy. The difference in the United States between the two categories of managers is especially impressive in the Security need area, where the standard scores of the two groups differ by more than 1.2.

The summary picture for need satisfaction is one which, in most need areas and in most countries, favors the large company. The most striking specific finding concerns the Security need area. Whatever else the large company supplies, it quite clearly satisfies Security needs of managers much better than does the smaller company.

### Need Importance

When managers from different-sized companies are asked to indicate the importance they attach to various needs, the results show that company size has relatively little effect on their answers, as can be seen in Table 28 and Figure 28, which present

| | Security | Social | Esteem | Autonomy | Self-Actualization | Number of Cases Small | Large |
|---|---|---|---|---|---|---|---|
| **Nordic-European Countries** | | | | | | | |
| Denmark | −.15 | .24 | −.10 | −.38 | −.21 | 69 | 80 |
| Germany | .10 | .01 | .15 | .15 | .04 | 126 | 453 |
| Norway | −.04 | .19 | .00 | .13 | .09 | 93 | 127 |
| Sweden | −.04 | −.11 | .16 | .07 | .13 | 100 | 242 |
| Average | −.03 | .08 | .05 | −.01 | .01 | | |
| **Latin-European Countries** | | | | | | | |
| Belgium | −.03 | .01 | .02 | .22 | −.03 | 177 | 199 |
| France | .36 | .12 | .04 | .08 | −.03 | 56 | 97 |
| Italy | −.01 | −.02 | .26 | .36 | .18 | 95 | 171 |
| Spain | −.05 | .20 | −.02 | −.05 | .01 | 131 | 69 |
| Average | .07 | .08 | .08 | .15 | .04 | | |
| **Anglo-American Countries** | | | | | | | |
| England | .11 | −.40 | −.21 | .36 | .01 | 24 | 213 |
| United States | .10 | −.07 | .05 | −.24 | .11 | 20 | 441 |
| Average | .11 | −.24 | −.08 | .06 | .06 | | |
| **Developing Countries** | | | | | | | |
| Argentina | .29 | .31 | .27 | −.07 | .08 | 111 | 86 |
| Chile | .13 | −.11 | .11 | −.01 | .13 | 83 | 76 |
| India | .04 | −.07 | .38 | .46 | −.07 | 6 | 107 |
| Average | .15 | .04 | .25 | .13 | .05 | | |
| Japan | .15 | −.13 | .37 | .37 | .12 | 61 | 103 |
| All Managers | .07 | .01 | .11 | .10 | .04 | | |

* Positive values indicate the need is more important for managers in smaller companies; negative values indicate it is more important for managers in larger companies.

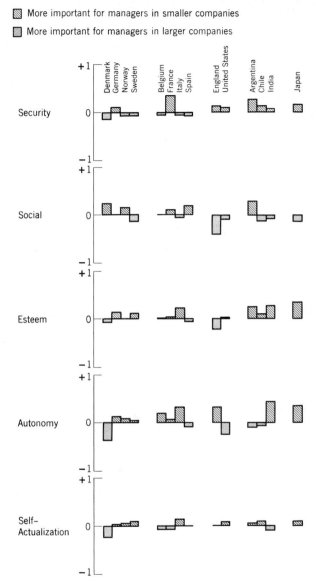

Figure 28. Need importance: managers in smaller versus larger companies.

the relevant data for such comparisons. Note that when the average of all countries is calculated, there is a slight trend for small-company managers to attach more importance to each of the five types of needs. This tendency is most pronounced in the Developing countries and in Japan. In the other groups of countries there are virtually no differences between small- and large-company managers. Overall, then, size seems to have a negligible effect on perceptions of need importance.

## Age of Managers

To obtain two groups approximately equal in numbers of managers when we classified managers by age, we chose age 40 as our dividing line. Those managers who were 39 years of age or younger, we have termed the "younger" group; and those 40 and over, the "older" group.

### Attitudes and Assumptions Underlying Management Practices

Table 29 and the accompanying Figure 29 show a generally inconsistent picture of relationships of age to attitudes and assumptions relevant to managerial practices. This can be seen quickly by a glance at the summary row at the bottom of the table. Only in the area of sharing information and objectives was there a consistent and fairly strong trend—this, in the direction of more favorable attitudes on the part of younger managers. In the other three areas, younger and older managers had about equivalent attitudes, considering all countries together.

The picture within individual countries is also an inconsistent one, with the exceptions of Sweden and the United States. In these two countries, younger managers consistently endorsed more democratic-participative stands.

All in all, age does not seem to have a very strong effect on attitudes toward managerial practices.

### Cognitive Descriptions of the Managerial Role

Since younger managers seem to have a very slight tendency to hold more democratic attitudes toward managerial practices, it might be anticipated they would see to *direct* and to *persuade*

TABLE 29. ATTITUDES TOWARD MANAGEMENT PRACTICES: YOUNGER
VERSUS OLDER MANAGERS (DIFFERENCES IN STANDARD SCORES) *

| | Capacity for Leadership and Initiative | Sharing Information and Objectives | Participation | Internal Control | Number of Cases | |
|---|---|---|---|---|---|---|
| | | | | | Younger | Older |
| Nordic-European Countries | | | | | | |
| Denmark | .22 | .50 | −.12 | .01 | 78 | 71 |
| Germany | −.05 | .16 | .00 | .14 | 333 | 253 |
| Norway | .19 | .07 | −.05 | −.19 | 48 | 173 |
| Sweden | .18 | .01 | .13 | .11 | 117 | 223 |
| Average | .14 | .19 | −.01 | .02 | | |
| Latin-European Countries | | | | | | |
| Belgium | −.03 | −.03 | −.03 | −.05 | 174 | 204 |
| France | −.03 | .13 | −.09 | −.11 | 66 | 88 |
| Italy | .35 | .21 | .17 | −.03 | 188 | 78 |
| Spain | −.05 | .35 | −.09 | .09 | 127 | 75 |
| Average | .06 | .17 | −.01 | −.03 | | |
| Anglo-American Countries | | | | | | |
| England | −.08 | .13 | .01 | .11 | 132 | 107 |
| United States | .08 | .01 | .13 | .11 | 117 | 223 |
| Average | .00 | .07 | .07 | .11 | | |
| Developing Countries | | | | | | |
| Argentina | −.07 | .01 | −.05 | −.12 | 117 | 81 |
| Chile | .20 | .28 | −.11 | .07 | 118 | 41 |
| India | .03 | −.07 | −.09 | .22 | 73 | 41 |
| Average | .03 | .07 | −.08 | .06 | | |
| Japan | −.05 | .27 | −.05 | .03 | 45 | 110 |
| All Managers | .06 | .14 | −.02 | .03 | | |

* Positive values indicate younger managers have more democratic attitudes; negative values indicate older managers have more democratic attitudes.

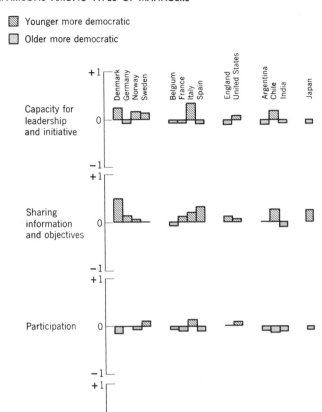

Figure 29. Attitudes toward management practices: younger versus older managers.

as more similar in meaning than do older managers; however, such is not the case, as is shown in Table 30. In ten of fourteen countries, it is the older managers who perceive greater similarity between these two concepts. Several of the individual countries, notably Denmark, Italy, and especially Chile, show very strong trends in that direction. On the other hand, several of the re-

TABLE 30. SIMILARITY OF THE CONCEPTS *To Direct* AND *To Persuade:*
YOUNGER VERSUS OLDER MANAGERS (DIFFERENCES
IN STANDARD SCORES)*

| | Differ-ences Between Means | Number of Cases | |
|---|---|---|---|
| | | Younger | Older |
| Nordic-European Countries | | | |
| Denmark | .47 | 68 | 61 |
| Germany | −.29 | 328 | 249 |
| Norway | .21 | 48 | 169 |
| Sweden | .14 | 115 | 218 |
| Average | .13 | | |
| Latin-European Countries | | | |
| Belgium | .12 | 171 | 203 |
| France | .09 | 67 | 86 |
| Italy | .48 | 183 | 80 |
| Spain | .15 | 127 | 74 |
| Average | .21 | | |
| Anglo-American Countries | | | |
| England | .07 | 132 | 107 |
| United States | −.21 | 186 | 271 |
| Average | −.07 | | |
| Developing Countries | | | |
| Argentina | .10 | 117 | 81 |
| Chile | .93 | 117 | 37 |
| India | −.01 | 72 | 39 |
| Average | .34 | | |
| Japan | −.25 | 43 | 106 |
| All Managers | .14 | | |

* Positive values indicate the two concepts are more similar for older
managers; negative values indicate they are more similar for younger
managers.

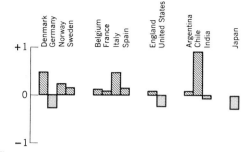

The two concepts more similar for older managers

The two concepts more similar for younger managers

Figure 30. Similarity of the concepts *to direct* and *to persuade:* younger versus older managers.

versals of the overall trend are fairly large, especially in Germany, the United States, and Japan. In these three countries, it is the younger managers who regard the two concepts as relatively more similar.

If we shift to Table 31, where the results for the relative similarity in perceptions of higher- and lower-status positions are given, we can see that age has little influence in this attitude area. Differences within each country tend to be quite small here, and the overall difference across all countries is negligible.

Taken together, the results presented in Tables 30 and 31, pertinent to managers' cognitive descriptions of the managerial role, show a slight but probably insignificant tendency for older managers to describe the role in a potentially less authoritarian manner. This tendency, as we indicated, is at variance with the results for the effects of age on attitudes and assumptions underlying managerial practices. However, all of the age trends so far mentioned are not very large, and it would be safe to conclude that age does not seem to be a very crucial variable in affecting the types of attitudes studied in at least two of the three parts of our questionnaire. We can therefore turn to the final attitude area covered in our study and see whether age seems to have any effect on motivations and satisfactions.

## TABLE 31. Similarity of Higher-Status Positions to Lower-Status Positions: Younger Versus Older Managers (Differences in Standard Scores)*

| | Differences Between Means | Number of Cases | |
|---|---|---|---|
| | | Younger | Older |
| Nordic-European Countries | | | |
| Denmark | .23 | 68 | 61 |
| Germany | .04 | 328 | 249 |
| Norway | −.03 | 48 | 169 |
| Sweden | .17 | 115 | 218 |
| Average | .10 | | |
| Latin-European Countries | | | |
| Belgium | .05 | 171 | 203 |
| France | .09 | 67 | 86 |
| Italy | −.05 | 183 | 80 |
| Spain | .07 | 127 | 74 |
| Average | .04 | | |
| Anglo-American Countries | | | |
| England | .08 | 132 | 107 |
| United States | .21 | 186 | 271 |
| Average | .15 | | |
| Developing Countries | | | |
| Argentina | −.05 | 117 | 81 |
| Chile | .00 | 117 | 37 |
| India | −.07 | 72 | 39 |
| Average | −.04 | | |
| Japan | −.05 | 43 | 106 |
| All Managers | .05 | | |

* Positive values indicate the two concepts are more similar for older managers; negative values indicate they are more similar for younger managers.

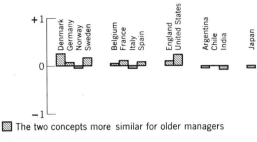

■ The two concepts more similar for older managers

▩ The two concepts more similar for younger managers

Figure 31. Similarity of higher-status positions to lower-status positions: younger versus older managers.

## Need Fulfillment

Younger managers report receiving less need fulfillment than older managers. This is the clear and unmistakable impression one gets from examining Table 32 and Figure 32, which present the relevant data for comparisons between the two age groups. However, it should be pointed out immediately that these results are not controlled for management level. Since we know from our demographic data that, on the average, older managers have higher-level positions, it is quite likely that the results are due more to management level than to age. In other words, what Table 32 and Figure 32 show is that older, higher-level managers receive more fulfillment than younger, lower-level managers. This is about equally the case for all need areas and for all the groups of countries.

Despite the overall similarity of the findings (from one type of need to another and from one group of countries to another) for differences between younger and older managers, there is some variability among the individual countries. For example, in Japan, age (in conjunction with managerial level) seems to make a considerable difference in perceived need fulfillment. Younger Japanese managers report receiving much less fulfillment, compared to older Japanese managers. Chile, Germany, and Spain also report strong trends in this same direction. On the other hand, in Norway, France, and India, the trend is generally reversed, with

TABLE 32. NEED FULFILLMENT: YOUNGER VERSUS OLDER MANAGERS
(DIFFERENCES IN STANDARD SCORES)*

| | Security | Social | Esteem | Autonomy | Self-Actualization | Number of Cases Younger | Older |
|---|---|---|---|---|---|---|---|
| **Nordic-European Countries** | | | | | | | |
| Denmark | −.24 | −.34 | −.51 | −.14 | −.08 | 78 | 71 |
| Germany | −.18 | −.25 | −.45 | −.29 | −.28 | 333 | 253 |
| Norway | .06 | .21 | −.06 | −.07 | .10 | 48 | 173 |
| Sweden | −.27 | −.26 | −.19 | −.26 | −.14 | 117 | 223 |
| Average | −.16 | −.16 | −.30 | −.19 | −.10 | | |
| **Latin-Europeon Countries** | | | | | | | |
| Belgium | −.16 | −.22 | −.35 | .09 | −.15 | 174 | 204 |
| France | .09 | −.29 | .10 | .19 | .21 | 66 | 88 |
| Italy | −.42 | −.17 | −.24 | −.24 | −.23 | 188 | 78 |
| Spain | −.31 | −.35 | −.48 | −.31 | −.17 | 127 | 75 |
| Average | −.20 | −.26 | −.24 | −.07 | −.09 | | |
| **Anglo-American Countries** | | | | | | | |
| England | .03 | −.17 | −.43 | −.07 | −.03 | 132 | 107 |
| United States | .14 | −.10 | −.11 | −.02 | .04 | 193 | 270 |
| Average | .09 | −.14 | −.27 | −.05 | .01 | | |
| **Developing Countries** | | | | | | | |
| Argentina | −.09 | .01 | −.27 | −.15 | −.15 | 117 | 81 |
| Chile | −.29 | −.09 | −.56 | −.09 | −.44 | 118 | 41 |
| India | .05 | −.08 | .00 | .32 | .15 | 73 | 41 |
| Average | −.11 | −.05 | −.28 | .03 | −.15 | | |
| Japan | −.34 | −.21 | −.71 | −.41 | −.37 | 45 | 110 |
| All Managers | −.14 | −.16 | −.30 | −.10 | −.11 | | |

* Positive values indicate younger managers have greater need fulfillment; negative values indicate older managers have greater need fulfillment.

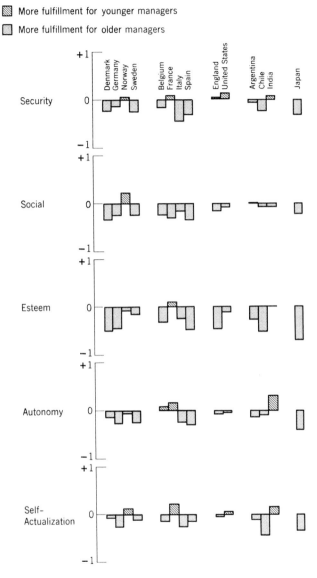

Figure 32. Need fulfillment: younger versus older managers.

the younger managers actually reporting more fulfillment than the older managers. In the United States, there appears to be relatively little difference between older and younger managers.

### Need Satisfaction

Given the results for need fulfillment, where there was a fairly consistent trend for older managers to report greater need fulfillment, the results for need satisfaction are somewhat surprising in that older managers evidence no greater satisfaction than younger managers. In fact, if there is any trend at all shown in Table 33 and Figure 33, which give the results for satisfaction differences among the two age groups, it is for the younger managers to express slightly greater satisfaction. Thus, although older managers feel they get more fulfillment from their jobs, this amount of fulfillment is no closer to their expectations than is the lower fulfillment of younger managers to that age group's expectations.

If we compare the age differences in satisfaction from country to country, we find that younger managers tend to be consistently more satisfied in Denmark, Norway, France, the United States, and India. Countries showing consistently greater satisfaction for older managers are Germany, Spain, and Argentina. In terms of groups of countries, younger managers seem to be relatively best off in the two Anglo-American countries, and worst off in the two South American Developing countries.

### Need Importance

Age seems to make some real differences in the importance attached to various needs. This fact is brought out in Table 34 and Figure 34 which give the differences between the two age groups for each need and for each country. As can be seen from the bottom row of Table 34, differences of any appreciable magnitude between the age groups, in the importance they attach to needs, are confined to the three lower-order needs: Security, Social, and Esteem. In each of these three areas, older managers attached more importance to the need. The average difference between the two age groups was greatest in the Security need area. As one might expect, considering the findings of a previous

TABLE 33. NEED SATISFACTION: YOUNGER VERSUS OLDER MANAGERS
(DIFFERENCES IN STANDARD SCORES) *

| | Secur-ity | Social | Esteem | Auton-omy | Self-Actu-aliza-tion | Number of Cases Younger | Older |
|---|---|---|---|---|---|---|---|
| Nordic-European Countries | | | | | | | |
| Denmark | −.14 | −.17 | −.38 | −.20 | −.12 | 78 | 71 |
| Germany | .06 | .02 | .06 | .12 | .17 | 333 | 253 |
| Norway | −.06 | −.28 | −.15 | .00 | −.16 | 48 | 173 |
| Sweden | .04 | −.08 | −.17 | .03 | −.01 | 117 | 223 |
| Average | −.03 | −.13 | −.16 | −.01 | −.03 | | |
| Latin-European Countries | | | | | | | |
| Belgium | .04 | −.01 | −.07 | −.14 | .04 | 174 | 204 |
| France | −.11 | .00 | −.37 | −.26 | −.30 | 66 | 88 |
| Italy | .02 | −.16 | −.09 | −.12 | .05 | 188 | 78 |
| Spain | .19 | .17 | .24 | .26 | .06 | 127 | 75 |
| Average | .04 | .00 | −.07 | −.07 | −.04 | | |
| Anglo-American Countries | | | | | | | |
| England | −.34 | −.09 | .05 | −.07 | −.16 | 132 | 107 |
| United States | −.39 | −.09 | −.13 | −.13 | −.20 | 193 | 270 |
| Average | −.37 | −.09 | −.04 | −.10 | −.18 | | |
| Developing Countries | | | | | | | |
| Argentina | .14 | .02 | .11 | .24 | .20 | 117 | 81 |
| Chile | .29 | −.18 | .28 | .03 | .24 | 118 | 41 |
| India | −.06 | −.10 | −.10 | −.45 | −.09 | 73 | 41 |
| Average | .12 | −.09 | .10 | −.06 | .12 | | |
| Japan | −.07 | −.10 | .13 | −.12 | .18 | 45 | 110 |
| All Managers | −.03 | −.08 | −.04 | −.06 | −.01 | | |

* Positive values indicate younger managers are more dissatisfied; nega-tive values indicate older managers are more dissatisfied.

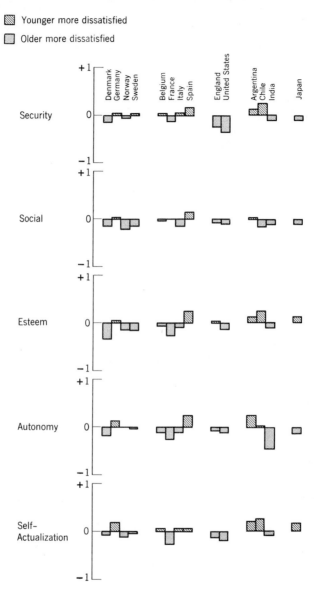

Figure 33. Need satisfaction: younger versus older managers.

TABLE 34. NEED IMPORTANCE: YOUNGER VERSUS OLDER MANAGERS
(DIFFERENCES IN STANDARD SCORES) *

| | Security | Social | Esteem | Autonomy | Self-Actualization | Number of Cases Younger | Older |
|---|---|---|---|---|---|---|---|
| **Nordic-European Countries** | | | | | | | |
| Denmark | −.74 | −.44 | −.49 | .10 | .06 | 78 | 71 |
| Germany | −.21 | −.17 | −.33 | −.10 | −.01 | 333 | 253 |
| Norway | .03 | .04 | −.07 | .02 | .24 | 48 | 173 |
| Sweden | −.47 | −.37 | −.29 | −.14 | −.10 | 117 | 223 |
| Average | −.35 | −.24 | −.30 | −.03 | .05 | | |
| **Latin-European Countries** | | | | | | | |
| Belgium | −.07 | −.12 | −.24 | .16 | −.03 | 174 | 204 |
| France | .21 | −.22 | .34 | .09 | −.04 | 66 | 88 |
| Italy | −.47 | −.17 | −.21 | −.07 | .09 | 188 | 78 |
| Spain | −.16 | −.30 | −.27 | −.18 | −.09 | 127 | 75 |
| Average | −.12 | −.20 | −.10 | .00 | −.02 | | |
| **Anglo-American Countries** | | | | | | | |
| England | −.47 | −.16 | −.22 | −.18 | .02 | 132 | 107 |
| United States | −.60 | −.22 | −.12 | .10 | .06 | 193 | 270 |
| Average | −.54 | −.19 | −.17 | −.04 | .04 | | |
| **Developing Countries** | | | | | | | |
| Argentina | .21 | .19 | −.19 | .07 | .04 | 117 | 81 |
| Chile | .10 | −.32 | −.36 | −.12 | −.12 | 118 | 41 |
| India | .06 | −.09 | .06 | .10 | .19 | 73 | 41 |
| Average | .12 | −.07 | −.16 | .02 | .04 | | |
| Japan | −.89 | −.18 | −.39 | −.25 | −.09 | 45 | 110 |
| All Managers | −.25 | −.18 | −.20 | −.03 | .02 | | |

* Positive values indicate the need is more important for younger managers; negative values indicate it is more important for older managers.

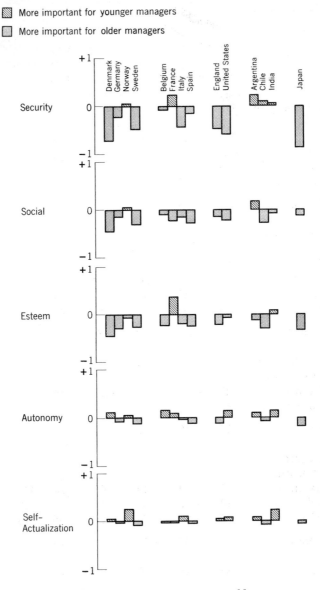

Figure 34. Need importance: younger versus older managers.

study of American managers,[11] older managers placed more—and often much more—importance on Security needs than did younger managers. This was especially the case in Japan, the two Anglo-American countries, and several of the European countries. In the Developing countries, on the other hand, there was a small reversal of this trend for Security needs, with the younger managers in these three countries putting more stress on Security. In both the Social and Esteem need areas, older managers consistently attached more importance to these needs. In each category, this was true in twelve of the fourteen countries.

For the two highest-order needs of Autonomy and Self-Actualization, there were no discernible trends in relation to the age of the manager.

[11] L. W. Porter, "Job Attitudes in Management II. Perceived Importance of Needs as a Function of Job Level," *Journal of Applied Psychology*, Vol. 47, 141–148 (1963).

# CHAPTER 6

# Conclusions

The summary of this book could take a variety of forms. The company operating in a foreign country and contemplating either exporting American managers or training foreign nationals will be interested in the detailed results of that particular country. For a country considering its own management development, the local results and their comparison with other countries' responses will have a special relevance. A manager can well afford to wonder why his national pattern is the way it is, how practices must be modified to fit it, and what its strengths and weaknesses are. But these concerns are all relatively specific to particular interests, and do not lend themselves to explicit summary here. On a more general level, there can be set down here a set of issues of broader interest to the student of management.

### The Nature of Human Nature

It is impossible to conceive of the structure of an industrial organization—much less the policies and practices by which it is operated—without making some assumptions about human behavior. What kind of people will we draw on to fill our slots? What motivates them, and how are they best led? These questions, and others like them, must be answered—though the assumptions about people are often implicit in structures and policies, and not faced squarely. These data give us a variety of indices of the assumptions about people made by managers across the world, and they present a clear, if somewhat perplexing, picture.

We have already pointed out the basic fact: Managers show relatively little faith in the capacity of others for initiative and leadership, but, surprisingly, approve of managerial practices presumably dependent on just these qualities. This point emerges clearly from their responses to direct questions about leadership, but it also appears elsewhere:

1. Taking all countries together, *to direct* has better connotations than *to persuade*. *To direct* has more *prestige, activity,* and *firmness.* It is closer to *to decide*. *To persuade,* on the other hand, is closer to making a mistake and cheating. We note that across the board, good management is still seen as deciding and directing—a much more centralized and unilateral view of the dynamics of the process than is often announced.

2. In addition to this overall character of unilaterality, the individual clusters stand out clearly here, too. The difference between *to direct* and *to persuade* is nearly three times as great for Norway, Denmark, Sweden, and Germany, as it is for the average of all the other countries. No country of the Nordic cluster shows a difference less than twice as big as the average of all the non-Nordic countries. Similarly, in estimating the capacity of subordinates, the countries in two clusters, Nordic and Latin, account for all the scores below the grand mean. All other countries—the two other clusters and Japan—are above the mean. Again, we have the pattern of a clear-cut overall characteristic of managers in general, and, within it, discriminably different patterns among the clusters of countries.

3. In evaluating the meaning of the concepts of "high-status positions" and "low-status positions" there is very little differ-

ence between the two for any country. All the countries cluster closely around the grand mean, and the groups of countries are virtually indistinguishable from one another. This failure to recognize the structural fact of the hierarchy fits oddly with the results, described earlier, regarding unilaterality and centralized command. In this way, the discrepancy is parallel to the findings on leadership. There, the faith in others was given a score only 70 percent as high as the approval of participative management practices, whereas the different practices differed among themselves only three percentage points. As far as these conceptual data are concerned, managers seem consistently to endorse egalitarian principles, vis-à-vis organizational structure, and yet seem to act as if they were part of an elite group.

It has already been suggested that the apparent espousal of more modern management practices may be merely a kind of lip service in the face of numerous management theorists insisting on it in recent years. Indeed, in the United States, though it is virtually "un-American" to declare oneself in favor of centralization, and though a public declaration in favor of unilaterality is anathema to most managers, the fact remains that the tremendous majority of American businesses are still run on a tight rein —highly centralized and closely supervised. Two problems arise from this discrepancy. In the first place, unwillingness to recognize the capacities of others may well be an outmoded vestige of a day when low standards of living and education, and a loose labor market, made this assumption more palatable to the general public than it is today. Times and ideas are changing, and it may be dangerous and expensive not to be sensitive to the shifts. This point will have to be developed a little further later on. The companion problem lies in the simple fact of the disparity between two integral parts of a philosophy of management. Ideas about structure and policy must necessarily be related to assumptions about the nature of human nature. To allow a wide gap to exist between them means a serious malfunction in the process of conceiving of a managerial philosophy. Part of this faulty conceptualization probably stems from an unwillingness to challenge highly personal and long-held notions about what people are like. Part of it, too, derives from management theorists' stressing action-panaceas in the form of practices, without closely examining their underpinnings. Whatever the reason, however, there is ample evidence here that management everywhere needs to examine implicit assumptions underlying policies and practices espoused. Further, the fact that this disparity between ideas about people and practice appears in the cluster-by-cluster analysis of the countries indicates that it is partly a cultural problem. This sympton calls for special examination in special cases, and a recognition of its roots in cultural traditions of good and bad, noble and peasant, and the needs of man.

## Kinds of Managers

It was possible to break the managers down into *old* and *young* (at 40), belonging to *large* and *small* companies (at 500), and occupying *higher-* and *lower-*level (at top third) positions. In a way, the remarkable thing is that these variables show relatively little influence on attitudes, motivation, or perceptions of the role of the manager. To be sure, there were differences, and they will be discussed, but the observed differences along these dimensions tend to be very much smaller than those associated with the clusters of countries. In overall terms, the general impact of the culture outweighs the effect of differentiating variable characteristics of the manager.

In spite of this tendency for the differences to be small, some exist, and are noteworthy. Democratic attitudes tend to appear in the young high-level managers in a large company. This may well be a kind of recognition on the part of a young successful group of a new role for the large corporation and a new possibility for management strategies. The higher-level managers in large companies tended to be more satisfied than the others. The higher-level managers tended to see more opportunities for need fulfillment in the job. So did older managers, but this may be partly because the older tend to be higher. Two patterns seem to stand out. The first has been mentioned—the possibility of a newer form of managerial practice with more democratic structure, more opportunity for satisfaction, and more actual satisfaction. The second pattern shows large companies to be higher in both satisfaction and democratic attitudes, and equal to smaller companies in seeing the necessity for satisfaction on the job. This pattern of response and its consistency seems directly contrary to the notion of the "Organization Man." Interdependence does not necessarily smother independence on the job.

### Social Philosophy and Managerial Motivation

In the area of motivation and the satisfaction of motives at work, there are a variety of points that need to be considered by everyone who is interested in management and in the way business as an institution is imbedded in society. A little pattern of important paradoxes that deserves our attention emerges. Let us restate the facts very simply:

1. There is little difference in the fulfillment of needs across countries. When asked how much there is, all managers —whether taken by countries or by clusters of countries—report similar degrees. The institution of industry is offering similar opportunities for people in various situations.

2. The satisfaction of needs measures the fulfillment provided against the expectations one brings to it. Across all countries, in general, two needs stand out as unsatisfied—Autonomy and Self-Actualization. Whatever opportunities business, as an institution, is offering, those who enter it are looking for more in these two areas.

3. The problem of high expectations shows up particularly when we look at countries and clusters of countries. The Developing countries (Argentina, Chile, and India) and two Latin-European countries (Spain and Italy) are highest in dissatisfaction. These five countries approach the fairly uniform motivational opportunities in industry with exceedingly high expectations.

4. When managers rank the importance of motivational possibilities, Argentina, Chile, and India are outstandingly and consistently high in their assessment of the importance of *all* needs. Spain and Italy are not far behind. These countries come to industry not only with high expectations, but also with the conviction that these are of prime importance. They

are also the most homogeneous in attitudes within their respective countries on this point among the fourteen-member family of nations sampled.

Two main issues stand out from these data: First, the motivational spectrum business provides, and, second, the meaning of heightened expectations in developing countries. To take up the first point first, the relative homogeneity of opportunities suggests that there is to some degree a common core in all business cultures. We do not get the picture—from the managers' view—of an archaic counting-house atmosphere in one place and consultative management in another. The problem of business, in motivational terms, is not one of bringing laggard countries up to a general standard.

However, the areas in which lack of fulfillment appears perhaps presage a problem. Across all countries, the needs least felt to be satisfied are Autonomy and Self-Actualization—the privileges of guiding oneself and of realizing one's capacities. Security is no longer a primary problem for these managers. Jobs have stabilized and Social satisfactions and Esteem are present. Lacking, are Autonomy and Self-Actualization. The deficit in Self-Actualization, for instance, is 1.8 times as great as in Esteem; the deficit in Self-Actualization and Autonomy combined is more than twice as large as the dissatisfaction in the other three areas combined. This pattern of relative satisfactions and dissatisfactions may be of considerable importance in the decision of people within a country to go into management. To recruit the ablest, and to secure their initiative and capacities for innovation, we will almost certainly have to come closer to meeting their expectations in the areas of Autonomy and Self-Actualization.

To some extent, we are at a turning point in historical development. Business was once seen as plagued by insecurity, barren of opportunities for social relationships, and lacking in recognition. From our study, the evidence of these three areas suggests that they are now reasonably cared for, at least in management. It is probably still true, however, that a capable youngster who wants to be master of his own fate will look to law, or to medicine, or to one of the traditionally autonomous professions. The specter of the "Organization Man" is currently large on most national business screens. Similarly, a talented man looking for an opportunity to realize his potential may well consider a commitment to artistic activity, look to an allied profession—architecture—or, in many cases, see government service, with its possibilities for changing the country, as a path to self-actualization. In principle, there doesn't seem to be any reason why industry cannot offer more of these opportunities for autonomy and self-actualization; and it seems clear that if it does not it will be at a competitive disadvantage in the labor market. Managerial philosophy and practices have changed over the years, probably in the direction of providing more opportunities of just this kind. However, this change in management thinking has not been as rapid as the change in the thinking of people from whom management must draw its new cadre, and it is just this disparity that is evident here.

This historical trend is even more sharply seen in the pattern of expectations of the countries with briefer histories of industrialization. Their expectations are uniformly high—higher, in fact, than those of the other countries. In the face of equal fulfillment, this means greater dissatisfaction. Further, these countries rank the satisfaction of all human needs as more important than do the older established countries. Things are happening in these newly industrialized countries that parallel what is going on in the even less developed ex-colonial African nations. First, like all managers in all countries, they respond to the "wind of change" that demands broader and broader enfranchisement—more autonomy and more opportunity for self-actualization. If anything is clear from recent history, it must be this sweep. All over the world, and in every kind of social institution, people and nations want the opportunity to determine their own fate and to realize their own potential. Second, they want it *now*. In all the rising countries, this immediacy of expectations is a familiar characteristic. The high expectations shown by the less-industrialized nations are characteristic of it. One is almost tempted to call them unreasonable expectations, but the assessment of what is reasonable is as culturally determined, and as shifting, as the old issue of what management's prerogative is. Third, the less-developed countries, in comparison with the other countries, uniformly rank the satisfactions of human needs as being of high importance. Business, as a social institution, is called upon to supply something quite different from, and more than, the means of production as defined in the traditional Marxist view of a factory. The implicit labor contract is no longer simply a provision of positively valued money in return for the disutility of work. The contract is more nearly a social contract in the Rousseauan sense. As the firm has grown big and stable, it has taken on the character of a social institution. And as it has done this, demands are being made of it that go well beyond a narrow economic-production definition of its function.

These three things—the demand for autonomy and self-actualization in all countries, the high expectations in the less-developed countries, and the relatively high level of importance these countries place on their satisfaction—have important implications for industry viewed as a social institution. First, in all countries, the demand for higher-order needs is closely related to the problem of who goes into management, and, consequently, to the role of the manager that is seen in a given culture. Everywhere, if business is to attract high levels of initiative and innovation, it probably must recast philosophies and practices to provide these satisfactions. Second, in all the developing countries in the world, we have a clue that this demand is made of business with a special urgency and immediacy. In attempts to foster industrial organizations in other countries, we must come to see them not merely as more or less successful productive organizations, but as part of the broad web of society, importantly charged with a responsibility to provide not only material production but also opportunities for human growth and development. If we fail to realize these expectations of business, we will miss an important part of the change in thinking that is going on. It is seductively easy to fall back on the simpler objective that the business of business is to produce goods and services, and that more cannot appropriately be demanded of it. However, this no longer seems to be a tenable position. Business has been so intimately connected with increases in the standard of living and the level of education, and has assumed such a stable role, that it is seen as a social institution; more, therefore, is demanded of it. To abdicate this responsibility would be to threaten the whole economic system. The conditions have been created for greater motivational demands. If they are not provided in industry, they will be sought elsewhere in social revolution of one form or another. If industry is narrowly viewed as the management of the means of production, it seems inevitable that it will be incorporated into, and become subservient to, the social institution that meets the human motivational demands.

Before we leave this point, it is worth noticing that it has seemed necessary in this discussion to deal with levels of industrialization as a means of uncovering the meaning of managers' responses—and this, in spite of the fact that previously we emphasized the approach of explaining managerial strategies by means of cultural forces. The data at hand are a good example of our suggestion that it is not an either-or choice. Typically, the two are jointly effective. An attempt to interpret the phenomena solely in terms on one or the other seems inevitably lopsided and inadequate.

### Internal and External Causal Factors

In looking over the findings shown in this book, two pairs of themes stand out, each of which seems, superficially, to contain a contradiction. The first is the rather considerable similarity of viewpoints across all managers, coupled with the strongly patterned diversity of the clusters of countries. This simultaneous existence of homogeneity and diversity reappears again and again in the data, and both sides of the phenomenon must be taken into account. On the one hand, there is an industrial culture, defined by the similarity of the responses of all managers. In this sense, the imperatives of the business situation and its values and traditions seem to bring about a uniform response to problems of management. On the other hand, in each country or group of countries, this industrial culture is re-evolved and adopted, with the stamp of national traditions clearly on it. The responses by clusters of countries are consistent, and clearly different from one another. It would be simpler if one could choose an either-or solution to these alternatives—if a respondent's answer could be explained simply by the fact that he is a manager or, say, a Frenchman. The explanation is not as simple as that, however. The response is due both to his managerial status and to his nationality, and any attempt to understand managerial behavior must include both facets of the problem.

The second apparently contradictory pair of themes recurring here is the simultaneous explanation in terms of level of industrialization and of cultural patterns in the groups of countries. Again, it would be tempting to look for—and find—an easier either-or solution. However, the data repeatedly force both influences on us simultaneously. For example, in considering motivations sought and found at work, the cultural clusters of countries stand clearly separate from one another, suggesting a one-sided explanation. At the same time, however, the cluster of Argentina, Chile, and India differs sharply from all the other clusters, suggesting the influence of levels of industrialization. Where there are differences within a cluster they follow the same pattern. Spain and Italy, less developed than Belguim and France, differ in the direction of agreement with Argentina, Chile, and India. Indeed, the very existence of the Argentina-Chile-India cluster is a sign of the same phenomenon. In the Latin or Nordic clusters, it is easy to point to common cultural links—language families, religious traditions, shared literary streams, and the like. In these terms, one might have expected India to be close to England; and Argentina and Chile to be close to the Latin cluster, especially Spain in our sample. Instead, they cross the faint cultural ties and form one of the tightest of all the clusters in terms of correlation with one another and lack of correlation with other countries.

Again, we must accept both factors as interrelated explanatory variables and eschew choosing one to the exclusion of the other. In any attempt to explain behavior, it is clear that the response is a complex function both of the way the person views and internalizes his world and of the pressures of his external situation. While no one quite explicitly denies this duality, in practice the emphasis has been heavily one-sided. Economists have tended to deal with structural situational variables—the size of the firm, the state of the labor market, concentration of capital, and the like. Psychologists, on the other hand, have turned toward more personally-oriented variables. With a tradition of research and theory dealing, for instance, with such internal factors as satisfactions, motives, and attitudes, they have tended to see causes in states of affairs grounded within the person. Neither approach seems to intend to deny the domain of the other; the exclusiveness is an accident of attention. However, these data re-emphasize the duality of the causal variables lying behind managerial behavior, and call again for a simultaneous recognition of the two factors and their complex interactions.

### The Moral of the Tale

If there is any one broad finding that emerges from this study, it must be the existence of recognizable cultural clusters of countries. We cannot consider the nature of international management without taking this factor into account. To some extent this must seem to be a truism—something which we all have always known and said. Indeed, it is true that it has been stated in general terms for a long time, but nothing has been done about it. Recognizing the existence of these cultural influences, but staggered by their diversity, we have tended to point to them and let them go. Now they are—albeit in the most preliminary fashion—identified, measured, and irrevocably set down. In this sense, the most important outcome of the study may well be the simple fact that it has been done. We make this suggestion without any intention of patting ourselves on the back. The importance of having done the study is not a tribute to its expertise or originality, but simply to its breaking the ice. So many times in the past one has recognized the existence of differences and patterns of differences; yet research workers have tended to feel it would be impossible to tease out the detail of national patterns. Now it is clear that identical questions *can* be asked across cultures without losing so much in translation as to blur the outlines. Foreign industrialists are at least as cooperative as our own in answering questions aimed at the comparative nature of managers. Present statistical techniques—with a boost from computer technology—make the data manageable. It is not at all suggested that the completion of this study ends the problem. On the contrary, the fact that such research can be done and has been done should stimulate additional work. We are ready—and techniques are available—for a host of comparative studies of managerial attitudes and behavior that will lead us into a detailed understanding of the role of national and cultural traditions in shaping managerial strategy and style.

Nothing seems clearer than the pressing need for data of this kind, and for the further understanding of comparative diversity in a world which, day by day, is growing rapidly smaller and more interdependent. None of us can any longer stand grandly in his isolation and feel that "they are undergoing the same kinds of change, but somehow they are different from us." We need to know the details of the way our developed neighbors see the process through their culturally-tinted spectacles. And if we are to help and nurture the growth of less-developed countries, we need infinitely more information about the way their traditional values and practices will interact with the culture of industrialization. This study is the merest beginning. If it points the way to a further collection of information, it will have done its job.

# English and Foreign-Language
# Questionnaires

On the following pages are the English and ten foreign-language versions of our questionnaire. All the translated versions are provided so that the exact wording of any part or parts of them may be easily reproduced.

It should be noted that, although there is no abridgment of the instructions or questions, the format has been condensed somewhat. In Part III of the actual questionnaire, for example, each of the fifteen concepts is followed by the same 9 rating scales. Here, however, the complete rating-scale pattern is shown for the first concept only. Also, in Part III of the actual questionnaire the instructions are worded in accordance with the original format of the questionnaire, where the instructions appeared on one page and the concepts and scales were presented on succeeding pages. Here, we have instead listed the concepts immediately following the instructions.

The questionnaires appear in the following order:

1. English
2. Danish
3. German
4. Norwegian
5. Swedish
6. Flemish
7. French
8. Italian
9. Spanish
10. South American Spanish (Argentina and Chile)
11. Japanese

INSTITUTE OF INDUSTRIAL RELATIONS

UNIVERSITY OF CALIFORNIA

BERKELEY, CALIFORNIA

# Research on Opinions in Industry

## PART I

In the section below you will see a series of statements. Please indicate your agreement or disagreement. Use the scale below each statement.

For Example:

It is easier to work in cool weather than in hot.

If you think it is easier to work in cool weather, put an (X) above "agree"; if you think it is much easier to work in cool weather, put a mark above "strongly agree." If you think it doesn't matter, put a mark over "undecided" and so on. Put your mark in a space, not on the boundaries.

There are no right or wrong answers. We are interested in your opinion about the statements which follow.

1. The average human being prefers to be directed, wishes to avoid responsibility, and has relatively little ambition.

2. Leadership skills can be acquired by most people regardless of their particular inborn traits and abilities.

3. The use of rewards (pay, promotion, etc.) and punishment (failure to promote, etc.) is **not** the best way to get subordinates to do their work.

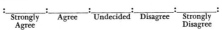

4. In a work situation, if the subordinates cannot influence me then I lose some influence on them.

5. A good leader should give detailed and complete instructions to his subordinates, rather than giving them merely general directions and depending upon their initiative to work out the details.

6. Group goal setting offers advantages that cannot be obtained by individual goal setting.

7. A superior should give his subordinates only that information which is necessary for them to do their immediate tasks.

8. The superior's authority over his subordinates in an organization is primarily economic.

**INSTRUCTIONS:**

On the following pages of Part II will be listed several characteristics or qualities connected with **your own position** in your firm. For each such characteristic, you are asked to give three ratings:

    a. **How much** of the characteristic **is there now** connected with **your position** in your firm?

    b. **How much** of the characteristic do you think **should be** connected with **your position** in your firm?

    c. **How important** is this position characteristic **to you?**

Each rating will be made on a seven-point scale, which will look like this:

    (minimum)   1      2      3      4      5      6      7   (maximum)

Please put a mark (X) above the number on the scale that represents the amount of the characteristic being rated. Low numbers represent low or minimum amounts, and high numbers represent high or maximum amounts. If you think there is "very little" or "none" of the characteristic presently associated with the position, you would place an X above number 1. If you think there is "just a little," you would place an X above number 2, and so on. If you think there is a "great deal but not a maximum amount," you would place an X above number 6. For each scale, place an X-mark above only one number.

**Please do not omit any scales.**

1. The **feeling of self-esteem** a person gets from being in my management position:

   a) How much is there now?

   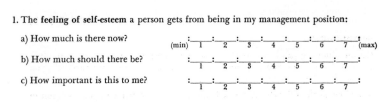

   b) How much should there be?

   c) How important is this to me?

2. The **authority** connected with my management position:

   a) How much is there now?

   b) How much should there be?

   c) How important is this to me?

3. The **opportunity for personal growth and development** in my management position:

   a) How much is there now?

   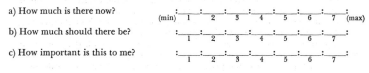

   b) How much should there be?

   c) How important is this to me?

4. The **prestige** of my management position **inside** the company (that is, the regard received from others **in** the company):

   a) How much is there now?

   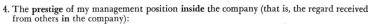

   b) How much should there be?

   c) How important is this to me?

5. The **opportunity for independent thought and action** in my management position:

   a) How much is there now?

   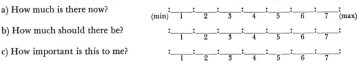

   b) How much should there be?

   c) How important is this to me?

6. The **feeling of security** in my management position:

   a) How much is there now?

   b) How much should there be?

   c) How important is this to me?

7. The **feeling of self-fulfillment** a person gets from being in my management position (that is, the feeling of being able to use one's own unique capabilities, realizing one's potentialities):

a) How much is there now?

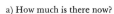
(min) 1　2　3　4　5　6　7 (max)

b) How much should there be?

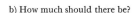
1　2　3　4　5　6　7

c) How important is this to me?

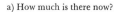
1　2　3　4　5　6　7


8. The **prestige** of my management position **outside** the company (that is, the regard received from others not in the company):

a) How much is there now?

(min) 1　2　3　4　5　6　7 (max)

b) How much should there be?

1　2　3　4　5　6　7

c) How important is this to me?

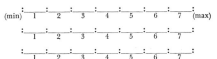
1　2　3　4　5　6　7


9. The **feeling of worthwhile accomplishment** in my management position:

a) How much is there now?

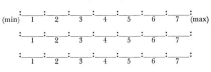
(min) 1　2　3　4　5　6　7 (max)

b) How much should there be?

1　2　3　4　5　6　7

c) How important is this to me?

1　2　3　4　5　6　7


10. The **opportunity, in my management position, to give help to other people:**

a) How much is there now?

(min) 1　2　3　4　5　6　7 (max)

b) How much should there be?

1　2　3　4　5　6　7

c) How important is this to me?

1　2　3　4　5　6　7


11. The **opportunity to develop close friendships** in my management position:

a) How much is there now?

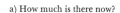
(min) 1　2　3　4　5　6　7 (max)

b) How much should there be?

1　2　3　4　5　6　7

c) How important is this to me?

1　2　3　4　5　6　7

## PART III

**INSTRUCTIONS:**

The purpose of this questionnaire is to obtain your impressions of a variety of things or ideas. For example, at the top of the next page is the word PHYSICIAN. You are to give your impression of what this means to you by placing an X on each of a series of scales which appear beneath it on the same page. Each of the scales is defined by a pair of words. (See the examples below.) Place an X on **each** scale in one of the seven spaces which most accurately describes the particular thing or idea, **in your opinion.** The following illustrate how you might mark the scales for a particular thing or idea.

large :_____:_____:__X__:_____:_____:_____:_____: small

unenjoyable :_____:_____:_____:_____:_____:__X__:_____: enjoyable

Please be sure to:

1. Place an X on every scale. **Do not omit any scales.**

2. Put only **one** X on each scale.

# PHYSICIAN

unimportant :____:____:____:____:____:____:____:____: important

profound :____:____:____:____:____:____:____:____: superficial

active :____:____:____:____:____:____:____:____: passive

narrow :____:____:____:____:____:____:____:____: wide

difficult :____:____:____:____:____:____:____:____: easy

good :____:____:____:____:____:____:____:____: bad

stable :____:____:____:____:____:____:____:____: changeable

interesting :____:____:____:____:____:____:____:____: uninteresting

weak :____:____:____:____:____:____:____:____: strong

COLONEL

TO DECIDE

TO PERSUADE

FACTORY FOREMAN

TO CREATE

TO CHEAT

PRIEST

TO MAKE A MISTAKE

SERGEANT

TO COOPERATE

BISHOP

TO DIRECT

TO REPRIMAND

FACTORY MANAGER

To help us with the statistical analysis of the data, please give the following information about yourself.

1. Country of citizenship:_____

2. Title of your present position in your company: _____

3. Present department in your company (check one):
   _____ Production
   _____ Sales, Marketing and Advertising
   _____ Finance and Accounting
   _____ Personnel and Training
   _____ Purchasing
   _____ Research and Development
   _____ General Administration
   _____ Other (please specify) _____

4. How many levels of supervision are there in your total company from the first-level supervisor to the head of the organization? (Give the number):
   _____

5. How many levels of supervision are there **above** your position? (Give the number):
   _____

6. How many years have you been working in business, industry or government? (Check one):
   _____ 0 to 1 year
   _____ 1 to 3 years
   _____ 3 to 5 years
   _____ 5 to 10 years
   _____ 10 to 20 years
   _____ 20 to 30 years
   _____ more than 30 years

7. Approximately how many employees (management and non-management) are there in your total company? (Check one):
   _____ 1 to 49
   _____ 50 to 99
   _____ 100 to 499
   _____ 500 to 999
   _____ 1,000 to 4,999
   _____ 5,000 to 9,999
   _____ 10,000 to 29,999
   _____ 30,000 to 99,999
   _____ 100,000 to 299,999
   _____ 300,000 or more

8. Do you own a major portion of your company? (Check one):
   _____ yes
   _____ no

9. Type of company you work for (check one):
   _____ Transportation and Shipping
   _____ Postal, Telegraph and Telephone
   _____ Power, Light and Electricity
   _____ Wholesale and Retail Trade
   _____ Finance and Insurance
   _____ Chemical and Petroleum
   _____ Mining
   _____ Steel and Metal Fabrication
   _____ Manufacturing
   _____ Other (please specify) _____

10. Your age (check one):
    _____ 20–24
    _____ 25–29
    _____ 30–34
    _____ 35–39
    _____ 40–44
    _____ 45–49
    _____ 50–54
    _____ 55–59
    _____ 60 or more

11. How many total years of formal education did you complete, including school, university, and technical school? (Give the number):
    _____

12. If you attended a university or a technical school, what was the specialty you studied? (Check one):
    _____ Engineering
    _____ Law
    _____ Economics
    _____ Arts and Philosophy
    _____ Other (please specify) _____

# Meningsundersøgelser Inden for Industrien

# FØRSTE DEL

I denne del af undersøgelsen vil De finde en række udtalelser. Vær så venlig at markete, om Deres egen opfattelse er i overensstemmelse med eller afviger fra disse udtalelser. Benyt skalaen under hver udtalelse.

For exempel:

Det er lettere at arbejde i køligt end i varmt vejr.

| Samtykker : | Samtykker | Kan ikke tage | Uenig | I høj grad |
|---|---|---|---|---|
| i høj grad | | bestemmelse | | uenig |

Hvis De mener, det er lettere at arbejde i et køligt klima, sæt så et (X) ovenover " samtykker "; hvis De mener, det er meget lettere at arbejde i et køligt klima, sæt så et mærke ovenover " samtykker i høj grad." Hvis De mener, at der er ingen forskel, sæt da et mærke ovenover " kan ikke tage bestemmelse," osv. Men sæt Deres mærke i en rubrik, ikke udenfor denne.

Der er ingen rigtige eller forkerte svar. Vi er interesseret i Deres mening vedrørende følgende udtalelser.

1. Gennemsnitsmennesket foretrækker at blive vejledet, ønsker at undgå et ansvar og har forholdsvis ringe ærgerrighed.

| Samtykker | Samtykker | Kan ikke tage | Uenig | I høj grad |
|---|---|---|---|---|
| i høj grad | | bestemmelse | | uenig |

2. Førerevner kan tilegnes af de fleste individer uanset deres særlige medfødte egenskaber og anlæg.

| Samtykker : | Samtykker | Kan ikke tage | Uenig | I høj grad |
|---|---|---|---|---|
| i høj grad | | bestemmelse | | uenig |

3. Benyttelsen af belønninger (gagepålæg, forfremmelse, esv.) og straf (undladelse af forfremmelse, osv.) er **ikke** den bedste metode til at få de underordnede til at udføre deres arbejde.

| Samtykker | Samtykker | Kan ikke tage | Uenig | I høj grad |
|---|---|---|---|---|
| i høj grad | | bestemmelse | | uenig |

4. Hvis de underordnede i en arbejdssituation ikke kan udøve indflydelse på mig, mister jeg noget af min indflydelse på dem.

| Samtykker : | Samtykker | Kan ikke tage | Uenig | I høj grad |
|---|---|---|---|---|
| i høj grad | | bestemmelse | | uenig |

5. En god leder bør hellere give detaljeret og komplet vejledning til sine underordnede end ved anvisninger i almindelighed at forlade sig på deres eget initiativ til selv at udarbejde enkelthederne.

| Samtykker | Samtykker | Kan ikke tage | Uenig | I høj grad |
|---|---|---|---|---|
| i høj grad | | bestemmelse | | uenig |

6. At en gruppe i fællesskab sætter sig et mål, den vil opfylde, rummer fordele, som ikke kan opnås ved, at de enkelte individer selv sætter sign tilsvarende mål.

| Samtykker : | Samtykker | Kan ikke tage | Uenig | I høj grad |
|---|---|---|---|---|
| i høj grad | | bestemmelse | | uenig |

7. En overordnet burde kun give sine underordnede de oplysninger, som er nødvendige for dem under udførelsen af deres umiddelbare hverv.

| Samtykker | Samtykker | Kan ikke tage | Uenig | I høj grad |
|---|---|---|---|---|
| i høj grad | | bestemmelse | | uenig |

8. Den overordnedes autoritet over sine underordnede i en organisation er hovedsagentlig af økonomisk art.

| Samtykker : | Samtykker | Kan ikke tage | Uenig | I høj grad |
|---|---|---|---|---|
| i høj grad | | bestemmelse | | uenig |

På de følgende sider af anden del vil blive opnoteret adskillige egenskaber forbundet med Deres egen stilling i Deres firma. For hver sådan egenskab beder vi Dem give tre bedømmelser:

a. **Hvor meget** af denne egenskab er **nu** knyttet til Deres stilling i Deres firma?

b. **Hvor meget** af denne egenskab mener De **burde** være forbundet med eller have tilknytning til Deres stilling i Deres firma?

c. **Hvor stor betydning** har denne stillings egenskab **for Dem**?

Hver bedømmelse vil blive vedføjet en skala med syv rubriker, der vil se ud som denne:

(minimum)  1     2     3     4     5     6     7  (maximum)

Vær så venlig at sætte et mærke (X) over det nummer på skalaen eller målestokken, som repræsenterer hvor meget af de egenskaber, der bliver vurderet. Lave tal repræsenterer små eller minimale værdier, og høje tal repræsenterer høje eller de højeste værdier. Hvis De mener, der er " meget lidt " eller " ingen " af disse egenskaber for tiden forbundet med stillingen, vil De sætte et " X " ovenover nummer 1. Hvis De mener, der er " en lille smule," vil De sætte et " X " over nummer 2, og så videre. Hvis De mener, der er en " hel del, men ikke maximum summen," vil De sætte et " X " over nummer 6. Men sæt kun eet mærke over et enkelt nummer på hver skala.

**Vær så venlig at tage hver skala i betragtning.**

1. Følelsen af **selvegtelse** en person kan få ved at være i min ledende stilling:

a) Hvor meget af den er der nu?  (min) 1  2  3  4  5  6  7 (max)

b) Hvor meget af den burde der være?  1  2  3  4  5  6  7

c) Af hvor stor betydning er denne følelse for mit vedkommende?  1  2  3  4  5  6  7

2. **Myndigheden** i forbindelse med min ledende stilling:

a) Hvor meget af den er der nu?  (min) 1  2  3  4  5  6  7 (max)

b) Hvor meget af den burde der være?  1  2  3  4  5  6  7

c) Af hvor stor betydning er denne følelse for mit vedkommende?  1  2  3  4  5  6  7

3. **Lejligheden for personlig vækst og udvikling** i min ledende stilling:

a) Hvor meget af den er der nu?  (min) 1  2  3  4  5  6  7 (max)

b) Hvor meget af den burde der være?  1  2  3  4  5  6  7

c) Af hvor stor betydning er denne følelse for mit vedkommende?  1  2  3  4  5  6  7

4. **Prestigen** i forbindelse med min ledende stilling **indenfor** firmaet (det vil sige agtelsen udvist fra andre **indenfor** firmaet).

a) Hvor meget af den er der nu?  (min) 1  2  3  4  5  6  7 (max)

b) Hvor meget af den burde der være?  1  2  3  4  5  6  7

c) Af hvor stor betydning er denne følelse for mit vedkommende?  1  2  3  4  5  6  7

5. **Lejligheden til selvstændig tænkning og handling** i min ledende stilling:

a) Hvor meget af den er der nu?  (min) 1  2  3  4  5  6  7 (max)

b) Hvor meget af den burde der være?  1  2  3  4  5  6  7

c) Af hvor stor betydning er denne følelse for mit vedkommende?  1  2  3  4  5  6  7

6. **Følelsen af sikkerhed** i min ledende stilling:

a) Hvor meget af den er der nu?  (min) 1  2  3  4  5  6  7 (max)

b) Hvor meget af den burde der være?  1  2  3  4  5  6  7

c) Af hvor stor betydning er denne følelse for mit vedkommende?  1  2  3  4  5  6  7

7. **Følelsen af virkeliggørelsen af ens muligheder,** en person kan få ved at være i min ledende stilling (det vil sige følelsen af at være i stand til at bruge ens særlige dygtighed og egenskaber samt at virkeliggøre ens muligheder):

a) Hvor meget af den er der nu?

(min) 1    2    3    4    5    6    7 (max)

b) Hvor meget af den burde der være?

1    2    3    4    5    6    7

c) Af hvor stor betydning er denne følelse for mit vedkommende?

1    2    3    4    5    6    7

8. **Prestigen** i forbindelse med min ledende stilling **udenfor** firmaet (det vil sige agtelsen udvist fra andre, som ikke er i firmaet):

a) Hvor meget af den er der nu?

(min) 1    2    3    4    5    6    7 (max)

b) Hvor meget af den burde der være?

1    2    3    4    5    6    7

c) Af hvor stor betydning er denne følelse for mit vedkommende?

1    2    3    4    5    6    7

9. **Følelsen af at udrette noget værdifuldt,** noget der er umagen værd, i min ledende stilling:

a) Hvor meget af den er der nu?

(min) 1    2    3    4    5    6    7 (max)

b) Hvor meget af den burde der være?

1    2    3    4    5    6    7

c) Af hvor stor betydning er denne følelse for mit vedkommende?

1    2    3    4    5    6    7

10. Den **lejlighed,** der gives i min ledende stilling **til at yde hjælp til andre mennesker:**

a) Hvor meget af den er der nu?

(min) 1    2    3    4    5    6    7 (max)

b) Hvor meget af den burde der være?

1    2    3    4    5    6    7

c) Af hvor stor betydning er denne følelse for mit vedkommende?

1    2    3    4    5    6    7

11. **Lejligheden til at knytte nære venskaber** i min ledende stilling:

a) Hvor meget af den er der nu?

(min) 1    2    3    4    5    6    7 (max)

b) Hvor meget af den burde der være?

1    2    3    4    5    6    7

c) Af hvor stor betydning er denne følelse for mit vedkommende?

1    2    3    4    5    6    7

**VEJLEDNING:**

Formålet med dette spørgeskema er at få Deres indtryk af forskellige ting og ideer. Øverst på næste side står f. eks. ordet **læge.** De vil give Deres indtryk af hvad dette ord betyder for Dem ved at sætte et X på hver af de serier af skalaer, som findes under ordet på samme side. (Se eksemplerne nedenunder.) Sæt et X i **hver skala** i den af de syv rubriker som efter **Deres mening** bedst beskriver den vedkommende ting eller idé. Det følgende illustrerer hvordan De sætter mærke ved skalaerne for at bedømme en særlig ting eller idé.

stor :____:____:____:____:____:____:____: lille

ubehagelig :____:____:____:____:____:_ X _:____: glædelig,
behagelig

1. Vær sikker på at sætte et X ved hver skala. **Overse ikke nogen af skalaerne.**

2. Sæt kun **eet** X på hver skala.

# LÆGE

uvigtig :___:___:___:___:___:___:___: vigtig

dybsindig :___:___:___:___:___:___:___: overfladisk

aktiv :___:___:___:___:___:___:___: passiv

snævert :___:___:___:___:___:___:___: bredt

vanskelig :___:___:___:___:___:___:___: let at omgås

god :___:___:___:___:___:___:___: dårlig

stabil :___:___:___:___:___:___:___: foranderlig

interessant :___:___:___:___:___:___:___: uinteressant

svag :___:___:___:___:___:___:___: stærk


OBERST

AT TRAEFFE BESTEMMELSE

AT OVERTALE

FABRIKSFORMAND

AT SKABE ELLER FREMBRINGE

AT SNYDE ELLER BEDRAGE

PRAEST

AT GØRE EN FEJLTAGELSE

SERGENT

AT SAMARBEJDE

BISKOP

AT DIRIGERE, ANVISE

AT IRETTESAETTE

FABRIKSDIREKTØR

For at hjælpe os med den statistiske analyse af oplysningerne, beder vi Dem give følgende underretning om Dem selv.

1. Af hvad land er De statsborger? _____

2. Titelen på Deres nuværende stilling i Deres firma:

_____

3. Nuværende afdeling i Deres firma (Sæt mærke ved een.):

_____ Produktion

_____ Afsætning og avertering

_____ Finanser og regnskaber

_____ Personale og uddannelse

_____ Indkøb

_____ Undersøgelse og udvikling

_____ Almindelig administration

_____ Andre (vær så venlig at specificere) _____

_____

4. På hvor mange niveauer er der opsyn eller tilsyn i Deres firma som helhed, fra inspektøren på første niveau og til firmaets leder? (Giv tallet):

_____

5. Hvor mange niveauer eller lag af inspektion og tilsyn er der over Deres stilling? (Giv antallet):

_____

6. I hvor mange år har De arbejdet i forretning, industri eller regering? (Sæt mærke ved eet):

_____ 0-1 år

_____ 1-3 år

_____ 3-5 år

_____ 5-10 år

_____ 10-20 år

_____ 20-30 år

_____ mere end 30 år

7. Hvor mange, omtrentlig, har beskæftigelse (ledende og ikkeledende) i Deres hele firma? (Sæt X ved et.):

_____ 1-49

_____ 50-99

_____ 100-499

_____ 500-999

_____ 1.000-4.999

_____ 5.000-9.999

_____ 10.000-29.999

_____ 30.000-99.999

_____ 100.000-299.999

_____ 300.000 eller flere

8. Ejer De en væsentlig del af Deres firma? (Sæt X ved et):

_____ yes

_____ no

9. Hvad slags firma arbejder De for? (Sæt X ved et):

_____ Transportation og skibsfart

_____ Post, telegraf og telefon

_____ Kraft, lys og elektricitet

_____ En gros og detajl handal

_____ Finans og forsikring

_____ Kemiske artikler og benzin, olje eller petroleum

_____ Minedrift

_____ Stål og metal-fabrikation

_____ Fabriksvirksomhed

_____ Andre (Vær så venlig at specificere)

_____

10. Deres alder (Sæt X ved et):

_____ 20-24

_____ 25-29

_____ 30-34

_____ 35-39

_____ 40-44

_____ 45-49

_____ 50-54

_____ 55-59

_____ 60 eller mere

11. Hvor mange fulde år af Deres formelle uddannelse fuldendte De, iberegnet skole, universitet og teknisk skole? (Giv tallet):

_____

12. Hvis De gik på universitet eller teknisk skole, hvad var det særlige fag De studerede? (Sæt X ved et):

_____ Ingeniør, maskinvæsen

_____ Jura

_____ Økonomi

_____ Kunst og filosofi

_____ Andre (Vær så venlig at specificere)

_____

# Internationale Erhebung über Führungskräfte der Wirtschaft

**ERKLÄRUNGEN:**

In dem folgenden Abschnitt lesen Sie eine Reihe von Feststellungen. Geben Sie hierzu bitte Ihre Zustimmung oder Ihren Widerspruch an. Benützen Sie dazu den Maßstab, den wir unterhalb jeder dieser Feststellungen aufgeführt haben.

Zum Beispiel: Schwierige Arbeiten erledigt man besser am Vormittag als am Nachmittag:

|    | X |    |    |    |
|---|---|---|---|---|
| Starke | Zustimmung | Unent- | Ablehnung | Starke |
| Zustimmung |  | schlossen |  | Ablehnung |

Falls Sie meinen, es sei besser, diese Arbeiten am Vormittag zu erledigen, schreiben sie ein X über »Zustimmung«; falls Sie glauben, es sei weitaus leichter, diese Arbeiten am Vormittag zu erledigen, schreiben Sie das Zeichen über »starke Zustimmung«. Wenn Sie meinen, es komme nicht darauf an, schreiben Sie das Zeichen über »unentschlossen« – und so weiter. Schreiben Sie bitte das X in *einen* der angegebenen Abschnitte, nicht zwischen zwei.

Es geht hier nicht um richtige oder falsche Antworten. Wir sind lediglich an *Ihrem* Urteil und *Ihrer* Meinung im Hinblick auf die folgenden Feststellungen interessiert.

**Bitte lassen Sie keinen der Maßstäbe aus.**

1. Der Durchschnittsmensch zieht es vor, geführt zu werden, möchte gerne der Verantwortung ausweichen und hat verhältnismässig wenig Ehrgeiz.

| :_____ | :_____ | :_____ | :_____ | :_____: |
|---|---|---|---|---|
| Starke Zustimmung | Zustimmung | Unent-schlossen | Ablehnung | Starke Ablehnung |

2. Fähigkeiten zur Führung können von den meisten Menschen erworben werden – gleichgültig, was ihre besonderen angeborenen Eigenschaften und Fähigkeiten sind.

| :_____ | :_____ | :_____ | :_____ | :_____: |
|---|---|---|---|---|
| Starke Zustimmung | Zustimmung | Unent-schlossen | Ablehnung | Starke Ablehnung |

3. Belohnungen (Bezahlung, Beförderung usw.) und Strafen (Ausbleiben von Beförderung usw.) sind *nicht das beste* Mittel, um Untergebene zur Erfüllung ihrer Arbeit zu bewegen.

| :_____ | :_____ | :_____ | :_____ | :_____: |
|---|---|---|---|---|
| Starke Zustimmung | Zustimmung | Unent-schlossen | Ablehnung | Starke Ablehnung |

4. Wenn in einer Arbeitssituation die Untergebenen keinen Einfluß auf mich ausüben können, dann verliere auch ich an Einfluß auf sie.

| :_____ | :_____ | :_____ | :_____ | :_____: |
|---|---|---|---|---|
| Starke Zustimmung | Zustimmung | Unent-schlossen | Ablehnung | Starke Ablehnung |

5. Ein guter Vorgesetzter sollte seinen Untergebenen ausführliche und vollständige Anweisungen geben, anstatt nur allgemeine Richtlinien zu geben und sich auf die Initiative der Untergebenen zu verlassen, die Einzelheiten selbst auszuarbeiten.

| :_____ | :_____ | :_____ | :_____ | :_____: |
|---|---|---|---|---|
| Starke Zustimmung | Zustimmung | Unent-schlossen | Ablehnung | Starke Ablehnung |

6. Die Erarbeitung von Zielsetzungen durch eine Gruppe bietet Vorteile, die mit der Erarbeitung der Zielsetzungen durch Einzelpersonen nicht erreicht werden.

| :_____ | :_____ | :_____ | :_____ | :_____: |
|---|---|---|---|---|
| Starke Zustimmung | Zustimmung | Unent-schlossen | Ablehnung | Starke Ablehnung |

7. Ein Vorgesetzter sollte seinen Untergebenen nur solche Informationen geben, die für sie nötig sind, damit sie ihre unmittelbare Arbeit leisten können.

| :_____ | :_____ | :_____ | :_____ | :_____: |
|---|---|---|---|---|
| Starke Zustimmung | Zustimmung | Unent-schlossen | Ablehnung | Starke Ablehnung |

8. Die Autorität des Vorgesetzten über seine Untergebenen in einer Organisation beruht hauptsächlich auf seiner wirtschaftlichen Macht.

| :_____ | :_____ | :_____ | :_____ | :_____: |
|---|---|---|---|---|
| Starke Zustimmung | Zustimmung | Unent-schlossen | Ablehnung | Starke Ablehnung |

**ERKLÄRUNGEN:**

Auf den folgenden Seiten des zweiten Teils sind mehrere mit **Ihrer eigenen Stellung** in Ihrer Firma verbundene Eigenschaften aufgeführt. Sie werden gebeten, für jede Eigenschaft drei Urteile abzugeben:

a. Inwieweit **ist** diese Eigenschaft **jetzt** mit Ihrer Stellung in Ihrer Firma verbunden?

b. Inwieweit **sollte** Ihrer Meinung nach diese Eigenschaft mit Ihrer Stellung in Ihrer Firma verbunden sein?

c. **Wie wichtig** ist diese Eigenschaft Ihrer Stellung für **Sie selbst?**

Tragen Sie Ihre Urteile jeweils auf einem Maßstab mit 7 Abschnitten ein. Dieser Maßstab sieht folgendermaßen aus:

|___:___:___:___:___:___:___:___|

(Minimum)   1     2     3     4     5     6     7   (Maximum)

Schreiben Sie bitte ein X über diejenige Ziffer des Maßstabes, die dem jeweils zutreffenden Grad der Eigenschaft entspricht.

Niedrige Ziffern bedeuten niedrige oder geringste Grade einer Eigenschaft, und hohe Ziffern bedeuten hohe oder höchste Grade. Wenn Sie beispielsweise meinen, daß zur Zeit die Eigenschaft »kaum« oder »gar nicht« mit Ihrer Stellung verbunden ist, so werden Sie das X über Ziffer 1 setzen; sind Sie der Ansicht, es sei »nur ein wenig«, so werden Sie das X über Ziffer 2 setzen – usw. Wenn Sie meinen, »in großem Maße, aber nicht im höchsten Maße«, würden Sie Ziffer 6 wählen.

Verwenden Sie bitte nur **ein** X für jeden der Maßstäbe.

**Bitte lassen Sie keinen der Maßstäbe aus.**

1. Das **Gefühl der Selbstachtung**, das man in meiner Führungsstellung erhält:

   a) Inwieweit ist es jetzt vorhanden?
   (min) 1   2   3   4   5   6   7 (max)

   b) Inwieweit sollte es vorhanden sein?
   1   2   3   4   5   6   7

   c) Wie wichtig ist es für mich selbst?
   1   2   3   4   5   6   7

2. Die mit meiner Führungsstellung verbundene **Autorität**:

   a) Inwieweit ist sie jetzt vorhanden?
   (min) 1   2   3   4   5   6   7 (max)

   b) Inwieweit sollte sie vorhanden sein?
   1   2   3   4   5   6   7

   c) Wie wichtig ist sie für mich selbst?
   1   2   3   4   5   6   7

3. Die **Gelegenheit zu persönlicher Entfaltung und Entwicklung** in meiner Führungsstellung:

   a) Inwieweit ist sie jetzt vorhanden?
   (min) 1   2   3   4   5   6   7 (max)

   b) Inwieweit sollte sie vorhanden sein?
   1   2   3   4   5   6   7

   c) Wie wichtig ist sie für mich selbst?
   1   2   3   4   5   6   7

4. Das **Ansehen**, das meine Führungsstellung innerhalb der Firma genießt (das heißt – die Achtung, die andere in der Firma ihr entgegenbringen):

   a) Inwieweit ist es jetzt vorhanden?
   (min) 1   2   3   4   5   6   7 (max)

   b) Inwieweit sollte es vorhanden sein?
   1   2   3   4   5   6   7

   c) Wie wichtig ist es für mich selbst?
   1   2   3   4   5   6   7

5. Die **Gelegenheit zu unabhängigem Denken und Handeln** in meiner Führungsstellung:

   a) Inwieweit ist sie jetzt vorhanden?
   (min) 1   2   3   4   5   6   7 (max)

   b) Inwieweit sollte sie vorhanden sein?
   1   2   3   4   5   6   7

   c) Wie wichtig ist sie für mich selbst?
   1   2   3   4   5   6   7

6. Das **Gefühl der Sicherheit** in meiner Führungsstellung:

   a) Inwieweit ist es jetzt vorhanden?
   (min) 1   2   3   4   5   6   7 (max)

   b) Inwieweit sollte es vorhanden sein?
   1   2   3   4   5   6   7

   c) Wie wichtig ist es für mich selbst?
   1   2   3   4   5   6   7

7. Das **Gefühl der Selbstverwirklichung**, das man in meiner Führungsstellung erhält (das Gefühl der Möglichkeit, die besonderen eigenen Fähigkeiten zu gebrauchen und die eigenen Entwicklungsmöglichkeiten zu verwirklichen):

a) Inwieweit ist es jetzt vorhanden?

(min) 1  2  3  4  5  6  7  (max)

b) Inwieweit sollte es vorhanden sein?

1  2  3  4  5  6  7

c) Wie wichtig ist es für mich selbst?

1  2  3  4  5  6  7

8. Das **Ansehen** meiner Führungsstellung **außerhalb** der Firma (das heißt – die Achtung von anderen, die nicht in der Firma sind):

a) Inwieweit ist es jetzt vorhanden?

(min) 1  2  3  4  5  6  7  (max)

b) Inwieweit sollte es vorhanden sein?

1  2  3  4  5  6  7

c) Wie wichtig ist es für mich selbst?

1  2  3  4  5  6  7

9. Das **Gefühl, wichtige Aufgaben zu erfüllen**, das man in meiner Führungsstellung hat:

a) Inwieweit ist es jetzt vorhanden?

(min) 1  2  3  4  5  6  7  (max)

b) Inwieweit sollte es vorhanden sein?

1  2  3  4  5  6  7

c) Wie wichtig ist es für mich selbst?

1  2  3  4  5  6  7

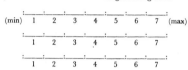

10. Die **Gelegenheit**, in meiner Führungsstellung **anderen Menschen zu helfen**:

a) Inwieweit ist sie jetzt vorhanden?

(min) 1  2  3  4  5  6  7  (max)

b) Inwieweit sollte sie vorhanden sein?

1  2  3  4  5  6  7

c) Wie wichtig ist sie für mich selbst?

1  2  3  4  5  6  7

11. Die **Gelegenheit** in meiner Führungsstellung, **enge Freundschaften zu schließen**:

a) Inwieweit ist sie jetzt vorhanden?

(min) 1  2  3  4  5  6  7  (max)

b) Inwieweit sollte sie vorhanden sein?

1  2  3  4  5  6  7

c) Wie wichtig ist sie für mich selbst?

1  2  3  4  5  6  7

# ERLÄUTERUNGEN:

Die folgenden Fragestellungen mögen Ihnen ungewöhnlich, ja befremdlich erscheinen. Es handelt sich jedoch um eine Art der Fragestellung, die sich bei Erhebungen in vielen Ländern bewährt hat – das sogenannte »Verfahren der Polaritätsprofile« (Semantic Differential).

Es ist die Absicht dieses Abschnittes unseres Fragebogens, **Ihre spontanen Reaktionen** zu einer Vielzahl von Dingen oder Ideen zu bekommen, wie z.B. »Arzt«, »Oberst«, »Entscheiden«, »Überreden«. Wie Sie sehen, handelt es sich um sehr verschiedene Arten von Begriffen. Jedem dieser Begriffe haben wir eine Anzahl von Maßstäben beigegeben, deren Enden durch ein Gegensatzpaar von Eigenschaften gekennzeichnet sind. Diese Maßstäbe sind in sieben Abschnitte eingeteilt, welche die unterschiedlichen Entfernungen von den Endpunkten der Maßstäbe wiedergeben sollen.

Wir möchten Sie nun um folgendes bitten:
Schreiben Sie **ein X** auf **jeden** der Maßstäbe, die unter den Begriffen angeführt sind. Wählen Sie auf den Maßstäben denjenigen der sieben Abschnitte, der **Ihrer** Meinung nach **am ehesten** Ihre Reaktion auf den jeweiligen Begriff wiedergibt.

Hier ein Beispiel:

Nehmen wir an, wir hätten gerne Ihre spontanen Reaktionen zu dem Begriff

»Reisen«

Hier sind nun einige Maßstäbe der Art, wie Sie sie auf den folgenden Seiten finden werden:

REISEN

schwierig :___:___:___:___: X :___:___: : leicht

hoch :___:___:___: X :___:___:___: : niedrig

hell :___: X :___:___:___:___:___: : dunkel

nahe :___:___:___:___:___:___: X : ferne

Bitte bedenken Sie, daß wir an Ihren **spontanen Reaktionen** interessiert sind. Tragen Sie diese Reaktionen auf **allen** Maßstäben ab – ob diese Maßstäbe eine offensichtliche Beziehung zu dem jeweiligen Begriff zu haben scheinen oder nicht.

## ARZT

unwichtig :___:___:___:___:___:___:___: wichtig

tiefgehend :___:___:___:___:___:___:___: oberflächlich

aktiv :___:___:___:___:___:___:___: passiv

eng :___:___:___:___:___:___:___: weit

schwierig :___:___:___:___:___:___:___: leicht

gut :___:___:___:___:___:___:___: schlecht

stabil :___:___:___:___:___:___:___: wechselhaft

interessant :___:___:___:___:___:___:___: uninteressant

schwach :___:___:___:___:___:___:___: stark

OBERST

ENTSCHEIDEN

ÜBERREDEN

WERKMEISTER

SCHÖPFERISCH SEIN

TÄUSCHEN

PFARRER

EINEN FEHLER MACHEN

FELDWEBEL

MITWIRKEN

BISCHOF

LEITEN

EINEN VERWEIS ERTEILEN

BETRIEBSLEITER

Um uns mit der statistischen Analyse der Aufzeichnungen zu helfen, geben Sie uns bitte noch die folgenden Auskünfte:

1. Staatsangehörigkeit: _____

2. Bezeichnung Ihrer jetzigen Stellung in dem Unternehmen: _____

3. Abteilung in Ihrem Unternehmen (bitte nur eine Angabe):
   _____ Produktion
   _____ Verkauf, Absatz, Werbung
   _____ Finanzwesen und Buchhaltung
   _____ Personalwesen und Ausbildungsprogramme
   _____ Einkauf
   _____ Forschung, Entwicklung
   _____ Allgemeine Verwaltung
   _____ Sonstiges (bitte erklären): _____

4. Wieviele Ebenen von Vorgesetzten-Stellungen gibt es in Ihrem *ganzen Unternehmen* – vom untersten Vorgesetzten-Grad (z.B. Werkmeister) bis zur obersten Leitung des Unternehmens? (Bitte die Zahl angeben):
   _____

5. Wieviele Ebenen von Vorgesetzten-Stellungen gibt es *über* Ihrer Stellung? (Anzahl):
   _____

6. Wieviele Jahre haben Sie insgesamt im Erwerbsleben gestanden, z.B. in der Wirtschaft oder der öffentlichen Verwaltung gearbeitet? (Bitte nur eine Angabe):
   _____ 0 bis zu 1 Jahr
   _____ 1 bis zu 3 Jahre
   _____ 3 bis zu 5 Jahre
   _____ 5 bis zu 10 Jahre
   _____ 10 bis zu 20 Jahre
   _____ 20 bis zu 30 Jahre
   _____ mehr als 30 Jahre

7. Wieviele Arbeitnehmer (leitende und untergeordnete) gibt es ungefähr in dem gesamten Unternehmen? (Bitte nur eine Angabe)
   _____ 1 bis 49
   _____ 50 bis 99
   _____ 100 bis 499
   _____ 500 bis 999
   _____ 1 000 bis 4 999
   _____ 5 000 bis 9 999
   _____ 10 000 bis 29 999
   _____ 30 000 bis 99 999
   _____ 100 000 bis 299 999
   _____ 300 000 oder mehr

8. Besitzen Sie einen größeren Kapitalanteil an dem Unternehmen?
   _____ ja
   _____ nein

9. Art des Unternehmens, in dem Sie arbeiten (bitte nur eine Angabe):
   _____ Transport, Schiffahrt
   _____ Post, Telefon, Telegraf, Kommunikation
   _____ Energie- und Elektrizitätswirtschaft
   _____ Groß- und Einzelhandel
   _____ Banken und Versicherungen
   _____ Chemische Industrie und Ölwirtschaft
   _____ Bergbau
   _____ Eisen- und Metallindustrie
   _____ Fabrikationsbetrieb
   _____ Sonstiges (bitte erklären) _____

10. Ihr Alter:
    _____ 20–24
    _____ 25–29
    _____ 30–34
    _____ 35–39
    _____ 40–44
    _____ 45–49
    _____ 50–54
    _____ 55–59
    _____ 60 oder darüber

11. Welche Schulen haben Sie besucht und wie lange?

    | Art der Schule: | Jahre: | Examen: |
    |---|---|---|
    | | | |
    | | | |
    | | | |
    | | | |

    Gesamtzahl der Jahre des Schulbesuchs: _____

12. Falls Sie eine Universität oder Technische Hochschule besucht haben: welches Fach haben Sie studiert? (Bitte Hauptstudienrichtung angeben):
    _____ Ingenieurwesen
    _____ Rechtswissenschaften
    _____ Wirtschaftswissenschaften
    _____ Geisteswissenschaften
    _____ Naturwissenschaften
    _____ Sonstiges (bitte angeben): _____

# Meningsmåling
# Blant
# Industriledere

VENNLIGST SKRIV IKKE DERES NAVN PÅ DETTE HEFTE

I avsnittet nedenfor vil De finne en serie påstander. Vennligst antyd om De er enig eller uenig i påstanden. Bruk skalaen nedenfor hver påstand.
Eks.: Det er lettere a arbeide i kjolig vaer enn i varmt vaer.

```
:_____:_____X_____:_____:_____:
Sterkt       Enig       Ubestemt   Uenig      Sterkt
Enig                                          Uenig
```

Hvis De mener det er lettere å arbeide i kjølig vaer, sett (X) over " enig." Hvis De mener det er mye lettere å arbeide i kjølig vaer, sett (X) over " absolutt enig." Hvis De mener det ikke spiller noen rolle, sett (X) over " ubestemt," osv. Sett (X) midt på linjen.
Det finnes ingen riktige eller gale svar. Vi er interessert i Deres mening om de følgende påstander:

1. Gjennomsnittsmennesket foretrekker å bli ledet, ønsker å unngå ansvar, og har forholdsvis små ambisjoner.

```
:_____:_____:_____:_____:_____:
Sterkt       Enig       Ubestemt   Uenig      Sterkt
Enig                                          Uenig
```

2. De fleste mennesker kan tilegne seg lederdyktighet, uansett deres spesielle medfødte egenskaper og evner.

```
:_____:_____:_____:_____:_____:
Sterkt       Enig       Ubestemt   Uenig      Sterkt
Enig                                          Uenig
```

3. Bruk av belønninger (betaling, forfremmelse osv.) og straff (unnlate å forfremme) er ikke den beste måte å få underordnede til å gjøre sitt arbeid på.

```
:_____:_____:_____:_____:_____:
Sterkt       Enig       Ubestemt   Uenig      Sterkt
Enig                                          Uenig
```

4. Hvis de underordnede ikke kan påvirke meg i en arbeidssituasjon, så mister jeg noe av min innflytelse på dem.

```
:_____:_____:_____:_____:_____:
Sterkt       Enig       Ubestemt   Uenig      Sterkt
Enig                                          Uenig
```

5. En god leder bør heller gi detaljerte og fullstendige instrukser til sine underordnede, enn bare å gi dem generelle retningslinjer, og stole på deres initiativ til å utarbeide detaljene.

```
:_____:_____:_____:_____:_____:
Sterkt       Enig       Ubestemt   Uenig      Sterkt
Enig                                          Uenig
```

6. Målsetting gjort av en gruppe gir fordeler som ikke kan oppnås ved indivduell målsetting.

```
:_____:_____:_____:_____:_____:
Sterkt       Enig       Ubestemt   Uenig      Sterkt
Enig                                          Uenig
```

7. En overordnet bør gi sine underordnede bare de opplysninger som er nødvendige for dem for å utføre de oppgaver de har i øyeblikket.

```
:_____:_____:_____:_____:_____:
Sterkt       Enig       Ubestemt   Uenig      Sterkt
Enig                                          Uenig
```

8. En overordnets autoritet overfor sine underordnede i en organisasjon er i første rekke av økonomisk art.

```
:_____:_____:_____:_____:_____:
Sterkt       Enig       Ubestemt   Uenig      Sterkt
Enig                                          Uenig
```

**INSTRUKSER**

På de følgende sider av Del II blir nevnt flere forskjellige karakteristiske egenskaper forbundet med Deres egen stilling i Deres firma. For hver enkel egenskap blir De bedt om å gi tre vurderinger:

a) I hvilken grad er vedkommende egenskap **nå** forbundet med Deres stilling i firmaet?

b) **Hvor mye** av vedkommende egenskap mener De **bør vaere** forbundet med Deres stilling i firmaet?

c) **Hvor viktig** er denne egenskap ved Deres stilling **for Dem?**

Hver vurdering blir gjort på en sjudelt skala, som ser slik ut:

(minimum)  1     2     3     4     5     6     7  (maksimum)

Sett (X) ovenfor det nummeret på skalaen som representerer mängden av den vurderte egenskap. Lave tall representerer små eller minimale mengder, og høye tall representerer store eller maksimale mengder. Hvis De mener at det er " meget lite " eller " intet " av egenskapen som nå er forbundet med stillingen, setter De en (X) ovenfor nr. 1. Hvis De mener det er " bare en liten del " setter De (X) ovenfor nr. 2, osv. Hvis De mener det er " en stor del " men ikke " maksimal mengde " setter De en (X) ovenfor nr. 6. For hver skala, sett bare **en** (X).

**Vennligst ikke utelat noen skala.**

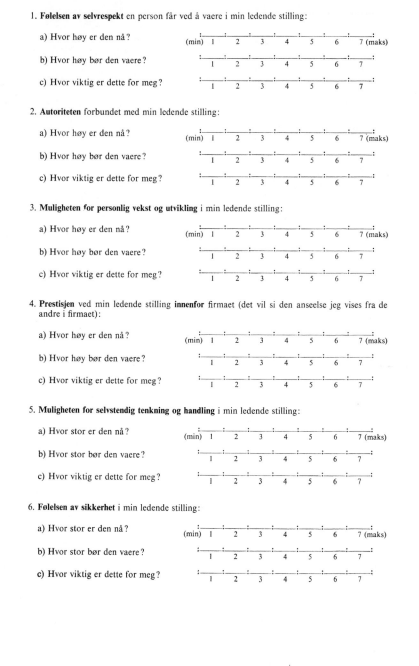

1. **Følelsen av selvrespekt** en person får ved å være i min ledende stilling:

   a) Hvor høy er den nå?

   (min) 1   2   3   4   5   6   7 (maks)

   b) Hvor høy bør den være?

   1   2   3   4   5   6   7

   c) Hvor viktig er dette for meg?

   1   2   3   4   5   6   7

2. **Autoriteten** forbundet med min ledende stilling:

   a) Hvor høy er den nå?

   (min) 1   2   3   4   5   6   7 (maks)

   b) Hvor høy bør den være?

   1   2   3   4   5   6   7

   c) Hvor viktig er dette for meg?

   1   2   3   4   5   6   7

3. **Muligheten for personlig vekst og utvikling** i min ledende stilling:

   a) Hvor høy er den nå?

   (min) 1   2   3   4   5   6   7 (maks)

   b) Hvor høy bør den være?

   1   2   3   4   5   6   7

   c) Hvor viktig er dette for meg?

   1   2   3   4   5   6   7

4. **Prestisjen** ved min ledende stilling **innenfor** firmaet (det vil si den anseelse jeg vises fra de andre i firmaet):

   a) Hvor høy er den nå?

   (min) 1   2   3   4   5   6   7 (maks)

   b) Hvor høy bør den være?

   1   2   3   4   5   6   7

   c) Hvor viktig er dette for meg?

   1   2   3   4   5   6   7

5. **Muligheten for selvstendig tenkning og handling** i min ledende stilling:

   a) Hvor stor er den nå?

   (min) 1   2   3   4   5   6   7 (maks)

   b) Hvor stor bør den være?

   1   2   3   4   5   6   7

   c) Hvor viktig er dette for meg?

   1   2   3   4   5   6   7

6. **Følelsen av sikkerhet** i min ledende stilling:

   a) Hvor stor er den nå?

   (min) 1   2   3   4   5   6   7 (maks)

   b) Hvor stor bør den være?

   1   2   3   4   5   6   7

   c) Hvor viktig er dette for meg?

   1   2   3   4   5   6   7

7. **Følelsen av selv-utfoldelse** en person får ved å vaere i min ledende stilling (det vil si følelsen av å kunne bruke sin spesielle dyktighet, virkeliggjøre sin intellektuelle styrke):

a) Hvor stor er den nå?

(min) 1   2   3   4   5   6   7 (maks)

b) Hvor stor bør den vaere?

1   2   3   4   5   6   7

c) Hvor viktig er dette for meg?

1   2   3   4   5   6   7

8. **Prestisjen** ved ledende stilling **utenfor** firmaet (det vil si den anseelse jeg får fra folk utenfor firmaet):

a) Hvor stor er den nå?

(min) 1   2   3   4   5   6   7 (maks)

b) Hvor stor bør den vaere?

1   2   3   4   5   6   7

c) Hvor viktig er dette for meg?

1   2   3   4   5   6   7

9. **Følelsen av å gjøre verdifullt arbeid** i min ledende stilling:

a) Hvor stor er den nå?

(min) 1   2   3   4   5   6   7 (maks)

b) Hvor stor bør den vaere?

1   2   3   4   5   6   7

c) Hvor viktig er dette for meg?

1   2   3   4   5   6   7

10. **Muligheten for**, i min ledende stilling, **å gi hjelp til andre mennesker:**

a) Hvor stor er den nå?

(min) 1   2   3   4   5   6   7 (maks)

b) Hvor stor bør den vaere?

1   2   3   4   5   6   7

c) Hvor viktig er dette for meg?

1   2   3   4   5   6   7

11. **Muligheten for å utvikle naert vennskap** i min ledende stilling:

a) Hvor stor er den nå?

(min) 1   2   3   4   5   6   7 (maks)

b) Hvor stor bør den vaere?

1   2   3   4   5   6   7

c) Hvor viktig er dette for meg?

1   2   3   4   5   6   7

**INSTRUKSER**

Hensikten med disse spørsmål er å få Deres inntrykk av forskjellige ting eller begreper. F. eks. øverst på neste side står ordet LEGE. De skal gi Deres inntrykk av hva dette begrepet betyr for Dem ved å sette en (X) på hver av skalaene som står nedenfor ordet på samme side. Hver av skalaene er forklart ved to ord. (Se eksemplene nedenfor.) Sett en (X) på **hver** skala på en av de 7 plassene som **etter Deres mening,** mest nøyaktig beskriver den spesielle ting eller idé. Det følgende viser hvordan De kan avmerke skalaene for en spesiell ting eller idé.

stor :_____:_____:___X___:_____:_____:_____:_____: liten

kjedelig :_____:_____:_____:_____:_____:___X___:_____: morsom

Vennligst:

1. Plaser en (X) på hver skala. **Ikke utelat noen av skalaene.**

2. Sett bare **en** (X) på hver skala.

# LEGE

lite viktig :____:____:____:____:____:____:____: viktig

dyp :____:____:____:____:____:____:____: overfladisk

aktiv :____:____:____:____:____:____:____: passiv

smal :____:____:____:____:____:____:____: vid

vanskelig :____:____:____:____:____:____:____: lett

god :____:____:____:____:____:____:____: dårlig

stabil :____:____:____:____:____:____:____: ustadig

interessant :____:____:____:____:____:____:____: uinteressant

svak :____:____:____:____:____:____:____: sterk


OBERST

Å BESTEMME

Å OVERTALE

FABRIKK-FORMANN

Å SKAPE

Å BEDRA, LURE.

PREST

Å GJØRE EN FEIL

SERSJANT

Å SAMARBEIDE

BISKOP

Å LEDE

Å IRETTESETTE

FABRIKK-LEDER

For å hjelpe oss med den statistiske behandlingen av disse data, vennligst gi følgende opplyaninger om Dem selv.

1. Nasjonalitet: _____

2. Tittelen på Deres nåværende stilling i Deres firma: _____

3. Nåværende avdeling i Deres firma (sett kryss):
_____ Produksjon
_____ Salg, markedsføring og reklame
_____ Budsjett og regnskapsførsel
_____ Personell og opplaering
_____ Innkjøp
_____ Forskning og utvikling
_____ Generell administrasjon
_____ Andre (specifiser) _____

4. Hvor mange lederniva har hele Deres firma, fra den laveste overordnede stilling, til sjefen for organisasjonen? (gi antallet):
_____

5. Hvor mange lederniva er der over Deres stilling? (Gi antallet):
_____

6. Hvor mange år har De vært i arbeid? (med forretningsvirksomhet, i industri, i staten eller andre steder) (Sett Kryss):
_____ o til 1 år
_____ 1 til 3 år
_____ 3 til 5 år
_____ 5 til 10 år
_____ 10 til 20 år
_____ 20 til 30 år
_____ mer enn 30 år

7. Omtrent hvor mange ansatte (underordnede og overordnede) er det totalt i Deres firma? (Sett kryss):
_____ 1 til 49
_____ 50 til 99
_____ 100 til 499
_____ 500 til 999
_____ 1,000 til 4,999
_____ 5,000 til 9,999
_____ 10,000 til 29,999
_____ 30,000 til 99,999
_____ 100,000 til 299,999
_____ 300,000 eller mer

8. Eier De en større del av Deres firma? (Sett kryss):
_____ ja
_____ nei

9. Den type firma De arbeider for (sett kryss):
_____ Transport og shipping
_____ Post, telegraf, telefon
_____ Kraft, lys, elektrisitet
_____ En gros- og detaljhandel
_____ Finansiering og assurance
_____ Kjemi- og olheindustri
_____ Gruvedrift
_____ Stål- og metallproduksjon
_____ Annen produksjon
_____ Andre (spesifiser) _____

10. Deres alder (sett kryss):
_____ 20-24
_____ 25-29
_____ 30-34
_____ 35-39
_____ 40-44
_____ 45-49
_____ 50-54
_____ 55-59
_____ 60 eller mer

11. Hvor mange års utdannelse har De totalt, inludert skole, universitet, teknisk skole/høyskole (gi antallet):
_____

12. Hvis De var student ved et universitet eller teknisk skole/høyskole, hvilket felt studerte De spesielt? (Sett kryss):
_____ Ingeniørfag
_____ Jus
_____ Økonomi
_____ Språk, Historie og Filosofi
_____ Andre (spesifiser) _____

# 5. Swedish

OPINIONSUNDERSÖKNING I FÖRETAG

Skriv inte Ert namn
på detta häfte

**Del I.**

I avsnittet nedan finner Ni en serie påståenden. Var god ange i vilken grad Ni instämmer eller ej. Använd för detta skalan under varje påstående.

Exempel:
Det är lättare att arbeta i svalt än i varmt väder.

:_____:_____._:_____:_____:_____

Instämmer    Instämmer    Tveksam    Instämmer    Instämmer
starkt                                ej           ej alls

Cm Ni anser att det är lättare att arbeta i svalt väder, sätt ett kryss
/  / ovanför "Instämmer"; om Ni anser att det är avsevärt mycket lättare att arbeta i svalt väder, sätt ett kryss ovanför "Instämmer starkt";
om Ni anser att det inte spelar någon roll, sätt ett kryss ovanför "Tveksam" osv. Sätt krysset mellan kolon.

Det finns inte något rätt eller fel svar. Vi är intresserade av Er
egen åsikt angående de påståenden som följer.

1.  Genomsnittsmänniskan föredrar att ledas, önskar undvika ansvar
    och har relativt svag ambition.

:_____:_____:_____:_____:_____

Instämmer    Instämmer    Tveksam    Instämmer    Instämmer
starkt                                ej           ej alls

2.  Skicklighet i ledarskap kan nås av de flesta, oberoende av anlag
    och medfödd förmåga.

:_____:_____:_____:_____:_____

Instammer    Instämmer    Tveksam    Instämmer    Instämmer
starkt                                ej           ej alls

3.  Bruket av belöningar /lön, befordran, osv./ och påföljder /ute-
    bliven befordran, osv./ är ej det bästa sättet för att få under-
    ordnade att utföra sina åligganden.

:_____:_____:_____:_____:_____

Instämmer    Instämmer    Tveksam    Instämmer    Instämmer
starkt                                ej           ej alls

4.  Om mina underordnade ej kan påverka mig i en arbetssituation,
    förlorar jag en del av mitt inflytande över dem.

:_____:_____:_____:_____:_____

Instämmer    Instämmer    Tveksam    Instämmer    Instämmer
starkt                                ej           ej alls

5.  En god ledare bör ge detaljerade och fullständiga instruktioner
    till sina underordnade hellre än att ge dem generella instruktio-
    ner och sedan lita på deras eget initiativ när det gäller detaljerna.

:_____:_____:_____:_____:_____

Instämmer    Instämmer    Tveksam    Instämmer    Instämmer
starkt                                ej           ej alls

6. Att en grupp sätter ett mål erbjuder fördelar som ej kan nås när en individ ensam sätter målet.

```
:_____:_____:_____:_____:_____:_____:
Instämmer  Instämmer  Tveksam  Instämmer  Instämmer
starkt                           ej        ej alls
```

7. En överordnad bör ge sina underordnade endast den information som är nödvändig för att de skall kunna utföra sina omedelbara åligganden.

```
:_____:_____:_____:_____:_____:_____:
Instämmer  Instämmer  Tveksam  Instämmer  Instämmer
starkt                           ej        ej alls
```

8. En överordnads auktoritet över sina underordnade beror huvudsakligen av ekonomiska förhållanden.

```
:_____:_____:_____:_____:_____:_____:
Instämmer  Instämmer  Tveksam  Instämmer  Instämmer
starkt                           ej        ej alls
```

## Del II.

### Instruktioner

På de sidor i Del II som följer kommer vi att räkna upp några av de karaktärsdrag eller egenskaper som är förknippade med Er egen position i Ert företag. Vi ber Er att ge tre omdömen för varje sådant karaktärsdrag:

a. Hur mycket av egenskapen är för närvarande förknippad med Er position inom Ert företag?

b. Hur mycket av egenskapen anser Ni borde vara förknippad med Er position i företaget?

c. Hur viktigt förefaller detta karaktärsdrag vara för Er?

Varje skattning skall Ni göra på en sjugradig skala, som ser ut så här:

```
:_____:_____:_____:_____:_____:_____:
/minimum/  1    2    3    4    5    6    7  /maximum/
```

Var god sätt ett kryss / X / ovanför den siffra på skalan som representerar Er skattning av den egenskap som värderas. Låga siffror representerar ringa eller minimal värdering och höga siffror representerar hög eller maximal värdering. Om Ni anser att "mycket litet" eller "inget" av egenskapen är förknippad med Er position för närvarande, sätt ett kryss ovanför siffran 1. Om Ni anser "litet", sätt ett kryss ovanför siffran 2, osv. Om Ni anser "mycket men ej maximum", sätt ett kryss ovanför siffran 6. För varje skala sätter Ni ett kryss ovanför endast en siffra.

### Hoppa ej över någon skala.

1. **Känslan av självaktning** jag får av att ha min position:
   a/ Hur mycket finns det nu?
   
   /min/ `1  2  3  4  5  6  7` /max/
   
   b/ Hur mycket borde det finnas?
   
   `1  2  3  4  5  6  7`
   
   c/ Hur mycket betyder det för mig?
   
   `1  2  3  4  5  6  7`

2. **Befogenheten** förknippad med min position:
   a/ Hur mycket finns det nu?
   
   /min/ `1  2  3  4  5  6  7` /max/
   
   b/ Hur mycket borde det finnas?
   
   `1  2  3  4  5  6  7`
   
   c/ Hur mycket betyder det för mig?
   
   `1  2  3  4  5  6  7`

3. **Tillfälle till personlig mognad och utveckling** förknippad med min position:
   a/ Hur mycket finns det nu?
   
   /min/ `1  2  3  4  5  6  7` /max/
   
   b/ Hur mycket borde det finnas?
   
   `1  2  3  4  5  6  7`
   
   c/ Hur mycket betyder det för mig?
   
   `1  2  3  4  5  6  7`

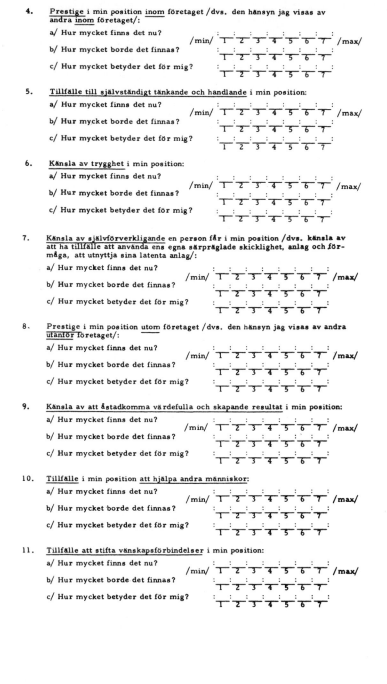

4. **Prestige i min position inom företaget** /dvs. den hänsyn jag visas av andra **inom** företaget/:

a/ Hur mycket finns det nu?
/min/ 1 2 3 4 5 6 7 /max/
b/ Hur mycket borde det finnas?
1 2 3 4 5 6 7

c/ Hur mycket betyder det för mig?
1 2 3 4 5 6 7

5. **Tillfälle till självständigt tänkande och handlande** i min position:

a/ Hur mycket finns det nu?
/min/ 1 2 3 4 5 6 7 /max/
b/ Hur mycket borde det finnas?
1 2 3 4 5 6 7

c/ Hur mycket betyder det för mig?
1 2 3 4 5 6 7

6. **Känsla av trygghet** i min position:

a/ Hur mycket finns det nu?
/min/ 1 2 3 4 5 6 7 /max/
b/ Hur mycket borde det finnas?
1 2 3 4 5 6 7

c/ Hur mycket betyder det för mig?
1 2 3 4 5 6 7

7. **Känsla av självförverkligande** en person får i min position /dvs. känsla av att ha tillfälle att använda ens egna särpräglade skicklighet, anlag och förmåga, att utnyttja sina latenta anlag/:

a/ Hur mycket finns det nu?
/min/ 1 2 3 4 5 6 7 /max/
b/ Hur mycket borde det finnas?
1 2 3 4 5 6 7

c/ Hur mycket betyder det för mig?
1 2 3 4 5 6 7

8. **Prestige i min position utom företaget** /dvs. den hänsyn jag visas av andra **utanför** företaget/:

a/ Hur mycket finns det nu?
/min/ 1 2 3 4 5 6 7 /max/
b/ Hur mycket borde det finnas?
1 2 3 4 5 6 7

c/ Hur mycket betyder det för mig?
1 2 3 4 5 6 7

9. **Känsla av att åstadkomma värdefulla och skapande resultat** i min position:

a/ Hur mycket finns det nu?
/min/ 1 2 3 4 5 6 7 /max/
b/ Hur mycket borde det finnas?
1 2 3 4 5 6 7

c/ Hur mycket betyder det för mig?
1 2 3 4 5 6 7

10. **Tillfälle i min position att hjälpa andra människor:**

a/ Hur mycket finns det nu?
/min/ 1 2 3 4 5 6 7 /max/
b/ Hur mycket borde det finnas?
1 2 3 4 5 6 7

c/ Hur mycket betyder det för mig?
1 2 3 4 5 6 7

11. **Tillfälle att stifta vänskapsförbindelser** i min position:

a/ Hur mycket finns det nu?
/min/ 1 2 3 4 5 6 7 /max/
b/ Hur mycket borde det finnas?
1 2 3 4 5 6 7

c/ Hur mycket betyder det för mig?
1 2 3 4 5 6 7

Instruktioner:

Andamålet med detta frågeformulär är att få Era intryck beträffande en mångfald ting och idéer. Exempel: överst på nästa sida står ordet LÄKARE. Vi ber Er återge Era intryck av detta ord genom att sätta ett kryss på var och en av den serie av skalor, vilka finns längre ned på samma sida. Varje skala definieras medelst ett ordpar. /Se exempel nedan./ Sätt ett kryss på varje skala ovanför ett av de sju avsnitten. Detta kryss markerar vad Ni anser om denna speciella sak eller idé. Följande exempel illustrerar, hur man kan markera i skalan för en speciell sak eller idé.

stor :____:____:____:____:____:____:____: liten

behaglig :____:____:____:____:____:____:____: obehaglig

Observera:
1. Sätt ett kryss på varje skala. Utelämna ej någon skala.
2. Sätt endast ett kryss på varje skala.

ÖVERSTE

oviktig :____:____:____:____:____:____:____: viktig

grundlig :____:____:____:____:____:____:____: ytlig

aktiv :____:____:____:____:____:____:____: passiv

smal :____:____:____:____:____:____:____: vid

svår :____:____:____:____:____:____:____: lätt

god :____:____:____:____:____:____:____: dålig

stabil :____:____:____:____:____:____:____: växlande

intressant :____:____:____:____:____:____:____: ointressant

svag :____:____:____:____:____:____:____: stark

LÄKARE
ATT FATTA BESLUT
ATT ÖVERTALA
VERKSTADSFÖRMAN
ATT SKAPA
ATT LURA, BEDRAGA
PRÄST
ATT GÖRA ETT MISSTAG
SERGEANT
ATT SAMARBETA
BISKOP
ATT VÄGLEDA, STYRA, DIRIGERA ETC.
ATT TILLRÄTTAVISA
FÖRETAGSCHEF

Del IV.

För att hjälpa oss med vår statistiska analys av dessa data, var god och lämna följande upplysningar om Er själv:

1. Nationalitet: _____

2. Beteckning på Er nuvarande befattning
/befattningstitel/ i Ert företag: _____

3. Avdelning i företaget /markera en rad/:

_____ Produktion
_____ Försäljning, Marketing och Reklam
_____ Ekonomi /Redovisning och Finansiering/
_____ Personal och Utbildning
_____ Inköp
_____ Forskning och Utveckling
_____ Administration
_____ Annan /specificera/ _____

4. Hur många nivåer av chefer finns det i hela Ert företag från den lägste till den högste chefen för företaget? Ange antalet:

_____

5. Hur många nivåer av chefer finns det över Er egen position? Ange antalet:

_____

6. Hur många år har Ni arbetat i affärsföretag, industri eller statligt företag? /Markera en rad/:

_____ 0 till 1 år
_____ 1 till 3 år
_____ 3 till 5 år
_____ 5 till 10 år
_____ 10 till 20 år
_____ 20 till 30 år
_____ över 30 år

7. Ungefär hur många anställda finns det i Ert företag? /Markera en rad/:

_____ 1 till 49
_____ 50 till 99
_____ 100 till 499
_____ 500 till 999
_____ 1.000 till 4.999
_____ 5.000 till 9.999
_____ 10.000 till 29.999
_____ 30.000 till 99.999
_____ 100.000 till 299.999
_____ 300.000 eller fler

8. Äger Ni en avsevärd del av Ert företag?

_____ ja
_____ nej

9. Typ av företag Ni arbetar i /markera en rad/:

_____ Transport och Rederi
_____ Post, Telegraf och Telefon
_____ Vattenkraft och Elektricitet och annan kraftförsörjning
_____ Gross- och Detaljhandel
_____ Bank och Försäkring
_____ Kemisk Industri och Olja
_____ Gruvindustri
_____ Järnindustri
_____ Mekanisk Verkstadsindustri
_____ Annat /specificera/ _____

10. Er ålder /markera en rad/:

_____ 20-24
_____ 25-29
_____ 30-34
_____ 35-39
_____ 40-44
_____ 45-49
_____ 50-54
_____ 55-59
_____ 60 eller äldre

11. Hur många års formell utbildning, inklusive folkskola, läroverk, universitet och teknisk skolning har Ni totalt bakom Er? /Ange antal år/:

_____

12. Om Ni har studerat vid universitet eller högskola, vilket område ägnade Ni Er åt? /Markera en rad/:

_____ Teknisk högskola
_____ Juridik
_____ Ekonomi
_____ Filosofi och Konsthistoria etc.
_____ Annan /specificera/ _____

# Opinie-Onderzoek
# Bij de
# Industrie

VERZOEKE NIET UW NAAM OP DIT BOEKJE TE SCHRIJVEN

In dit hoofdstuk vindt U een aantal meningen vermeld. U wordt verzocht middels de onder iedere mening afgedrukte schaal aan te geven of U het met deze mening eens bent of oneens.

Voorbeeld: Het is makkelijker te werken bij koel dan bij warm weder.

| Geheel | Mee eens | Twijfel | Niet mee | Geheel niet |
| mee eens | | | eens | mee eens |

Indien U denkt dat het makkelijker werken is bij koel weder, zet dan een kruis boven " Mee eens "; indien U denkt dat het veel makkelijker te werken is bij koel weder, zet dan een kruis boven " Geheel mee eens." Indien U vindt dat de temperatuur van geen belang is, zet dan een kruis boven " Twijfel " enz. Zet het kruis in een vak, niet tussen twee vakken. Er bestaan geen juiste of foute antwoorden; wij stellen slechts belang in Uw mening omtrent de hierna volgende verklaringen.

1. Het gemiddelde menselijk wezen geeft er de voorkeur aan geleid te worden, wenst verantwoordelijkheid te vermijden en bezit betrekkelijk weinig ambitie.

| Geheel | Mee eens | Twijfel | Niet mee | Geheel niet |
| mee eens | | | eens | mee eens |

2. Het vermogen om leiding te geven kan door de meeste mensen verkregen worden, welke ook hun aangeboren kenmerken en bekwaamheden mogen zijn.

| Geheel | Mee eens | Twijfel | Niet mee | Geheel niet |
| mee eens | | | eens | mee eens |

3. De toepassing van beloningen (betaling, bevordering, enz.) en van straffen (de ontzegging van bevordering, enz.) is niet de juiste manier om ondergeschikten ertoe te krijgen hun werk naar behoren te verrichten.

| Geheel | Mee eens | Twijfel | Niet mee | Geheel niet |
| mee eens | | | eens | mee eens |

4. Indien mijn ondergeschikten bij de behandeling van vraagstukken het werk betreffende op mij geen invloed kunnen uitoefenen, dan gaat dit enigszins ten koste van de invloed welke ik op hen uitoefen.

| Geheel | Mee eens | Twijfel | Niet mee | Geheel niet |
| mee eens | | | eens | mee eens |

5. Een goede chef dient zijn ondergeschikten uitvoerige en volledige aanwijzigingen te verstrekken in plaats van algemene richtlijnen zonder meer om het daarna aan hun initiatief over te laten de bijzonderheden zelf uit te werken.

| Geheel | Mee eens | Twijfel | Niet mee | Geheel niet |
| mee eens | | | eens | mee eens |

6. Het doel dat een groep werkers zichzelf stelt biedt voordelen welke niet verkregen worden indien een enkele werker zich een doel stelt.

| Geheel | Mee eens | Twijfel | Niet mee | Geheel niet |
| mee eens | | | eens | mee eens |

7. Een superieur dient zijn ondergeschikten slechts die gegevens te verstrekken welke zij voor het verrichten van hun huidige taak nodig hebben.

| Geheel | Mee eens | Twijfel | Niet mee | Geheel niet |
| mee eens | | | eens | mee eens |

8. Bij een organisatie is het gezag van een superieur over zijn ondergeschikten in de eerste plaats van economische aard.

| Geheel | Mee eens | Twijfel | Niet mee | Geheel niet |
| mee eens | | | eens | mee eens |

**AANWIJZINGEN**

Op de volgende bladzijden van Hoofdstuk II vindt U een lijst van verscheidene karakteristieken of factoren welke betrekking hebben op de functie welke U bij Uw firma bekleedt. U wordt verzocht voor iedere karakteristiek drie waarderingen te geven:

a) In welke mate bestaat er verband tussen de karakteristiek en de functie welke U bij Uw firma bekleedt?

b) In welke mate dient er verband te bestaan tussen de karakteristiek en de functie welke U bij Uw firma bekleedt, volgens Uw mening?

c) Hoeveel belang hecht U aan deze functie-karakteristiek?

Iedere waardering wordt tot uitdrukking gebracht op een schaal met 7 punten, welke er uit ziet alsvolgt:

(minimum) 1    2    3    4    5    6    7 (maximum)

U wordt verzocht een kruis te zetten boven het nummer op de schaal dat Uw waardering van de karakteristiek tot uitdrukking brengt. Lage nummers drukken een geringe of minimum waardering uit; hoge nummers drukken een aanzienlijke of maximum waardering uit. Indien U van mening zijt dat er slechts een zeer gering of geen verband bestaat tussen de karakteristiek en Uw huidige functie, dan zoudt U een kruis boven nummer 1 dienen to plaatsen. Indien er volgens Uw mening een gering verband aanwezig is, dan zoudt U een kruis boven nummer 2 dienen te plaatsen, enz. Indien U denkt dat er een aanzienlijk doch geen maximum verband aanwezig is, dan zoudt U een kruis boven nummer 6 dienen te plaatsen. Bij iedere schaal mag men slechts een kruis boven een nummer plaatsen.

Men wordt verzocht geen schaal over te slaan.

1. Het gevoel van zelfrespect dat men in mijn functie verkrijgt:

a) In welke mate is dit thans aanwezig?  (min) 1  2  3  4  5  6  7 (max)

b) In welke mate dient dit aanwezig te zijn?  1  2  3  4  5  6  7

c) Van hoeveel belang is dit voor mij?  1  2  3  4  5  6  7

2. Het gezag dat met mijn functie gepaard gaat:

a) In welke mate is dit thans aanwezig?  (min) 1  2  3  4  5  6  7 (max)

b) In welke mate dient dit aanwezig te zijn?  1  2  3  4  5  6  7

c) Van hoeveel belang is dit voor mij?  1  2  3  4  5  6  7

3. De gelegenheid voor persoonlijke vervolmaking en ontwikkeling welke mijn functie biedt:

a) In welke mate is deze thans aanwezig?  (min) 1  2  3  4  5  6  7 (max)

b) In welke mate dient deze aanwezig te zijn?  1  2  3  4  5  6  7

c) Van hoeveel belang is deze voor mij?  1  2  3  4  5  6  7

4. Het prestige dat voortspruit uit mijn functie binnen de onderneming, (de achting welke ik van anderen in dienst van de onderneming ondervind):

a) In welke mate is dit thans aanwezig?  (min) 1  2  3  4  5  6  7 (max)

b) In welke mate dient dit aanwezig te zijn?  1  2  3  4  5  6  7

c) Van hoeveel belang is dit voor mij?  1  2  3  4  5  6  7

5. De gelegenheid voor onafhankelijk denken en handelen welke mijn functie biedt:

a) In welke mate is deze thans aanwezig?  (min) 1  2  3  4  5  6  7 (max)

b) In welke mate dient deze aanwezig te zijn?  1  2  3  4  5  6  7

c) Van hoeveel belang is deze voor mij?  1  2  3  4  5  6  7

6. Het gevoel van zekerheid dat me mijn functie gepaard gaat:

a) In welke mate is dit thans aanwezig?  (min) 1  2  3  4  5  6  7 (max)

b) In welke mate dient dit aanwezig te zijn?  1  2  3  4  5  6  7

c) Van hoeveel belang is dit voor mij?  1  2  3  4  5  6  7

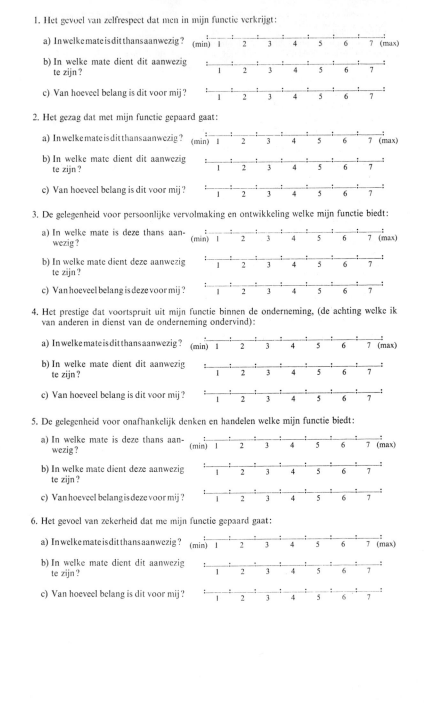

7. De zelfvoldoening welke met mijn functie gepaard gaat (het gevoel in staat te zijn eigen unieke bekwaamheden toe te passen zich daarbij rekenschap gevende van hetgeen binnen zijn macht ligt):

a) In welke mate is deze thans aanwezig?   (min) 1   2   3   4   5   6   7   (max)

b) In welke mate dient deze aanwezig te zijn?   1   2   3   4   5   6   7

c) Van hoeveel belang is deze voor mij?   1   2   3   4   5   6   7

8. Het prestige dat voortspruit uit mijn functie buiten de onderneming (de achting welke ik van anderen niet in dienst van de onderneming ondervind):

a) In welke mate is dit thans aanwezig?   (min) 1   2   3   4   5   6   7   (max)

b) In welke mate dient dit aanwezig te zijn?   1   2   3   4   5   6   7

c) Van hoeveel belang is dit voor mij?   1   2   3   4   5   6   7

9. Het gevoel in mijn functie iets tot stand te hebben gebracht dat de moeite waard is:

a) In welke mate is dit thans aanwezig?   (min) 1   2   3   4   5   6   7   (max)

b) In welke mate dient dit aanwezig te zijn?   1   2   3   4   5   6   7

c) Van hoeveel belang is dit voor mij?   1   2   3   4   5   6   7

10. De gelegenheid welke mijn functie biedt om anderen behulpzaam te zijn:

a) In welke mate is deze thans aanwezig?   (min) 1   2   3   4   5   6   7   (max)

b) In welke mate dient deze aanwezig te zijn?   1   2   3   4   5   6   7

c) Van hoeveel belang is deze voor mij?   1   2   3   4   5   6   7

11. De gelegenheid welke mijn functie biedt om hecht vriendschappen te sluiten:

a) In welke mate is deze thans aanwezig?   (min) 1   2   3   4   5   6   7   (max)

b) In welke mate dient deze aanwezig te zijn?   1   2   3   4   5   6   7

c) Van hoeveel belang is deze voor mij?   1   2   3   4   5   6   7

**AANWIJZIGINGEN**

Het doel van de navolgende vragenlijst is Uw indrukken te verkrijgen betreffende verscheidene zaken of ideen. Bovenaan de volgende bladzijde vindt U bijvoorbeeld het woord ARTS. U wordt verzocht een indruk te geven van hetgeen dit voor U betekent door een kruis te plaatsen op ieder van een reeks schalen welke onder dit woord op dezelfde bladzijde zijn afgedrukt. De betekenis van iedere schaal wordt vertolkt door twee woorden. (Zie de hieronder gegeven voorbeelden.) Plaats in een van de zeven vakken op iedere schaal een kruis dat Uw waardering betreffende de zaak of idee op de meest nauwkeurige wijze tot uitdrukking brengt. Het volgende voorbeeld toont aan op welke wijze U de schaal zoudt kunnen merken met betrekking tot een zekere zaak of idee:

groot :____:_X_:____:____:____:____:____ : klein

vervelend :____:____:____:____:____:_X_:____: vermakelijk

N.B.

1. Plaats een kruis op iedere schaal. Slaat geen schalen over.

2. Plaats slechts een kruis op iedere schaal.

ARTS

onbelangrijk :____:____:____:____:____:____:____: belangrijk

diepgaand :____:____:____:____:____:____:____: oppervlakkig

bedrijvig :____:____:____:____:____:____:____: passief

nauw :____:____:____:____:____:____:____: breed

moeilijk :____:____:____:____:____:____:____: gemakkelijk

goed :____:____:____:____:____:____:____: slecht

bestendig :____:____:____:____:____:____:____: veranderlijk

belangwekkend :____:____:____:____:____:____:____: onbelangwekkend

zwak :____:____:____:____:____:____:____: sterk

KOLONEL

BESLISSEN

OVERREDEN

FABRIEKSBAAS

SCHEPPEN

BEDRIEGEN

PRIESTER

EEN FOUT BEGAAN

SERGEANT

SAMENWERKING

BISSCHOP

LEIDING GEVEN

BERISPEN

FABRIEKSDIRECTEUR

Teneinde ons bij te staan bij de verrichting van de statistische analyse van de voorgaande gegevens, wordt U verzocht de volgende inlichtingen betreffende Uzelf te verstrekken.

1. Nationaliteit _____

2. Titel van Uw huidige functie bij Uw Firma

_____

3. De afdeling van Uw Firma waarbij U thans werkzaam zijt (een aanstrepen):

_____ Productie

_____ Verkoop, Marketing en Reclame

_____ Financieen en Boekhouding

_____ Personeel en Opleiding

_____ Inkoop

_____ Onderzoek en Ontwikkeling

_____ Algemene Administratie

_____ Andere Afdeling (verzoeke to specificeren) _____

4. Hoeveel rangen bestaan er bij Uw Firma, te rekenen vanaf de laagste opzichter tot de Directeur Generaal? (Vermeld het aantal rangen):

_____

5. Hoeveel rangen staan er boven Uw functie? (Vermeld het aantal):

_____

6. Gedurende hoeveel jaren zijt gij werkzaam geweest in het zakenleven, bij de industrie of bij de regering? (een aanstrepen):

_____ 0 tot 1 jaar

_____ 1 tot 3 jaar

_____ 3 tot 5 jaar

_____ 5 tot 10 jaar

_____ 10 tot 20 jaar

_____ 20 tot 30 jaar

_____ meer dan 30 jaar

7. Hoeveel werknemers (in leidende en in nietleidende functies) zijn er werkzaam bij Uw Firma? (een aanstrepen):

_____ 1 tot 49

_____ 50 tot 99

_____ 100 tot 499

_____ 500 tot 999

_____ 1000 tot 4999

_____ 5000 tot 9999

_____ 10000 tot 29999

_____ 30000 tot 99999

_____ 1000000 tot 299999

_____ 300000 of meer

8. Vormt een belangrijk gedeelte van Uw Firma Uw eigen bezit? (een aanstrepen):

_____ ja

_____ neen

9. Soort onderneming waar U bij werkzaam bent (een aanstrepen):

_____ Vervoer en Scheepvaart

_____ Post, Telegraaf en Telefoon

_____ Gas en Electriciteit

_____ Groothandel en Kleinhandel

_____ Financieen en Verzekeringswezen

_____ Chemische Producten en Petroleum

_____ Mijnbouw

_____ Ijzer- en Staalfabricage

_____ Verwerkende Industrie

_____ Andere onderneming (verzoeke te specificeren):

10. Uw leeftijd (een aanstrepen):

_____ 20-24

_____ 25-29

_____ 30-34

_____ 35-39

_____ 40-44

_____ 45-49

_____ 50-54

_____ 55-59

_____ 60 of ouder

11. Hoeveel jaren onderwijs hebt gij genoten met inbegrip van lager, middelbaar, hoger onderwijs en technische school? (Vermeld het aantal jaren):

12. Indien U een universiteit of technische hogeschool bezocht, aan welke faculteit volgde U dan de colleges? (een aanstrepen):

_____ Techniek

_____ Rechten

_____ Economie

_____ Letteren en Wijsbegeerte

_____ Andere faculteit (verzoeke te specificeren)_____

# Enquête sur quelques Opinions chez les Dirigeants dans l'Entreprise

VEUILLEZ NE PAS INSCRIRE VOTRE NOM SUR CE DOCUMENT

Vous trouverez ci-après une série d'opinions. Veuillez indiquer si vous êtes d'accord ou non au moyen des réponses imprimées sous chaque phrase.

Par exemple:

" Il est plus facile de travailler dans la fraîcheur que dans la chaleur."

| :_____: | :_____: | :_____: | :_____: | :_____: |
|---|---|---|---|---|
| Entièrement d'accord | D'accord | Hésitant | Contre | Absolument contre |

Si vous pensez qu'il est plus facile de travailler dans la fraîcheur, placez une croix au-dessus du mot " d'accord," si vous pensez qu'il est beaucoup plus facile de travailler dans la fraîcheur, placez une croix au-dessus de " entièrement d'accord." Si vous estimez que la température n'est pas un facteur important, placez une croix au-dessus de " hésitant." Ne placez de croix que dans une seule case par opinion.

Il n'y a pas de réponses correctes ou erronées; nous désirons simplement connaître votre point de vue sur les opinions qui suivent.

1. Les hommes préfèrent en général être dirigés;ils cherchent à éviter les responsabilités et ont relativement peu d'ambition.

| :_____: | :_____: | :_____: | :_____: | :_____: |
|---|---|---|---|---|
| Entièrement d'accord | D'accord | Hésitant | Contre | Absolument contre |

2. L'art de commander peut être acquis par la plupart des hommes, quels que soient leur caractère et leurs capacités innées.

| :_____: | :_____: | :_____: | :_____: | :_____: |
|---|---|---|---|---|
| Entièrement d'accord | D'accord | Hésitant | Contre | Absolument contre |

3. L'emploi de récompenses (salaire, promotion, etc.) et de sanctions (refus d'avancement, etc.) **n'est pas** le meilleur moyen d'amener les subordonnés à faire leur travail.

| :_____: | :_____: | :_____: | :_____: | :_____: |
|---|---|---|---|---|
| Entièrement d'accord | D'accord | Hésitant | Contre | Absolument contre |

4. Si mes subordonnés ne peuvent pas m'influencer dans les questions professionnelles je perds un peu de l'influence que j'ai sur eux.

| :_____: | :_____: | :_____: | :_____: | :_____: |
|---|---|---|---|---|
| Entièrement d'accord | D'accord | Hésitant | Contre | Absolument contre |

5. Un bon chef doit donner à ses subordonnés des instructions détaillées et complètes, plutôt que de leur donner simplement des directives générales, laissant ensuite à leur initiative le soin de mettre au point les détails.

| :_____: | :_____: | :_____: | :_____: | :_____: |
|---|---|---|---|---|
| Entièrement d'accord | D'accord | Hésitant | Contre | Absolument contre |

6. Le fait qu'un objectif est fixé par un groupe apporte des avantages qu'on ne peut obtenir lorsque l'objectif est fixé par une seule personne.

| :_____: | :_____: | :_____: | :_____: | :_____: |
|---|---|---|---|---|
| Entièrement d'accord | D'accord | Hésitant | Contre | Absolument contre |

7. Le supérieur ne devrait donner à ses subordonnés que les informations nécessaires à l'accomplissement de leur travail immédiat.

| :_____: | :_____: | :_____: | :_____: | :_____: |
|---|---|---|---|---|
| Entièrement d'accord | D'accord | Hésitant | Contre | Absolument contre |

8. Dans une organisation, l'autorité d'un supérieur sur ses subordonnés est surtout d'ordre économique.

| :_____: | :_____: | :_____: | :_____: | :_____: |
|---|---|---|---|---|
| Entièrement d'accord | D'accord | Hésitant | Contre | Absolument contre |

## DEUXIÈME PARTIE

Dans les pages suivantes vous trouverez une liste de facteurs ou de caractéristiques se rapportant au poste que vous occupez dans votre entreprise. Pour chacune de ces caractéristiques, nous vous demandons d'apprécier:

a. quelle est la part de cette caractéristique attachée actuellement au poste que vous occupez (situation actuelle)?

b. quelle est la part de cette caractéristique qui devrait être selon vous attachée à ce poste (situation idéale)?

c. quelle importance attribuez-vous personnellement à cet aspect de la vie professionnelle (importance personnelle)?

Chacune des appréciations se fera au moyen d'une échelle graduée de 1 à 7, qui se présentera de la façon suivante:

(minimum) 1    2    3    4    5    6    7 (maximum)

Veuillez mettre une croix au-dessus du nombre qui représente la part attribuée à la caractéristique étudiée. Les nombre voisins de 1 représentent des parts faibles ou minimes. Un nombre élevé indique la présence (actuelle ou idéale) importante de la caractéristique en question. En d'autres termes, si vous pensez que cette caractéristique est très peu ou pas du tout associée en ce moment avec votre position, vous placeriez une croix au-dessus du nombre 1. Si vous pensez qu'il y en a un peu, vous placeriez une croix au-dessus du nombre 2, et ainsi de suite. Si vous estimez qu'il y en a beaucoup (sans atteindre le maximum) vous placeriez une croix au-dessus du nombre 6. Veuillez n'utiliser qu'un seul nombre par échelle.

**Prière de répondre à toutes les questions.**

1. **L'estime de soi** qu'on acquiert dans mon poste:

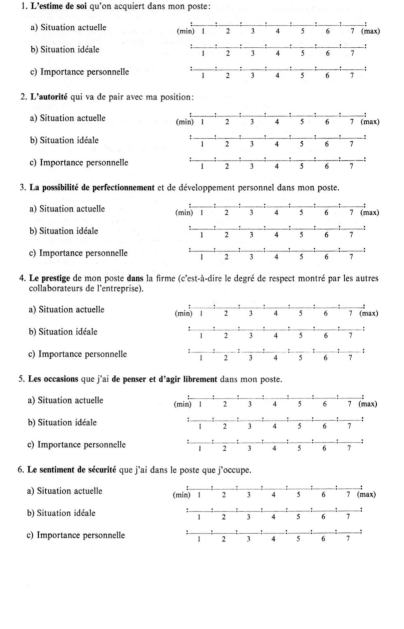

a) Situation actuelle

(min) 1   2   3   4   5   6   7 (max)

b) Situation idéale

1   2   3   4   5   6   7

c) Importance personnelle

1   2   3   4   5   6   7

2. **L'autorité** qui va de pair avec ma position:

a) Situation actuelle

(min) 1   2   3   4   5   6   7 (max)

b) Situation idéale

1   2   3   4   5   6   7

c) Importance personnelle

1   2   3   4   5   6   7

3. **La possibilité de perfectionnement** et de développement personnel dans mon poste.

a) Situation actuelle

(min) 1   2   3   4   5   6   7 (max)

b) Situation idéale

1   2   3   4   5   6   7

c) Importance personnelle

1   2   3   4   5   6   7

4. **Le prestige** de mon poste **dans** la firme (c'est-à-dire le degré de respect montré par les autres collaborateurs de l'entreprise).

a) Situation actuelle

(min) 1   2   3   4   5   6   7 (max)

b) Situation idéale

1   2   3   4   5   6   7

c) Importance personnelle

1   2   3   4   5   6   7

5. **Les occasions** que j'ai **de penser et d'agir librement** dans mon poste.

a) Situation actuelle

(min) 1   2   3   4   5   6   7 (max)

b) Situation idéale

1   2   3   4   5   6   7

c) Importance personnelle

1   2   3   4   5   6   7

6. **Le sentiment de sécurité** que j'ai dans le poste que j'occupe.

a) Situation actuelle

(min) 1   2   3   4   5   6   7 (max)

b) Situation idéale

1   2   3   4   5   6   7

c) Importance personnelle

1   2   3   4   5   6   7

7. **Le sentiment d'épanouissement personnel** qu'on éprouve à mon poste (c'est-à-dire la conscience de pouvoir employer ses capacités individuelles et de réaliser tout ce dont on est capable.

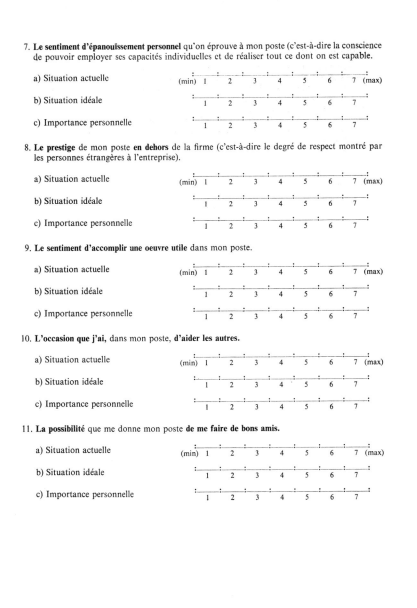

a) Situation actuelle    (min) 1   2   3   4   5   6   7 (max)

b) Situation idéale            1   2   3   4   5   6   7

c) Importance personnelle      1   2   3   4   5   6   7

8. **Le prestige** de mon poste **en dehors** de la firme (c'est-à-dire le degré de respect montré par les personnes étrangères à l'entreprise).

a) Situation actuelle    (min) 1   2   3   4   5   6   7 (max)

b) Situation idéale            1   2   3   4   5   6   7

c) Importance personnelle      1   2   3   4   5   6   7

9. **Le sentiment d'accomplir une oeuvre utile** dans mon poste.

a) Situation actuelle    (min) 1   2   3   4   5   6   7 (max)

b) Situation idéale            1   2   3   4   5   6   7

c) Importance personnelle      1   2   3   4   5   6   7

10. **L'occasion que j'ai,** dans mon poste, **d'aider les autres.**

a) Situation actuelle    (min) 1   2   3   4   5   6   7 (max)

b) Situation idéale            1   2   3   4   5   6   7

c) Importance personnelle      1   2   3   4   5   6   7

11. **La possibilité** que me donne mon poste **de me faire de bons amis.**

a) Situation actuelle    (min) 1   2   3   4   5   6   7 (max)

b) Situation idéale            1   2   3   4   5   6   7

c) Importance personnelle      1   2   3   4   5   6   7

**INSTRUCTIONS:**

Cette partie du questionnaire a pour but de recueillir vos impressions sur différents termes ou idées. Par exemple, au haut de la page suivante vous trouverez le mot MEDECIN. Nous vous demandons de traduire l'impression que ce mot évoque en vous en mettant une croix sur chacune des échelles se trouvant sous le mot MEDECIN et sur la même page. Chaque échelle est definie par deux mots. (Voir les exemples ci-dessous.) Mettez une croix sur **chaque** échelle dans celui des sept espaces qui décrit, **selon vous**, le plus exactement le terme ou l'idée. Les exemples suivants montrent comment vous pourriez marquer les échelles pour un des termes ou une des idées.

grand :_____:_____:___X___:_____:_____:_____:_____: petit

amusant :_____:_____:_____:_____:_____:___X___:_____:ennuyeux

Veuillez ne mettre qu'**une** croix sur **chaque** échelle.

## MEDECIN

peu important :____:____:____:____:____:____:____: important

profond :____:____:____:____:____:____:____: superficiel

actif :____:____:____:____:____:____:____: passif

étroit :____:____:____:____:____:____:____: large

difficile :____:____:____:____:____:____:____: facile

bon :____:____:____:____:____:____:____: mauvais

stable :____:____:____:____:____:____:____: variable

intéressant :____:____:____:____:____:____:____: peu intéressant

faible :____:____:____:____:____:____:____: fort

COLONEL

DECIDER

PERSUADER

CONTREMAITRE

CREER

TRICHER

PRÊTRE

SE TROMPER

SERGENT

COOPERER

EVÊQUE

DIRIGER

REPRIMANDER

DIRECTEUR D'USINE

# QUATRIEME PARTIE

Pour nous aider à faire l'étude statistique des résultats veuillez donner les renseignements suivants vous concernant:

1. Nationalité: _____

2. Position actuelle dans votre firme: _____

3. Service actuel dans votre firme (marquez d'une croix):

_____ Production

_____ Ventes, Service Commercial et Publicité

_____ Finances et Comptabilité

_____ Personnel et Formation

_____ Approvisionnements

_____ Recherches et Innovations

_____ Administration Générale

_____ Autre (Prière de spécifier):_____

4. Combien y a-t-il d'échelons hiérarchiques dans votre société depuis le chef d'équipe jusqu'au directeur général?

_____ (Donnez le nombre.)

5. Combien y a-t-il d'échelons au-dessus de vous?

6. Depuis combien de temps travaillez-vous dans les affaires, l'industrie ou l'administration publique? (Marquez d'une croix):

_____ 0 à 1 année

_____ 1 à 3 années

_____ 3 à 5 années

_____ 5 à 10 années

_____ 10 à 20 années

_____ 20 à 30 années

_____ plus de 30 années

7. Environ combien d'employés y a-t-il dans votre compagnie, direction comprise?

_____ 1 à 49

_____ 50 à 99

_____ 100 à 499

_____ 500 à 999

_____ 1000 à 4999

_____ 5000 à 9999

_____ 10,000 à 29,999

_____ 30,000 à 99,999

_____ 100,000 à 299,999

_____ 300,000 ou plus.

8. Etes-vous propriétaire d'une partie importante de votre entreprise?

_____ oui

_____ non

9. Pour quel genre d'entreprise travaillez-vous? (Marquez d'une croix):

_____ Transports et affrètement

_____ Postes Télégraphes Téléphones

_____ Gaz et électricité

_____ Commerce de gros ou de détail

_____ Finances et assurances

_____ Produits chimiques et pétrole

_____ Mines

_____ Métallurgie

_____ Industries de transformation

_____ Autre (Prière de spécifier):_____

10. Votre âge (marquez d'une croix):

_____ 20-24

_____ 25-29

_____ 30-34

_____ 35-39

_____ 40-44

_____ 45-49

_____ 50-54

_____ 55-59

_____ 60 ou plus.

11. Combien d'années d'études (primaires, secondaires et supérieures) avez-vous fait en tout? (Donnez le nombre d'années):

_____

12. Si vous avez fait des études supérieures quelle fut votre spécialité?

_____ Ingénieur

_____ Droit

_____ Sciences politiques et économiques

_____ Arts et philosophie

_____ Autre (veuillez spécifier):_____

# Ricerca sulle Opinioni nell' Industria

Qui di seguito troverete una serie di affermazioni. Per favore, indicate se siete in accordo o in disaccordo. A questo fine, usate la scala che si trova al di sotto di ciascuna affermazione.

Per esempio:

È più facile lavorare quando fà freddo che quando fà caldo.

```
:_____:_____X___:_____:_____:_____:
decisamente   d'accordo   indeciso   in disaccordo   decisamente
in accordo                                           in disaccordo
```

Se pensate che sia più facile lavorare quando fà freddo, segnate una (X) sopra " d'accordo "; se pensate che sia molto più facile lavorare quando fà freddo, segnate la (X) al di sopra di " decisamente in accordo." Se pensate che la cosa non ha alcun rilievo, segnate la (X) sopra " indeciso," e così via. Segnate la (X) nello spazio apposito, non sui punti di separazione.

Non esistono risposte esatte o risposte sbagliate. Siamo unicamente interessati alla vostra opinione sulle seguenti affermazioni:

1. Le persona media preferisce essere guidata, desidera di evitare le responsabilità e nutre poche ambizioni.

```
:_____:_____:_____:_____:_____:
decisamente   d'accordo   indeciso   in disaccordo   decisamente
in accordo                                           in disaccordo
```

2. La capacità di dirigere può venire acquistata dalla maggior parte della gente, indipendentemente da particolari caratteristiche e capacità innate.

```
:_____:_____:_____:_____:_____:
decisamente   d'accordo   indeciso   in disaccordo   decisamente
in accordo                                           in disaccordo
```

3. L'uso di incentivi (aumento della retribuzione, promozioni, ecc.) e di sanzioni (mancate promozioni, ecc.), non è il modo migliore per ottenere che i subordinati eseguano il loro compito.

```
:_____:_____:_____:_____:_____:
decisamente   d'accordo   indeciso   in disaccordo   decisamente
in accordo                                           in disaccordo
```

4. In una situazione di lavoro, il fatto che i subordinati non riescano ad influenzarmi, significa che stò perdendo la mia influenza su di loro.

```
:_____:_____:_____:_____:_____:
decisamente   d'accordo   indeciso   in disaccordo   decisamente
in accordo                                           in disaccordo
```

5. Un buon dirigente dovrebbe dare istruzioni dettagliate e complete ai suoi subordinati, piuttosto che dar loro solamente direttive generali, e far dipendere dalla loro iniziativa la messa a punto dei dettagli.

```
:_____:_____:_____:_____:_____:
decisamente   d'accordo   indeciso   in disaccordo   decisamente
in accordo                                           in disaccordo
```

6. Il fissare un obbiettivo collettivamente presenta vantaggi che non sono ottenibili individualmente.

```
:_____:_____:_____:_____:_____:
decisamente   d'accordo   indeciso   in disaccordo   decisamente
in accordo                                           in disaccordo
```

7. Un superiore dovrebbe informare i suoi subordinati solo di quanto è necessario perchè essi possano eseguire i loro compiti immediati.

```
:_____:_____:_____:_____:_____:
decisamente   d'accordo   indeciso   in disaccordo   decisamente
in accordo                                           in disaccordo
```

8. In una organizzazione, l'autorità del superiore sopra i suoi subordinati è soprattutto di carattere economico.

```
:_____:_____:_____:_____:_____:
decisamente   d'accordo   indeciso   in disaccordo   decisamente
in accordo                                           in disaccordo
```

Nelle pagine seguenti sono elencate alcune caratteristiche o qualità correlate con la posizione che ricoprite nella vostra ditta. Per ciascuna di dette caratteristiche, siete pregati di rispondere alle seguenti domande:

a) **In quale misura** la caratteristica è **attualmente** associata con la posizione che ricoprite nella vostra azienda?

b) **In quale misura** pensate che la caratteristica **dovrebbe** essere associata con la posizione che ricoprite nella vostra azienda?

c) **Quale importanza** riveste **per voi** questa caratteristica?

Per ciascuna domanda darete una valutazione su una scala di valori da 1 a 7, simile a quella riprodotta qui di seguito:

(minimo)   1      2      3      4      5      6      7   (massimo)

Per favore, segnate la (X) sul numero che stà a rappresentare in quale misura è presente la caratteristica da valutarsi. Valori bassi rappresentano un'importanza bassa o minima, e valori alti un'importanza alta o massima. Se ritenete che la caratteristica sia presente in piccola o nessuna misura, segnate una (X) sul numero 1. Se ritenete che essa sia presente in misura appena sufficiente, segnate una (X) sul numero 2, e così di seguito. Se pensate che essa sia presente in grande, ma non nella massima misura, segnate una (X) sul numero 6. In ogni caso, per ciascuna scala, segnate una (X) su un numero solamente.

Per favore, attribuite le vostre valutazioni **a tutte le scale.**

1. **La sensazione di stima in se stessi** che deriva dall'occupare la mia posizione.

a) In che misura è presente ora? (min.) 1 2 3 4 5 6 7 (mas.)

b) In che misura dovrebbe essere presente? 1 2 3 4 5 6 7

c) Che importanza riveste per me? 1 2 3 4 5 6 7

2. **L'autorità** associata con la mia posizione.

a) In che misura è presente ora? (min.) 1 2 3 4 5 6 7 (mas.)

b) In che misura dovrebbe essere presente? 1 2 3 4 5 6 7

c) Che importanza riveste per me? 1 2 3 4 5 6 7

3. **La possibilità di avanzamento e miglioramento personale** nella mia posizione.

a) In che misura è presente ora? (min.) 1 2 3 4 5 6 7 (mas.)

b) In che misura dovrebbe essere presente? 1 2 3 4 5 6 7

c) Che importanza riveste per me? 1 2 3 4 5 6 7

4. **Il prestigio** della mia posizione **all'interno** della mia azienda (vale a dire, la stima goduta presso altri **nell'** azienda).

a) In che misura è presente ora? (min.) 1 2 3 4 5 6 7 (mas.)

b) In che misura dovrebbe essere presente? 1 2 3 4 5 6 7

c) Che importanza riveste per me? 1 2 3 4 5 6 7

5. **La possibilità di pensare ed agire indipendentemente** nella mia posizione.

a) In che misura è presente ora? (min.) 1 2 3 4 5 6 7 (mas.)

b) In che misura dovrebbe essere presente? 1 2 3 4 5 6 7

c) Che importanza riveste per me? 1 2 3 4 5 6 7

6. **La sensazione di sicurezza** nella mia posizione.

a) In che misura è presente ora? (min.) 1 2 3 4 5 6 7 (mas.)

b) In che misura dovrebbe essere presente? 1 2 3 4 5 6 7

c) Che importanza riveste per me? 1 2 3 4 5 6 7

7. **La sensazione di auto-realizzazione** che si può ottenere occupando la mia posizione (vale a dire, la sensazione di essere in grado di usare le proprie capacità individuali, e di realizzare le proprie potenzialità).

a) In che misura è presente ora?  (min.) 1    2    3    4    5    6    7 (mas.)

b) In che misura dovrebbe essere presente?     1    2    3    4    5    6    7

c) Che importanza riveste per me?     1    2    3    4    5    6    7

8. **Il prestigio** della mia posizione **all'esterno** della mia azienda (vale a dire, la stima goduta presso altri **pon appartenenti** all'azienda).

a) In che misura è presente ora?  (min.) 1    2    3    4    5    6    7 (mas.)

b) In che misura dovrebbe essere presente?     1    2    3    4    5    6    7

c) Che importanza riveste per me?     1    2    3    4    5    6    7

9. **La sensazione di ottenere risultati di valore** nella mia posizione.

a) In che misura è presente ora?  (min.) 1    2    3    4    5    6    7 (mas.)

b) In che misura dovrebbe essere presente?     1    2    3    4    5    6    7

c) Che importanza riveste per me?     1    2    3    4    5    6    7

10. **La possibilità,** data la mia posizione, **di aiutare altre persone.**

a) In che misura è presente ora?  (min.) 1    2    3    4    5    6    7 (mas.)

b) In che misura dovrebbe essere presente?     1    2    3    4    5    6    7

c) Che importanza riveste per me?     1    2    3    4    5    6    7

11. **La possibilità di instaurare rapporti di stretta amicizia** nella mia posizione.

a) In che misura è presente ora?  (min.) 1    2    3    4    5    6    7 (mas.)

b) In che misura dovrebbe essere presente?     1    2    3    4    5    6    7

c) Che importanza riveste per me?     1    2    3    4    5    6    7

**ISTRUZIONI**

Lo scopo che questo questionario si propone, è ottenere le vostre impressioni su un certo numero di cose e idee. Per esempio, in cima alla prossima pagina, leggerete la parola MEDICO. Dateci la vostra impressione di ciò che detta parola significa per voi. A questo scopo segnerete una (X) su ciascuna di una serie di scale che appaiono nella stessa pagina. Ciascuna scala è delimitata da una coppia di aggettivi (vedi gli esempi qui sotto). Ogni scala dispone di sette spazi; segnate la (X) su quello che, **secondo voi,** descrive nel modo più accurato la particolare cosa o idea. Il seguente esempio illustra come voi potreste contrassegnare le scale per una particolare cosa o idea.

grande : ___ : ___ : ___ : ___ : ___ : ___ : piccolo

spiacevole : ___ : ___ : ___ : ___ : ___ : ___ : piacevole

Per favore, siate ben certi di:

1. Segnare una (X) su ciascuna scala. **Non** omettetene alcuna.

2. Segnare solamente una (X) su ciascuna scala.

## MEDICO

poco importante :_____:_____:_____:_____:_____:_____:_____: importante

profondo :_____:_____:_____:_____:_____:_____:_____: superficiale

attivo :_____:_____:_____:_____:_____:_____:_____: passivo

stretto :_____:_____:_____:_____:_____:_____:_____: largo

difficile :_____:_____:_____:_____:_____:_____:_____: facile

buono :_____:_____:_____:_____:_____:_____:_____: cattivo

stabile :_____:_____:_____:_____:_____:_____:_____: mutevole

interessante :_____:_____:_____:_____:_____:_____:_____: poco interessante

debole :_____:_____:_____:_____:_____:_____:_____: forte


COLONNELLO

DECIDERE

PERSUADERE

CAPOSQUADRA

CREARE

INGANNARE

PRETE

COMMETTERE UN ERRORE

SERGENTE

COOPERARE

VESCOVO

DIRIGERE

RIMPROVERARE

DIRIGENTE AZIENDALE

Ai fini dell'analisi statistica dei dati, per favore forniteci le seguenti informazioni:

1. Cittadinanza——————————————

2. Titolo della posizione che occupate attualmente

——————————————————————

3. Sezione nella vostra azienda:

——— Produzione

——— Vendite e pubblicità

——— Finanza e contabilità

——— Personale ed addestramento

——— Acquisti

——— Ricerche

——— Amministrazione generale

——— Altro (per favore specificare)———

4. Quanti livelli di controllo esistono in totale nella vostra organizzazione, dal più basso al capo dell'organizzazione stessa? (Date il numero):

———

5. Quanti livelli di controllo esistono al di sopra della vostra posizione? (Date il numero):

———

6. Per quanti anni avete lavorato in imprese commerciali, industriali o pubbliche?

——— da 0 a 1 anno

——— da 1 a 3 anni

——— da 3 a 5 anni

——— da 5 a 10 anni

——— da 10 a 20 anni

——— da 20 a 30 anni

——— più di 30 anni

7. Approssimativamente, quante persone sono impiegate in totale (impieghi direttivi e non direttivi) nella vostra azienda?

——— da 1 a 49

——— da 50 a 99

——— da 100 a 499

——— da 500 a 999

——— da 1000 a 4999

——— da 5000 a 9999

——— da 10.000 a 29.999

——— da 30.000 a 99.999

——— da 100.000 a 299.999

——— più di 300.000

8. Esercitate un controllo finanziario determinante nella vostra azienda?

——— sì

——— no

9. Tipo di azienda per la quale lavorate:

——— Trasporti e spedizioni

——— Poste, telegrafi e telefoni

——— Industria elettrica

——— Commercio all'ingrosso e al dettaglio

——— Finanziaria ed assicuratrice

——— Chimica e petrolifera

——— Mineraria

——— Metallurgica

——— Manifatturiera

——— Altro (per favore specificare)———

10. La vostra età:

——— 20-24

——— 25-29

——— 30-34

——— 35-39

——— 40-44

——— 45-49

——— 50-54

——— 55-59

——— 60 o più

11. Quanti anni di istruzione scolastica avete completato, includendo scuola elementare, media e università:

———

12. Se avete frequentato un'università, o una scuola media[1] superiore, quale è stata la vostra specializzazione:

——— Ingegneria

——— Giurisprudenza

——— Scienze Economiche e Commerciali

——— Lettere e Filosofia

——— Altra (per favore specificare)———

# Investigacion sobre Opiniones en la Industria

NO ESCRIBA SU NOMBRE EN ESTE FOLLETO

En la sección de abajo encontrará una serie de affrmaciones. Haga el favor de indicar si está de acuerdo o en desacuerdo. Use la escala debajo de cada afirmación. Por ejemplo:
Es má fácil trabajar en un clima templado que en un clima cálido.

|  | | X | | | |
|---|---|---|---|---|---|
| muy de acuerdo | de acuerdo | indeciso | en desacuerdo | muy en desacuerdo | |

Si cree que es más fácil trabajar en un clima templado, ponga una (X) sobre " de acuerdo "; si cree que es mucho más fácil trabajar en clima templado, ponga una marca sobre " muy de acuerdo." Si Vd. piensa que no existe diferencia, ponga la marca sobre " indeciso," (etc.). Ponga la marca en el centro del espacio, no en los **extremos**.

No hay respuestas correctas o incorrectas. Estamos interesados en su opinión sobre las afiirmaciones que siguen:

1. El individuo medio prefiere ser dirigido, elude la responsabilidad, y tiene, relativamente, poca ambición.

| muy de acuerdo | de acuerdo | indeciso | en desacuerdo | muy en desacuerdo |
|---|---|---|---|---|

2. La habilidad de dirigir puede ser adquirida por la mayor parte de las personas, independientemente de sus rasgos y habilidades innatas.

| muy de acuerdo | de acuerdo | indeciso | en desacuerdo | muy en desacuerdo |
|---|---|---|---|---|

3. El uso de recompensas (pagas, promoción, etc.) y castigos (dejar de promover, etc.) **no** es el mejor medio para que los subordinados trabajen.

| muy de acuerdo | de acuerdo | indeciso | en desacuerdo | muy en desacuerdo |
|---|---|---|---|---|

4. Si en el trabajo los subordinados no pueden ejercer su influencia sobre mí, pierdo entonces cierta influencia sobre ellos.

| muy de acuerdo | de acuerdo | indeciso | en desacuerdo | muy en desacuerdo |
|---|---|---|---|---|

5. Un buen líder debería dar instrucciones completas y detalladas a sus subordinados, en vez de darles simplemente instrucciones generales y depender de su iniciativa para realizar los detalles.

| muy de acuerdo | de acuerdo | indeciso | en desacuerdo | muy en desacuerdo |
|---|---|---|---|---|

6. El establecimiento de metas de equipo ofrece ventajas que no pueden ser obtenidas por el establecimiento de metas individuales.

| muy de acuerdo | de acuerdo | indeciso | en desacuerdo | muy en desacuerdo |
|---|---|---|---|---|

7. Un superior debe dar a sus subordinados solamente la información necesaria para que ellos puedan hacer su trabajo inmediato.

| muy de acuerdo | de acuerdo | indeciso | en desacuerdo | muy en desacuerdo |
|---|---|---|---|---|

8. La autoridad de un superior sobre sus subordinados, en unaorganización, es primordialmente económica.

| muy de acuerdo | de acuerdo | indeciso | en desacuerdo | muy en desacuerdo |
|---|---|---|---|---|

**INSTRUCCIONES**

En las siguientes páginas de esta segunda parte se enumerán varias características o cualidades relacionadas con **su propia posición** en su empresa. Para cada una de estas características, se le pide dar tres juicios:

a) ¿ **Que grado** de la característica **hay en este momento** relacionada con **su posición** en la empresa?

b) ¿ **Que grado** de la característica cree usted que **debiera estar** relacionada con **su posición** en la empresa?

c) ¿ **Que importancia** tiene esta característica de su posición **parausted**?

Cada juicio se hará en una escala de siete puntos, que aparecerá así:

(mnimo)   1     2     3     4     5     6     7     (mximo)

Haga el favor de marcar con una (X) encima del número de la escala que representa la cantidad de la característica que se enjuicia. Los números bajos representan cantidades bajas o mínimas, y los nomeros altos representan cantidades altas o máximas. Se cree que hay " muy poco " o " nada " de la característica relacionado ahora con la posición, ponga una X sobre el número 1. Si cree que hay " sólo un poco," ponga una X sobre el número 2, y así sucesivamente. Si cree que hay " mucho pero no un máximo," ponga una X sobre el número 6. En cada escala, ponga la marca X solamente sobre un nomero.

**Por favor no omita ninguna escala.**

1. El **sentimiento de propia estima** que una persona obtiene por estar en mi posición de directivo:

a) ¿Qué grado alcanza ahora?

(min) 1   2   3   4   5   6   7 (max)

b) ¿Qué grado debería alcanzar?

1   2   3   4   5   6   7

c) ¿Qué importancia tiene esto para mí?

1   2   3   4   5   6   7

2. La **autoridad** relacionada con mi posición de directivo:

a) ¿Qué grado alcanza ahora?

(min) 1   2   3   4   5   6   7 (max)

b) ¿Qué grado debería alcanzar?

1   2   3   4   5   6   7

c) ¿Qué importancia tiene esto para mí?

1   2   3   4   5   6   7

3. La **oportunidad para la formación y perfeccionamiento personal** en mi posición de director:

a) ¿Qué grado alcanza ahora?

(min) 1   2   3   4   5   6   7 (max)

b) ¿Qué grado debería alcanzar?

1   2   3   4   5   6   7

c) ¿Qué importancia tiene esto para mí?

1   2   3   4   5   6   7

4. El **prestigio** de mi posición de directivo dentro de la empresa (es decir, el respeto que se recibe de otros **en la empresa**):

a) ¿Qué grado alcanza ahora?

(min) 1   2   3   4   5   6   7 (max)

b) ¿Qué grado debería alcanzar?

1   2   3   4   5   6   7

c) ¿Qué importancia tiene esto para mí?

1   2   3   4   5   6   7

5. La **oportunidad para pensar y actuar libremente** en mi posición de directivo:

a) ¿Qué grado alcanza ahora?

(min) 1   2   3   4   5   6   7 (max)

b) ¿Qué grado debería alcanzar?

1   2   3   4   5   6   7

c) ¿Qué importancia tiene esto para mí?

1   2   3   4   5   6   7

6. El **sentimiento de seguridad** en mi posición de directivo:

a) ¿Qué grado alcanza ahora?

(min) 1   2   3   4   5   6   7 (max)

b) ¿Qué grado debería alcanzar?

1   2   3   4   5   6   7

c) ¿Qué importancia tiene esto para mí?

1   2   3   4   5   6   7

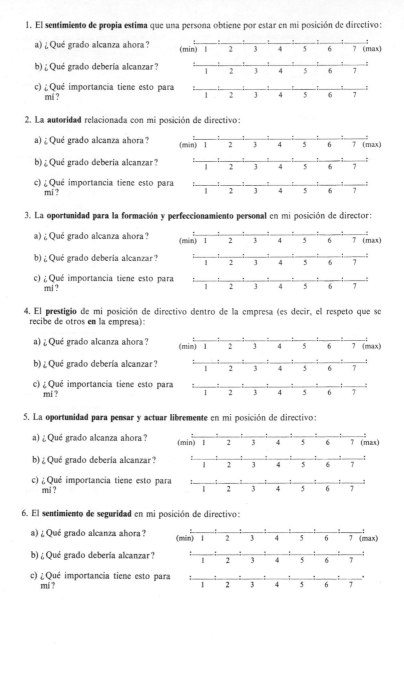

7. El **sentimiento de autorealización** que alcanza una persona al estar en mi posición de directivo (es decir, el sentimiento de poder usar las capacidades de uno mismo, realizando las propias potencias):

a) ¿Qué grado alcanza ahora?

(min) 1   2   3   4   5   6   7 (max)

b) ¿Qué grado debería alcanzar?

1   2   3   4   5   6   7

c) ¿Qué importancia tiene esto para mí?

1   2   3   4   5   6   7

8. El **prestigio** de mi posición de directivo **fuera** de la compañia (es decir, el respeto que se recibe de otros que no están en la empresa):

a) ¿Qué grado alcanza ahora?

(min) 1   2   3   4   5   6   7 (max)

b) ¿Qué grado debería alcanzar?

1   2   3   4   5   6   7

c) ¿Qué importancia tiene esto para mí?

1   2   3   4   5   6   7

9. El **sentimiento de estar haciendo algo importante** en mí posición de directivo:

a) ¿Qué grado alcanza ahora?

(min) 1   2   3   4   5   6   7 (max)

b) ¿Qué grado debería alcanzar?

1   2   3   4   5   6   7

c) ¿Qué importancia tiene esto para mí?

1   2   3   4   5   6   7

10. La **oportunidad**, en mi posición, **de ayudar a otras personas:**

a) ¿Qué grado alcanza ahora?

(min) 1   2   3   4   5   6   7 (max)

b) ¿Qué grado debería alcanzar?

1   2   3   4   5   6   7

c) ¿Qué importancia tiene esto para mí?

1   2   3   4   5   6   7

11. La **oportunidad de establecer amistades firmes** en mi posición de directivo:

a) ¿Qué grado alcanza ahora?

(min) 1   2   3   4   5   6   7 (max)

b) ¿Qué grado debería alcanzar?

1   2   3   4   5   6   7

c) ¿Qué importancia tiene esto para mí?

1   2   3   4   5   6   7

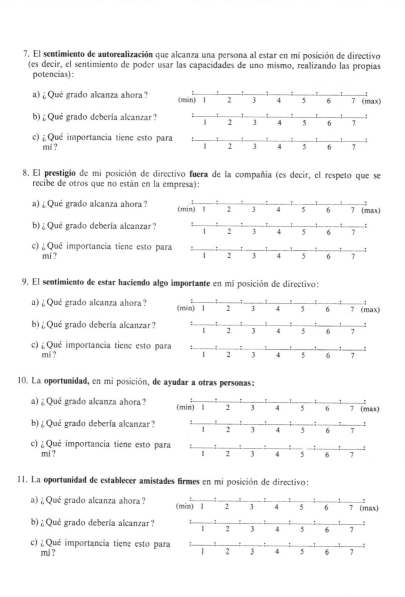

**INSTRUCCIONES**

El proposito de este cuestionario es obtener sus impresiones acerca de una variedad de cosas o ideas. Por ejemplo, encabezando la siguiente página está la palabra MEDICO. Debe dar su impresión de lo que esto significa para usted por medio de una X que pondrá en cada una de la serie de escalas que aparecen debajo en la misma página. Cada escala está definida por un par de palabras. (Vea los ejemplos abajo.) Ponga una X en **cada** escala, en aquél de los siete espacios que describa con mayor exactitud la cosa o idea, específica, **en su opinión.** A continuación se dá un ejemplo de como marcar las escalas para una cosa o idea particular.

grande :_____:_____:___X__:_____:_____:_____:_____: pequeño

aburrido :_____:_____:_____:_____:_____:___X__:_____: divertido

Por favor, esté seguro de:

1. Poner una X en cada escala. **No omita ninguna escala.**

2. Poner solamente **una** X en cada escala.

MÉDICO

sin importancia :____:____:____:____:____:____:____: importante

profundo :____:____:____:____:____:____:____: superficial

activo :____:____:____:____:____:____:____: pasivo

reducido :____:____:____:____:____:____:____: amplio

difícil :____:____:____:____:____:____:____: fácil

bueno :____:____:____:____:____:____:____: malo

estable :____:____:____:____:____:____:____: cambiable

interesante :____:____:____:____:____:____:____: sin interés

débil :____:____:____:____:____:____:____: fuerte


CORONEL

DECIDIR

PERSUADIR

CAPATAZ DE TALLER

CREAR

ENGAÑAR

SACERDOTE

COMETER UN ERROR

SARGENTO

COOPERAR

OBISPO

DIRIGIR

CORREGIR

SUPERVISOR DE TALLER

Para ayudarnos en el análisis estadístico de los datos, dé, por favor, la siguiente información:

1. Ciudadanía ⎯⎯⎯⎯⎯⎯⎯⎯⎯⎯

2. Título de su actual posición en la empresa⎯⎯

⎯⎯⎯⎯⎯⎯⎯⎯⎯⎯⎯⎯⎯⎯⎯⎯

3. Departamento a que pertenece usted en la empresa (marque uno):

⎯⎯⎯ Producción

⎯⎯⎯ Ventas, Mercado y Propaganda

⎯⎯⎯ Finanza y Contabilidad

⎯⎯⎯ Personal e Instrucción

⎯⎯⎯ Compras

⎯⎯⎯ Investigación y Desarrollo

⎯⎯⎯ Dirección General

⎯⎯⎯ Otro (especifique) ⎯⎯⎯⎯⎯⎯

4. ¿Cuántos niveles de supervisión hay en su empresa desde el supervisor del primer nivel hasta la cabeza de la organización? (Dé el número):

⎯⎯⎯

5. ¿Cuántos niveles de supervisión hay por encima de su posición?

⎯⎯⎯

6. ¿Cuántos años ha estado trabajando en comercio, industria, o gobierno? (Marque uno):

⎯⎯⎯ 0 a 1 año

⎯⎯⎯ 1 a 3 años

⎯⎯⎯ 3 a 5 años

⎯⎯⎯ 5 a 10 años

⎯⎯⎯ 10 a 20 años

⎯⎯⎯ 20 a 30 años

⎯⎯⎯ más de 30 años

7. Aproximadamente, ¿cuántos empleados (directivo y no directivo) hay en su empresa? (marque uno):

⎯⎯⎯1 a 49

⎯⎯⎯ 50 a 99

⎯⎯⎯ 100 a 499

⎯⎯⎯ 500 a 999

⎯⎯⎯ 1.000 a 4.999

⎯⎯⎯ 5.000 a 9.999

⎯⎯⎯ 10.000 a 299.999

⎯⎯⎯ 300.000 ó más

8. ¿Es usted dueño de una gran parte de la empresa? (Marque uno):

⎯⎯⎯ sí

⎯⎯⎯ no

9. Clase de la empresa donde trabaja (Marque uno):

⎯⎯⎯ Transporte y expedición

⎯⎯⎯ Correo, Telégrafo y Teléfono

⎯⎯⎯ Fuerza, Luz y Electricidad

⎯⎯⎯ Por Mayor y Por Menor

⎯⎯⎯ Finanza y Seguro

⎯⎯⎯ Química y Petroleo

⎯⎯⎯ Minería

⎯⎯⎯ Acero y Fabricaciones Metálicas

⎯⎯⎯ Manufacturas

⎯⎯⎯ Otra (especifique, por favor)⎯⎯

10. Su edad (Marque uno):

⎯⎯⎯ 20-24

⎯⎯⎯ 25-29

⎯⎯⎯ 30-34

⎯⎯⎯ 35-39

⎯⎯⎯ 40-44

⎯⎯⎯ 45-49

⎯⎯⎯ 50-54

⎯⎯⎯ 55-59

⎯⎯⎯ 60 ó más

11. ¿Cuántos años de estudios realizó usted, incluyendo escuela, universidad y escuela técnica? (Dé el número):

⎯⎯⎯

12. Si fué a una universidad o escuela técnica, ¿En que se especializó? (Marque uno):

⎯⎯⎯ Ingeniería

⎯⎯⎯ Abogacía

⎯⎯⎯ Económía

⎯⎯⎯ Artes y Filosofía

⎯⎯⎯ Otra (especifique, por favor)⎯⎯

# 10. South American Spanish

# Investigación sobre Opiniones en la Industria

NO ESCRIBA SU NOMBRE EN ESTE FOLLETO

En la sección de abajo encontrará una serie de afirmaciones. Haga el favor de indicar si está de acuerdo o en desacuerdo. Use la escala debajo de cada afirmación.

Por ejemplo:
Es más fácil trabajar en un clima templado que en un clima cálido.

| :_____ | :_____X | :_____ | :_____ | :_____ : |
| muy de acuerdo | de acuerdo | indeciso | en desacuerdo | muy en desacuerdo |

Si cree que es más fácil trabajar en un clima templado, ponga una (X) sobre "de acuerdo"; si cree que es mucho más fácil trabajar en clima templado, ponga una marca sobre "muy de acuerdo." Si Vd. piensa que no existe diferencia, ponga la marca sobre "indeciso," (etc.). Ponga la marca en el centro del espacio, no en los **extremos**.

No hay respuestas correctas o incorrectas. Estamos interesados en su opinión sobre las afirmaciones que siguen:

1. El individuo medio prefiere ser dirigido, elude responsabilidades, y tiene, relativamente, poca ambición.

| :_____ | :_____ | :_____ | :_____ | :_____ : |
| muy de acuerdo | de acuerdo | indeciso | en desacuerdo | muy en desacuerdo |

2. La habilidad de dirigir puede ser adquirida por la mayor parte de las personas, independientemente de sus rasgos y habilidades innatas.

| :_____ | :_____ | :_____ | :_____ | :_____ : |
| muy de acuerdo | de acuerdo | indeciso | en desacuerdo | muy en desacuerdo |

3. El uso de recompensas (pagas, promoción, etc.) y castigos (dejar de promover, etc.) **no** es el mejor medio para que los subordinados trabajen.

| :_____ | :_____ | :_____ | :_____ | :_____ : |
| muy de acuerdo | de acuerdo | indeciso | en desacuerdo | muy en desacuerdo |

4. Si en el trabajo los subordinados no pueden ejercer su influencia sobre mí, pierdo entonces cierta influencia sobre ellos.

| :_____ | :_____ | :_____ | :_____ | :_____ : |
| muy de acuerdo | de acuerdo | indeciso | en desacuerdo | muy en desacuerdo |

5. Un buen líder debería dar instrucciones completas y detalladas a sus subordinados, en vez de darles simplemente instrucciones generales y depender de su iniciativa para realizar los detalles.

| :_____ | :_____ | :_____ | :_____ | :_____ : |
| muy de acuerdo | de acuerdo | indeciso | en desacuerdo | muy en desacuerdo |

6. El establecimiento de metas de equipo ofrece ventajas que no pueden ser obtenidas por el establecimiento de metas individuales.

| :_____ | :_____ | :_____ | :_____ | :_____ : |
| muy de acuerdo | de acuerdo | indeciso | en desacuerdo | muy en desacuerdo |

7. Un superior debería dar a sus subordinados solamente la información necesaria para que ellos puedan hacer su trabajo inmediato.

| :_____ | :_____ | :_____ | :_____ | :_____ : |
| muy de acuerdo | de acuerdo | indeciso | en desacuerdo | muy en desacuerdo |

8. La autoridad de un superior sobre sus subordinados, en una organización, es primordialmente económica.

| :_____ | :_____ | :_____ | :_____ | :_____ : |
| muy de acuerdo | de acuerdo | indeciso | en desacuerdo | muy en desacuerdo |

**INSTRUCCIONES**

En las siguientes páginas de esta segunda parte se enumeran varias características o cualidades relacionadas con **su propia posición** en su empresa. Para cada una de estas características, se le pide dar tres juicios:

a) ¿**Que grado** de la característica **hay en este momento** relacionada con **su posición** en la empresa?

b) ¿**Que grado** de la característica cree usted que **debiera estar** relacionada con **su posición** en la empresa?

c) ¿**Que importancia** tiene esta característica de su posición **para usted?**

Cada juicio se hará en una escala de siete puntos, que aparecerá así:

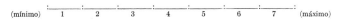

(mínimo)    1     2     3     4     5     6     7     (máximo)

Haga el favor de marcar con una (X) encima del número de la escala que representa la cantidad de la característica que se enjuicia. Los números bajos representan cantidades bajas o mínimas, y los números altos representan cantidades altas o máximas. Si cree que hay "muy poco" o "nada" de la característica relacionado ahora con la posición, ponga una X sobre el número 1. Si cree que hay "sólo un poco," ponga una X sobre el número 2, y así sucesivamente. Si cree que hay "mucho pero no un máximo," ponga una X sobre el número 6. En cada escala, ponga la marca X solamente sobre un número.

**Por favor no omita ninguna escala.**

1. El **sentimiento de propia estima** que una persona obtiene por estar en mi posición directiva:

   a) ¿Qué grado alcanza ahora?  (mín) 1   2   3   4   5   6   7 (máx)

   b) ¿Qué grado debería alcanzar?  1   2   3   4   5   6   7

   c) ¿Qué importancia tiene esto para mí?  1   2   3   4   5   6   7

2. La **autoridad** relacionada con mi posición directiva:

   a) ¿Qué grado alcanza ahora?  (mín) 1   2   3   4   5   6   7 (máx)

   b) ¿Qué grado debería alcanzar?  1   2   3   4   5   6   7

   c) ¿Qué importancia tiene esto para mí?  1   2   3   4   5   6   7

3. La **oportunidad para la formación y perfeccionamiento personal** en mi posición directiva:

   a) ¿Qué grado alcanza ahora?  (mín) 1   2   3   4   5   6   7 (máx)

   b) ¿Qué grado debería alcanzar?  1   2   3   4   5   6   7

   c) ¿Qué importancia tiene esto para mí?  1   2   3   4   5   6   7

4. El **prestigio** de mi posición directiva dentro de la empresa (es decir, el respeto que se recibe de otros **en** la empresa):

   a) ¿Qué grado alcanza ahora?  (mín) 1   2   3   4   5   6   7 (máx)

   b) ¿Qué grado debería alcanzar?  1   2   3   4   5   6   7

   c) ¿Qué importancia tiene esto para mí?  1   2   3   4   5   6   7

5. La **oportunidad para pensamiento y acción independientes** en mi posición directiva:

   a) ¿Qué grado alcanza ahora?  (mín) 1   2   3   4   5   6   7 (máx)

   b) ¿Qué grado debería alcanzar?  1   2   3   4   5   6   7

   c) ¿Qué importancia tiene esto para mí?  1   2   3   4   5   6   7

6. El **sentimiento de seguridad** en mi posición directiva:

   a) ¿Qué grado alcanza ahora?  (mín) 1   2   3   4   5   6   7 (máx)

   b) ¿Qué grado debería alcanzar?  1   2   3   4   5   6   7

   c) ¿Qué importancia tiene esto para mí?  1   2   3   4   5   6   7

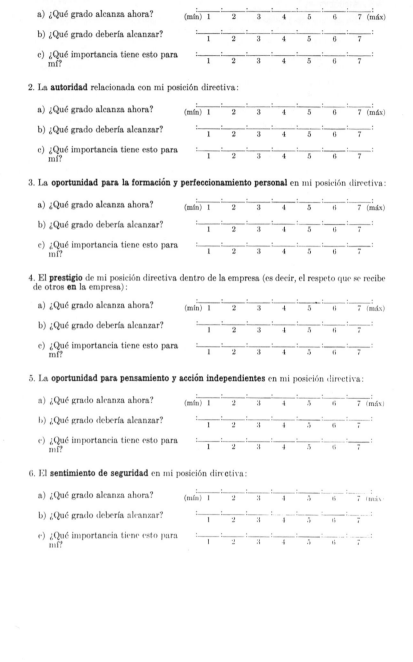

7. El **sentimiento de autorealización** que alcanza una persona al estar en mi posición directiva (es decir, el sentimiento de poder utilizar la singular capacidad de uno mismo, realizando las propias potencialidades):

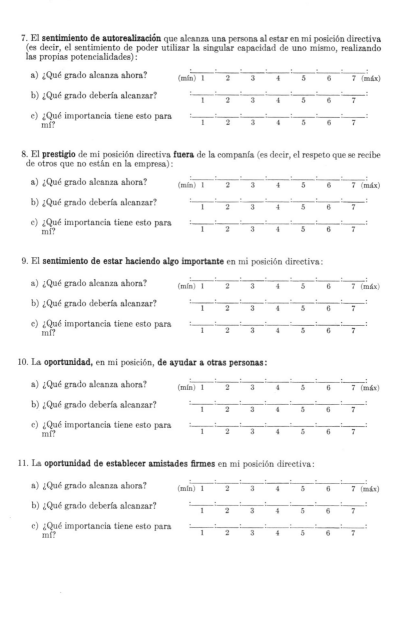

a) ¿Qué grado alcanza ahora?  (mín) 1  2  3  4  5  6  7 (máx)

b) ¿Qué grado debería alcanzar?  1  2  3  4  5  6  7

c) ¿Qué importancia tiene esto para mí?  1  2  3  4  5  6  7

8. El **prestigio** de mi posición directiva **fuera** de la companía (es decir, el respeto que se recibe de otros que no están en la empresa):

a) ¿Qué grado alcanza ahora?  (mín) 1  2  3  4  5  6  7 (máx)

b) ¿Qué grado debería alcanzar?  1  2  3  4  5  6  7

c) ¿Qué importancia tiene esto para mí?  1  2  3  4  5  6  7

9. El **sentimiento de estar haciendo algo importante** en mi posición directiva:

a) ¿Qué grado alcanza ahora?  (mín) 1  2  3  4  5  6  7 (máx)

b) ¿Qué grado debería alcanzar?  1  2  3  4  5  6  7

c) ¿Qué importancia tiene esto para mí?  1  2  3  4  5  6  7

10. La **oportunidad, en mi posición, de ayudar a otras personas**:

a) ¿Qué grado alcanza ahora?  (mín) 1  2  3  4  5  6  7 (máx)

b) ¿Qué grado debería alcanzar?  1  2  3  4  5  6  7

c) ¿Qué importancia tiene esto para mí?  1  2  3  4  5  6  7

11. La **oportunidad de establecer amistades firmes** en mi posición directiva:

a) ¿Qué grado alcanza ahora?  (mín) 1  2  3  4  5  6  7 (máx)

b) ¿Qué grado debería alcanzar?  1  2  3  4  5  6  7

c) ¿Qué importancia tiene esto para mí?  1  2  3  4  5  6  7

**INSTRUCCIONES**

El propósito de este cuestionario es obtener sus impresiones acerca de una variedad de cosas o ideas. Por ejemplo, encabezando la sigueinte página está la palabra MEDICO. Se le pide que dé su impresión de lo que esto significa para usted por medio de una X que pondrá en cada una de la serie de escalas que aparecen debajo en la misma página. Cada escala está definida por un par de palabras. (Vea los ejemplos abajo.) Ponga una X en **cada** escala, en aquél de los siete espacios que describa con mayor exactitud la cosa o idea, específica, **en su opinión.** A continuación se dá un ejemplo de como marcar las escalas para una cosa o idea particular.

grande :_____:_____:____X___:_____:_____:_____:_____: pequeño

aburrido :_____:_____:_____:_____:_____:___X___:_____: divertido

Por favor, esté seguro de:

1. Poner una X en cada escala. **No omita ninguna escala.**

2. Poner solamente **una** X en cada escala.

## MÉDICO

sin importancia :___:___:___:___:___:___:___: importante

profundo :___:___:___:___:___:___:___: superficial

activo :___:___:___:___:___:___:___: pasivo

estrecho :___:___:___:___:___:___:___: amplio

difícil :___:___:___:___:___:___:___: fácil

bueno :___:___:___:___:___:___:___: malo

estable :___:___:___:___:___:___:___: cambiable

interesante :___:___:___:___:___:___:___: sin interés

débil :___:___:___:___:___:___:___: fuerte


CORONEL

DECIDIR

PERSUADIR

CAPATAZ DE FABRICA

CREAR

ENGAÑAR

SACERDOTE

COMETER UN ERROR

SARGENTO

COOPERAR

OBISPO

DIRIGIR

AMONESTAR

GERENTE DE FABRICA

Para ayudarnos en el análisis estadístico de los datos, dé, por favor, la siguiente información

1. Ciudadanía _____

2. Título de su actual posición en la empresa _____

_____

3. Departamento a que pertenece usted en la empresa (marque uno):

_____ Producción

_____ Ventas, Mercado y Propaganda

_____ Finanza y Contabilidad

_____ Personal e Instrucción

_____ Compras

_____ Investigación y Desarrollo

_____ Administración General

_____ Otro (especifique) _____

4. ¿Cuántos niveles de supervisión hay en su empresa desde el supervisor del primer nivel hasta la cabeza de la organización? (Dé el número):

_____

5. ¿Cuántos niveles de supervisión hay por encima de su posición?

_____

6. ¿Cuántos años ha estado trabajando en comercio, industria, o gobierno? (Marque uno):

_____ 0 a 1 año

_____ 1 a 3 años

_____ 3 a 5 años

_____ 5 a 10 años

_____ 10 a 20 años

_____ 20 a 30 años

_____ más de 30 años

7. Aproximadamente, ¿cuántos empleados (directivos y no directivos) hay en su empresa? (marque uno):

_____ 1 a 49

_____ 50 a 99

_____ 100 a 499

_____ 500 a 999

_____ 1.000 a 4.999

_____ 5.000 a 9.999

_____ 10.000 a 299.999

_____ 300.000 ó más

8. ¿Es usted dueño de una gran parte de la empresa? (Marque uno):

_____ sí

_____ no

9. Clase de empresa donde trabaja (Marque uno):

_____ Transporte y expedición

_____ Correo, Telégrafo y Teléfono

_____ Fuerza, Luz y Electricidad

_____ Comercio mayorista y minorista

_____ Finanza y Seguro

_____ Química y Petroleo

_____ Minería

_____ Acero y Fabricaciones Metálicas

_____ Manufacturas

_____ Otra (especifique, por favor) _____

10. Su edad (Marque uno):

_____ 20–24

_____ 25–29

_____ 30–34

_____ 35–39

_____ 40–44

_____ 45–49

_____ 50–54

_____ 55–59

_____ 60 ó más

11. ¿Cuántos años de estudios realizó usted, incluyendo escuela, universidad y escuela técnica? (Dé el número):

_____

12. Si fué a una universidad o escuela técnica, ¿En qué se especializó? (Marque uno):

_____ Ingeniería

_____ Abogacía

_____ Economía

_____ Artes y Filosofía

_____ Otra (especifique, por favor) _____

# 11. Japanese

産業關係研究所
カリフオルニヤ大學
バークレイ・カリフオルニヤ

産業における意見調査

この冊子には 名前を書かないで 下さい

第一部

　　　下に一連の意見が述べてあります。それらの意見に對して，賛成か反對かを　各意見の下にある尺度を用いて記入して下さい。

例
　暑い日に働くよりも，涼しい日に働く方が容易である。

    :_____:_____:_____:_____:_____:
    絶對　　　賛成　　どちらとも　　反對　　　絶對
    賛成　　　　　　　いえない　　　　　　　　反對

　　　もし，涼しい日に働く方が容易であると思われるならば，"賛成"の上に（X）を記入して下さい。もし，涼しい日に働く方が極めて容易であると思われるならば，"絶對賛成"の上に X印を記入して下さい。　もし，どちらでもかまわないと思われるならば，"どちらともいえない"の上に印をして下さい。反對の場合も同様です。なお，X印は必ず空白の所に書き込み，境界線にまたがらないよう注意して下さい。

　　　回答は，正しいとか誤りだとかいうような中のではありません。下に述べてある意見に對して，あなたがどう思っているかを知ろうとするものです。

1. 他人から指導されることを好む人たちは, 一般に 自分に
責任がかかることを避けようとする人たちであり, 相對的に
云って, あまり野望を持たない人たちである。

```
   :_____:_____:_____:_____:_____:
   絶 對      賛 成    どちらとも    反 對    絶 對
   賛 成             いえない            反 對
```

2. 指導(リーダーシップ)の技術は, 生れつきもっている特性や能力
とは無關係に, ほとんどの人が獲得できるものである。

```
   :_____:_____:_____:_____:_____:
   絶 對      賛 成    どちらとも    反 對    絶 對
   賛 成             いえない            反 對
```

3. 賞(昇給・昇進等)や罰(昇進をおくらす等)を用いることは, 部下
を使う最上の方法ではない。

```
   :_____:_____:_____:_____:_____:
   絶 對      賛 成    どちらとも    反 對    絶 對
   賛 成             いえない            反 對
```

4. 作業事態で, 部下が上司に意見を述べたり, いろいろ進言した
りして, 上司を動かすことが不可能な場合は, 上司もまた,
部下を充分動かすことができないものである。

```
   :_____:_____:_____:_____:_____:
   絶 對      賛 成    どちらとも    反 對    絶 對
   賛 成             いえない            反 對
```

5. 良い指導者は、 一般的な 指示だけをして、 仕事の細部
は部下にまかせるようなな指導はしないで、寧ろ細部に亘って
完全に指示すべきである.

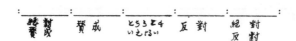

絶對
賛成　　賛成　　どちらとも　　反對　　絶對
　　　　　　　いえない　　　　　　反對

6. 集團で目標を設定すれば、 個人が目標設定しても得られない
ようなな 利益が 得られる わけである.

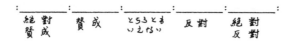

絶對
賛成　　賛成　　どちらとも　　反對　　絶對
　　　　　　　いえない　　　　　　反對

7. 上司は部下に、 仕事に直接必要である情報だけを與えるべ
きである.

絶對
賛成　　賛成　　どちらとも　　反對　　絶對
　　　　　　　いえない　　　　　　反對

8. 組織体(會社)内において、 上司が部下に對して權威がある
のは、 主として、 部下の給與の昇給や昇給停止の權限
を持っているからである.

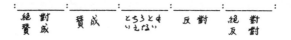

絶對
賛成　　賛成　　どちらとも　　反對　　絶對
　　　　　　　いえない　　　　　　反對

第二部

　　次の第二部には，あなたの會社で，現在あなたが占めている
地位について，いろいろ特性や特質が述べられています。各特性
について，三つの観点から評定しなければなりません。

A. そこに述べられている特性は，あなたの會社において，あなたがついて
　　いる地位に　現在　どれほど関連がありますか。

B. そこに述べられている特性は，あなたの會社において，あなたが
　　ついている地位に，本来なら，どれほど関連がなければなら
　　ないと思いますか。

C. あなたの地位が持っているその特性は，あなたにとって，どれ
　　ほど重要ですか。

　　各評定は，下に示されているような七段階評定尺度で行なわれ
ます。

(最低) 1 : 2 : 3 : 4 : 5 : 6 : 7 (最高 )

　　上記の尺度上の数値は，評定される特性がどれくらいあるか
という量を示しており，その数値上の空間に（X）印をつけるのです。

数値が低いのは、その特性が少いことを意味し、数値が高いのは、その特性が多いことを意味します。若し、あなたの地位と、そこに述べられている特性とが、現在事実上、"ほとんど関係がないが"、あるいは、"全く関係がない"と思われたら、数値1の上にX印を記入して下さい。"ほんの少しだけ"関係があると思われたら、数値2の上にX印をつけて下さい。若し、"非常に関係はあるが、最高とまではいかない"と思われたら、数値6の上にX印をつけて下さい。各尺度に必ず一つだけX印をつけて下さい。二つ以上つけてはいけません。どの尺度にも見落しのないように注意して下さい。

**1.** あなたが現在ついている管理上の地位に他人がついた場合, どれくらいの誇りや自尊感情をもつと思いますか.

**A)** 現在, どれくらいの誇りや自尊感情がありますか.

(最低) 1 : ___ : ___ : ___ : ___ : ___ : ___ : 7 (最高)
            2    3    4    5    6

**B)** 本来なら, どれくらいあるべきだと思いますか.

(最低) 1 : ___ : ___ : ___ : ___ : ___ : ___ : 7 (最高)
            2    3    4    5    6

**C)** あなたにとって, 誇りや自尊感情はどれくらい重要なものですか.

(最低) 1 : ___ : ___ : ___ : ___ : ___ : ___ : 7 (最高)
            2    3    4    5    6

**2.** あなたが現在ついている管理上の地位には, どれくらいの権限がありますか.

**A)** 現在, どれくらい権限がありますか.

(最低) 1 : ___ : ___ : ___ : ___ : ___ : ___ : 7 (最高)
            2    3    4    5    6

**B)** 本来なら, どれくらいあるべきだと思いますか.

(最低) 1 : ___ : ___ : ___ : ___ : ___ : ___ : 7 (最高)
            2    3    4    5    6

**C)** あなたにとって, その権限はどれくらい重要なものですか.

(最低) 1 : ___ : ___ : ___ : ___ : ___ : ___ : 7 (最高)
            2    3    4    5    6

**3.** あなたは，現在の管理上の地位について，どれくらい個人的な成長発達の機會にめぐまれますか。

**A)** 現在，どれくらい機會がありますか。

(最低) 1 : 2 : 3 : 4 : 5 : 6 : 7 (最高)

**B)** 本來なら，どれくらいの機會があるべきたと思いますか。

(最低) 1 : 2 : 3 : 4 : 5 : 6 : 7 (最高)

**C)** あなたにとって，個人的發展の機會はどれくらい重要だと思いますか。

(最低) 1 : 2 : 3 : 4 : 5 : 6 : 7 (最高)


**4.** 會社内においては，あなたの管理上の地位は，どれくらい威光がありますか。(すなわち，會社内において他人から受ける尊敬の度合)

**A)** 現在，どれくらい威光がありますか。

(最低) 1 : 2 : 3 : 4 : 5 : 6 : 7 (最高)

**B)** 本來なら，どれくらいあるべきたと思いますか。

(最低) 1 : 2 : 3 : 4 : 5 : 6 : 7 (最高)

**C)** あなたにとって，その威光はどれくらい重要ですか。

(最低) 1 : 2 : 3 : 4 : 5 : 6 : 7 (最高)

5. あなたは，現在の管理上の地位について，独自の思考や行為が
   とれる機会はどれくらいありますか。

   A) 現在，どれくらいの機会がありますか。

   (最低) 1 : 2 : 3 : 4 : 5 : 6 : 7 (最高)

   B) 本来なら，どれくらいあるべきだと思いますか。

   (最低) 1 : 2 : 3 : 4 : 5 : 6 : 7 (最高)

   C) あなたにとって，独自の思考や行為がとれることは，どれ
   くらい重要ですか。
   (最低) 1 : 2 : 3 : 4 : 5 : 6 : 7 (最高)


6. あなたは，現在の管理上の地位について，どれくらい安定感
   がありますか。

   A) 現在，どれくらい安定感がありますか。

   (最低) 1 : 2 : 3 : 4 : 5 : 6 : 7 (最高)

   B) 本来なら，どれくらいあるべきだと思いますか。

   (最低) 1 : 2 : 3 : 4 : 5 : 6 : 7 (最高)

   C) あなたにとって，安定感はどれくらい重要ですか。

   (最低) 1 : 2 : 3 : 4 : 5 : 6 : 7 (最高)

7. あなたが現在ついている管理上の地位に，他人がついた場合，その人は，どれくらい自己達成の感情(すなわち，自己特有の能力を發揮したり，自己の可能性を実現できるという感情)を抱くでしょうか.

A) 現在，どれくらい自己達成の感情がありますか.

(最低)——1——:——2——:——3——:——4——:——5——:——6——:——7——(最高)

B) 本来なら，どれくらいあるべきだと思いますか.

(最低)——1——:——2——:——3——:——4——:——5——:——6——:——7——(最高)

C) あなたにとって，自己達成の感情はどれくらい重要ですか.

(最低)——1——:——2——:——3——:——4——:——5——:——6——:——7——(最高)

8. 會社外において，あなたの管理上の地位はどれくらい威光がありますか.(すなわち，會社外で他人から受ける尊敬の度合)

A) 現在，どれくらい威光がありますか.

(最低)——1——:——2——:——3——:——4——:——5——:——6——:——7——(最高)

B) 本来なら，どれくらいあるべきたと思いますか.

(最低)——1——:——2——:——3——:——4——:——5——:——6——:——7——(最高)

C) あなたにとって，その威光はどれくらい重要ですか.

(最低)——1——:——2——:——3——:——4——:——5——:——6——:——7——(最高)

9. あなたが現在ついている管理上の地位は、どれくらいやり甲斐のある仕事だと思いますか。

A) 現在、どれくらいやり甲斐がありますか。

(最低) <u>1 : 2 : 3 : 4 : 5 : 6 : 7</u> (最高)

B) 本来なら、どれくらいあるべきだと思いますか。

(最低) <u>1 : 2 : 3 : 4 : 5 : 6 : 7</u> (最高)

C) あなたにとって、やり甲斐のある仕事だという感情はどれくらい重要ですか。

(最低) <u>1 : 2 : 3 : 4 : 5 : 6 : 7</u> (最高)


10. あなたが現在ついている管理上の地位には、どれくらい他人を助けてやる機會がありますか。

A) 現在、どれくらいの機會がありますか。

(最低) <u>1 : 2 : 3 : 4 : 5 : 6 : 7</u> (最高)

B) 本来なら、どれくらいあるべきだと思いますか。

(最低) <u>1 : 2 : 3 : 4 : 5 : 6 : 7</u> (最高)

C) あなたにとって、他人を助けてやる機會はどれくらい重要ですか。

(最低) <u>1 : 2 : 3 : 4 : 5 : 6 : 7</u> (最高)

11. あなたが現在 ついている管理上の地位には、親密な交友関係を発展させる機會がどれくらいありますか.

A) 現在、どれくらい機會がありますか.

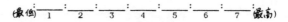
(最低) 1 : 2 : 3 : 4 : 5 : 6 : 7 (最高)

B) 本來なら、どれくらいあるべきだと思いますか.

(最低) 1 : 2 : 3 : 4 : 5 : 6 : 7 (最高)

C) あなたにとって、親密な交友関係を発展させる機會はどれくらい重要ですか.

(最低) 1 : 2 : 3 : 4 : 5 : 6 : 7 (最高)

第三部

　　この質問紙の目的は、いろいろな事物や観念について、あなたがどんな印象をおもちであるかを知ろうとするものです。例えば次のページの如きに「医者」という言葉があります。この言葉について、あなたが感じられる印象を同じページの下方にある一組の尺度にそれぞれ XEP でもって答え下さい。（下の例をみて下さい）自分自身の考えに従って、そこに提示された事物、あるいは観念について、七段階の尺度の中から、もっとも正しく言い表わしていると思われる所の空欄に XEP をつけて下さい。

　　次に示す例は、提示された事物や観念に対して、尺度上にどのように答えたらよいかを示したものです。

　　　　:____:_X_:____:____:____:____:____:
　　　　:____:____:____:____:____:_X_:____:

注意：

　　1. どの尺度にも答えて下さい。飛ばさないように注意すること。

　　2. 一つの尺度に必ず一つだけ XEP をつけて下さい。二つ以上つけてはいけません。

# 醫　者

取るに足らない :＿＿:＿＿:＿＿:＿＿:＿＿:＿＿: 重要な

深遠な :＿＿:＿＿:＿＿:＿＿:＿＿:＿＿: 表面的な

能動的な :＿＿:＿＿:＿＿:＿＿:＿＿:＿＿: 受動的な

狹い :＿＿:＿＿:＿＿:＿＿:＿＿:＿＿: 廣い

難がしい :＿＿:＿＿:＿＿:＿＿:＿＿:＿＿: 易しい

良い :＿＿:＿＿:＿＿:＿＿:＿＿:＿＿: 悪い

安定した :＿＿:＿＿:＿＿:＿＿:＿＿:＿＿: 變化し易い

興味のある :＿＿:＿＿:＿＿:＿＿:＿＿:＿＿: 興味のない

弱い :＿＿:＿＿:＿＿:＿＿:＿＿:＿＿: 強い


陸軍大佐

決定すること

説得すること

職場における一線監督者

創造すること

欺くこと

僧侶

誤ちをおかすこと

軍曹

協力すること

大僧正

指導すること

叱責すること

工場管理者

第四部

統計分析のため，下記の項目に御記入をお願致します。

1. 國籍
2. 會社における地位
3. 自分の属する部又は 課（職種）（一つにチェックして下さい）
____ 生産
____ 販賣宣傳
____ 會計
____ 人事又は 職員訓練
____ 購入
__ _ 研究所
____ 一般管理
____ その他 （記入） _____

4. あなたの會社には，第一線監督から社長に至るまで，
   どれほどの監督の 段階がありますか。（段階の数を記入して
   下さい。）

   _____

5. あなたの地位の上には，どれだけの監督の段階があり
   ますか。（段階の数を記入して下さい。）

   _____

6. あなたは，これまで，商社，工場及び官庁で合計何年

働きましたか. (一つに チェック して下さい.)

_____ 0 — 1年　　　_____ 1 — 3年　　　_____ 3 — 5年

_____ 5 — 10年　　_____ 10 — 15年　　_____ 20 — 30年

_____ 30年以上

7. あなたの會社には, 従業員(管理部分の人も 一般従業員も 含めて)は 大体 何名 ぐらい いますか (一つに チェックして下さい.)

_____ 1 — 49人　　　　_____ 50 — 99人　　　　_____ 100 — 499人

_____ 500 — 999人　　_____ 1,000 — 4,999人　_____ 5,000 — 9,999人

_____ 10,000—29,000人　_____ 30,000—99,999人　_____ 100,000—299,999人

_____ 300,000人以上

8. あなたは, 會社の 重要な 部分を 担当 していますか. (一つに チェック して下さい.)

——— はい　　　　——— いいえ

9. あなたが 勤めている 會社の 種類は 何ですか. (一つだけ チェック して下さい.)

——— 陸上, 海上 輸送

——— 郵便, 電信 電話

——— 電力, 電氣

——— 卸賣 又は 小賣

——— 金融, 保險

——— 化學製品, 油

_____ 鑛業

_____ 鉄鋼業

_____ 製造業

_____ 其他 （記入）_____

10.

| _____ 20 -- 24才 | _____ 25 -- 29才 | _____ 30 -- 34才 |
|---|---|---|
| _____ 35 -- 39才 | _____ 40 -- 44才 | _____ 45 -- 49才 |
| _____ 50 -- 54才 | _____ 55 -- 59才 | _____ 60才以上 |

11. 教育を受けた總年數，すなわち，小學校から大學或は
專門學校までの合計年數（年數を記入して下さい）

_____

12. 大學或は專門學校にいかれた方に對して，自分の專門として
學ばれた學科に一っだけ チエックをつけて下さい。

_____ 工業 （土木，電氣，機械等を含む。）

_____ 法律

_____ 經濟

_____ 文學或は哲學

_____ 其他 （記入）——————————

# Breakdown of Sample

TABLE B-1. AGE

| | Denmark | Germany | Norway | Sweden | Belgium | France | Italy | Spain | England | U. S. | Argentina | Chile | India | Japan |
|---|---|---|---|---|---|---|---|---|---|---|---|---|---|---|
| 20 to 24 | 0 | 1 | 0 | 0 | 1 | 0 | 1 | 4 | 0 | 0 | 3 | 7 | 13 | 0 |
| 25 to 29 | 6 | 7 | 0 | 1 | 3 | 1 | 17 | 12 | 7 | 2 | 9 | 16 | 19 | 2 |
| 30 to 34 | 19 | 25 | 2 | 9 | 20 | 10 | 28 | 20 | 20 | 15 | 21 | 23 | 32 | 10 |
| 35 to 39 | 28 | 24 | 19 | 25 | 23 | 31 | 25 | 27 | 28 | 25 | 27 | 28 | 20 | 17 |
| 40 to 44 | 27 | 14 | 32 | 28 | 16 | 20 | 11 | 16 | 23 | 26 | 17 | 17 | 6 | 12 |
| 45 to 49 | 11 | 9 | 24 | 22 | 12 | 19 | 8 | 10 | 15 | 14 | 11 | 6 | 10 | 23 |
| 50 to 54 | 7 | 8 | 15 | 11 | 12 | 10 | 7 | 5 | 6 | 9 | 8 | 3 | 0 | 24 |
| 55 to 59 | 2 | 6 | 4 | 3 | 9 | 5 | 2 | 2 | 0 | 7 | 3 | 0 | 0 | 9 |
| 60 or over | 1 | 5 | 3 | 1 | 4 | 3 | 1 | 3 | 0 | 3 | 3 | 0 | 0 | 4 |

Figures rounded off to nearest percentage.

## TABLE B-2. YEARS OF FORMAL EDUCATION

| | Denmark | Germany | Norway | Sweden | Belgium | France | Italy | Spain | England | U.S. | Argentina | Chile | India | Japan |
|---|---|---|---|---|---|---|---|---|---|---|---|---|---|---|
| 8 or less | 4 | 4 | 3 | 2 | 1 | 0 | 1 | 9 | 1 | 1 | 5 | 2 | 1 | 1 |
| 9 to 12 | 25 | 48 | 11 | 11 | 10 | 11 | 5 | 25 | 38 | 9 | 25 | 27 | 6 | 15 |
| 13 to 16 | 32 | 33 | 35 | 57 | 34 | 52 | 18 | 36 | 36 | 53 | 39 | 34 | 55 | 43 |
| 17 and more | 39 | 15 | 51 | 30 | 55 | 37 | 76 | 29 | 25 | 37 | 30 | 37 | 38 | 41 |

## TABLE B-3. SPECIALIZATION IN EDUCATION

| | Denmark | Germany | Norway | Sweden | Belgium | France | Italy | Spain | England | U.S. | Argentina | Chile | India | Japan |
|---|---|---|---|---|---|---|---|---|---|---|---|---|---|---|
| Engineering | 60 | 26 | 50 | 26 | 49 | 50 | 24 | 33 | 44 | 45 | 34 | 41 | 44 | 28 |
| Law | 3 | 14 | 16 | 4 | 13 | 21 | 23 | 15 | 2 | 4 | 13 | 6 | 3 | 17 |
| Economics | 21 | 44 | 25 | 65 | 22 | 13 | 29 | 33 | 8 | 15 | 25 | 17 | 10 | 38 |
| Humanities and Other | 16 | 15 | 9 | 5 | 16 | 15 | 23 | 19 | 46 | 37 | 28 | 35 | 44 | 17 |

Figures rounded off to nearest percentage.

## TABLE B-4. Type of Company

| | Denmark | Germany | Norway | Sweden | Belgium | France | Italy | Spain | England | U.S. | Argentina | Chile | India | Japan |
|---|---|---|---|---|---|---|---|---|---|---|---|---|---|---|
| Transportation and Shipping | 1 | 1 | 9 | 4 | 2 | 2 | 1 | 1 | 3 | 1 | 0 | 0 | 7 | 0 |
| Postal, Telegraph and Telephone | 11 | 1 | 4 | 0 | 0 | 0 | 3 | 1 | 0 | 24 | 1 | 2 | 1 | 0 |
| Power, Light and Electricity | 1 | 5 | 5 | 2 | 3 | 0 | 3 | 3 | 8 | 1 | 1 | 7 | 11 | 4 |
| Wholesale and Trade | 4 | 5 | 8 | 14 | 7 | 9 | 7 | 5 | 13 | 7 | 12 | 14 | 1 | 6 |
| Finance and Insurance | 2 | 12 | 6 | 7 | 11 | 1 | 7 | 4 | 1 | 4 | 6 | 3 | 7 | 4 |
| Chemical and Petroleum | 5 | 9 | 15 | 9 | 10 | 16 | 23 | 7 | 12 | 11 | 18 | 18 | 20 | 15 |
| Mining | 0 | 2 | 2 | 3 | 3 | 1 | 1 | 1 | 0 | 0 | 1 | 6 | 0 | 5 |
| Steel and Metal Fabrication | 11 | 29 | 12 | 4 | 11 | 9 | 9 | 11 | 6 | 5 | 8 | 11 | 3 | 7 |
| Manufacturing | 45 | 24 | 25 | 18 | 26 | 38 | 19 | 35 | 42 | 36 | 26 | 19 | 42 | 45 |
| Other | 20 | 12 | 16 | 38 | 27 | 23 | 27 | 35 | 16 | 11 | 28 | 20 | 7 | 13 |

Figures rounded off to nearest percentage.

# Intercorrelations among Countries and Clusters

## Table C-1. Intercorrelations Among Countries

| | Denmark | Germany | Norway | Sweden | Belgium | France | Italy | Spain | England | U.S. | Argentina | Chile | India | Japan |
|---|---|---|---|---|---|---|---|---|---|---|---|---|---|---|
| Denmark | | .40 | .37 | .33 | -.03 | -.25 | -.61 | -.53 | .04 | -.13 | -.31 | -.36 | -.33 | .20 |
| Germany | | | .19 | .18 | .01 | -.26 | -.05 | -.32 | -.50 | -.53 | -.04 | -.11 | -.05 | -.14 |
| Norway | | | | .77 | .20 | -.01 | -.35 | -.52 | .43 | .13 | -.75 | -.75 | -.76 | .31 |
| Sweden | | | | | .26 | -.03 | -.34 | -.50 | .35 | .01 | -.53 | -.62 | -.76 | .32 |
| Belgium | | | | | | .62 | .07 | .14 | -.01 | -.20 | -.33 | -.48 | -.49 | -.07 |
| France | | | | | | | .23 | .22 | .11 | .20 | -.42 | -.44 | -.25 | -.22 |
| Italy | | | | | | | | .53 | -.29 | -.11 | .23 | .20 | .34 | -.55 |
| Spain | | | | | | | | | -.46 | -.28 | .37 | .38 | .30 | -.37 |
| England | | | | | | | | | | .76 | -.49 | -.49 | -.29 | .16 |
| U.S. | | | | | | | | | | | -.32 | -.25 | -.11 | .18 |
| Argentina | | | | | | | | | | | | .89 | .66 | -.23 |
| Chile | | | | | | | | | | | | | .69 | -.19 |
| India | | | | | | | | | | | | | | -.40 |
| Japan | | | | | | | | | | | | | | |

| | Nordic-European | Latin-European | Anglo-American | Developing | Japan |
|---|---|---|---|---|---|
| Nordic-European | .37 | −.21 | −.03 | −.45 | .17 |
| Latin-European | | .30 | −.13 | −.05 | −.30 |
| Anglo-American | | | .76 | −.33 | .17 |
| Developing | | | | .72 | −.27 |
| Japan | | | | | |

# Factor Loadings

TABLE D-1. LOADINGS OF THE NINE SEMANTIC DIFFERENTIAL
SCALES ON THE FIVE FACTORS

| | Factors | | | | |
|---|---|---|---|---|---|
| Scales | Prestige | Scope | Activity | Firmness | Difficulty |
| Important | .88 | .16 | .20 | .14 | .10 |
| Profound | .73 | .26 | .26 | .28 | .17 |
| Active | .33 | .12 | .87 | .15 | .12 |
| Wide | .27 | .91 | .15 | .13 | .08 |
| Difficult | .17 | .09 | .13 | .11 | .96 |
| Good | .33 | .36 | .32 | .61 | .22 |
| Stable | .17 | .04 | .09 | .92 | .04 |
| Interesting | .54 | .37 | .37 | .33 | .19 |
| Strong | .22 | .34 | .53 | .53 | .17 |

# Index